Gideon's Gang

Gideon's Gang

A Case Study of the
Church in Social Action

JEFFREY K. HADDEN
and
CHARLES F. LONGINO, JR.

with the assistance of
Myer S. Reed, Jr.

A Pilgrim Press Book
from
United Church Press
Philadelphia

Library of Congress Cataloging in Publication Data

Hadden, Jeffrey K
  Gideon's gang: a case study of the church in
social action.

  "A Pilgrim Press book."
  Includes bibliographical references.
  1. Congregation for Reconciliation, Dayton, Ohio.
2. Congregation for Reconciliation, Cincinnati.
3. Social action—Case studies. I. Longino, Charles
F., 1938–   joint author. II. Title.
BX9886.Z7D3944   261.8′3   74-6156
ISBN 0-8298-0275-4 Cloth
ISBN 0-8298-0279-7 Paper

The chart on page 218, " 'Strong' and 'Weak' Groups," is from *Why Conservative
Churches Are Growing* by Dean M. Kelley, p. 84. Copyright © 1972 by Dean M.
Kelley. Used by permission of Harper & Row, Publishers, Inc.

United Church Press, 1505 Race Street,
Philadelphia, Pennsylvania 19102

Contents

Foreword

Only yesterday, it seems, in 1965, Dick Righter was a crusading pastor in Philadelphia, and I was a reforming bureaucrat in that city's Anti-Poverty Program. In those years we believed, along with many other activists, that we could help achieve permanent change in the structure of racial and economic injustices of American society. Now, almost a decade later, the national administration and the Philadelphia city administration both stand for a reversal of all that we believed in and worked for. And many former activists have modified their expectations and abandoned their high ideals for a smaller scale of achievement.

Today in Dayton, Ohio, the Congregation for Reconciliation under Righter's leadership stands for the best that the 1960s had to offer: clear analysis of racism as a basic social evil, intelligent and concerted action, and a faith that human life can be lived in wholeness and equality. It also stands squarely within the Western tradition of religious dissent. It combines degrees of rationalism and enthusiasm, anti-institutionalism and institutional seriousness, work and play. It has lived longer than many other social-activist attempts to encounter racism from a biblical basis. We need to ask why from two perspectives. One is the perspective of social scientific curiosity. How does a small congregation manage to meet its own needs and still confront the principalities and powers of the surrounding community? The other perspective is that of mission strategy. How is the drive for social justice, with its multitude of motivations and expectations, given an ongoing institutional framework?

The modern phenomenon of religious dissent has both Greek and Hebrew antecedents. The followers of Pythagoras, rebelling against the stultifying conformity in the Greek city-state, set up their own community built upon the mathematical representation of cosmic order. The history of the Hebrews as a people summoned to be a light unto the nations is one of continual tension between establishment, in the name of order, and prophecy, in the name of compassion. The early church, born of both traditions, sought to embody a new alternative to prevailing political and economic practice. Its survival is the result, in large measure, of its ability to live in, but not of, the world—to accept the limitations of its cultural environment only with faith in the promise that wholeness and peace would one day be established throughout the earth.

But what about the future? Can the Congregation for Reconciliation succeed and, more importantly, can it be a leader for that part of the American church which sees itself continually addressing social issues from the perspective of the Gospel?

The paradox of religious dissent is that it is both anti-institutional and proto-institutional. The act of exposing oppression and injustice challenges basic institutional arrangements. Yet commonly held notions of ethical right and human possibility can become patterns of social behavior, and thus the foundation for new institutions. Because of this paradox, success is difficult to measure; success won too quickly may indicate a less than adequate approach to the problem. Yet perseverance can lead to a series of subtle and perhaps unintended consequences. Old issues fade away, fresh problems are uncovered, and new people are recruited to the cause. The Puritan movement, with its wide variety of dissenting groups, survived two hundred years of struggle, finally achieving a lasting impact on the political and economic structure of American society.

The challenge facing religiously sensitive persons today is not only to find an authentic personal faith. The genius of religious faith is not that it inspires adherence but that it engineers critical judgment and creativity. In a democratic society there can be no enduring sense of personal identity without involvement in a process of continually examining the circumstances of equality. The challenge is one of finding ways by which creative possibilities are expressed and embodied in all our institutions. Our society

10

has a stake in the success and influence of the Congregation for Reconciliation.

This book is the product of a too rare collaboration among self-reflective leaders of a congregation, perceptive social analysts, and denominational executives with an ongoing concern for accurate evaluation. In this time of institutional change, the practical problems which the Congregation for Reconciliation has faced with imaginative solutions are of wide interest to all church leaders. We are deeply grateful to Richard Righter and "Gideon's Army" and to Jeffrey Hadden and Chuck Longino. We hope this book can stimulate further solid research efforts within the traditions of religious dissent.

Theodore H. Erickson, Jr.

United Church Board for Homeland Ministries

11

Preface

Doing sociology is not so easy as it used to be. Once upon a time—not very long ago, really—sociologists believed in the doctrine of "value free" social research. This creed served many useful functions, not the least of which was to lend an aura of legitimacy to the enterprise. It convinced most of us that we were really scientists and at the same time persuaded a fair proportion of a grateful and unsuspecting public this was so. But perhaps the most important function of this doctrine was that it saved us from having to ask a lot of difficult questions of how, in one way or another, our own value presuppositions, those of our discipline, and those of our culture affect the outcome of our work.

The convulsions which rocked our society during the 1960s also sent tremors through the discipline of sociology, and we shall probably never be the same. Sociologists are now in their most serious period of self-appraisal since the inception of the discipline. The traditional distinctions between pure and applied research have grown dim. A few among our ranks now argue for the abandonment of any effort to be "objective," contending that all knowledge, sociological or otherwise, is ultimately political rhetoric. We don't buy this viewpoint, but we do believe that the efforts of sociologists, as well as of social scientists in other disciplines, to be more self-conscious about how their own value presuppositions alter their work, are long overdue.

If sociology passed through a period of excess in its commitment to a "value free" posture, as many of us now believe, there is every reason to guard against the pendulum swing to excess in the other direction. If there is merit in trying to be explicit about our value presuppositions, there is also danger in such confessions' providing license for abandoning the search for those elusive but empirically true relationships in the social world. The danger may be even greater for the consumers of sociological research; that is, our admission of the complexity of our task may provide added reason for consumers to reject any sociological knowledge which does not conform to their own values.

What we are, we bring to our research. Our presuppositions about social reality constitute a screen through which we filter our observations. We do not believe this means that "objective" social research is impossible. Rather, it means we need to understand the concept of objectivity in a framework more realistically reflective of the process of doing research. It also means that researchers should attempt to be honest with themselves and their readers in making known the value presuppositions impinging on the research and interpretative processes. We shall try to do this, but obviously one's own value assumptions are evasive; that which one takes for granted is not easily articulated.

The reader, then, has two awesome responsibilities. The first is careful attention so as to better understand how our value presuppositions have affected what we have done and said. In short, our values are raw data the reader must process before beginning to come to grips with the implications of this sociological inquiry.

The secondary responsibility is a serious effort to comprehend how one's own value presuppositions affect the reading and interpretation of this volume. The first task is partially a natural reaction in all interaction situations. Most of us, though, seldom fulfill the second responsibility. We typically do not question how *our own* values distort or block our understanding of what we see, hear, and read. Without self-conscious reflection on the biases of our own values, however, neither learning nor communication can take place. Observing, analyzing, and evaluating reality as perceived by others is the key to knowledge and intellectual growth.

There are a number of ways in which one might attempt to identify one's own value presuppositions for the benefit of an audience. One would be to write a long autobiographic essay which attempts self-analysis. Another is simply to specify one's values as they become relevant to the process of interpreting data. With the exception of a few autobiographic comments in the paragraphs which immediately follow, we have opted for the latter. This does not always take an explicit form. That is, we don't periodically say, "STOP . . . take note, for we are now going to tell you about ourselves." Rather, we simply attempt not to hide our values when they become relevant. We are in substantial agreement with Rémy De Gourmont, who wrote in his preface to *Le Livre des Masques*, "The only excuse a man has for writing is to write himself—to reveal to others the kind of world reflected in his individual mirror." [1]

Both of us come out of a conservative tradition of Protestantism. Through the process of our education and socialization we came to see the individual racial prejudice and structural arrangements of our society which fostered and perpetuated discrimination as morally and intellectually reprehensible. Each of us, at a fairly early age, saw an incongruity between the principles of love and brotherhood which were taught by our faith and the indifference and discrimination so often practiced by our churches and so many of those who call themselves Christians.

Neither of us has ever been closely aligned with radical social-protest groups, although we have often been sympathetic with their objectives and sometimes appreciative of their efforts. That we see our own roles as working within the "system" probably says a great deal about how we view the discipline of sociology. We see the social order as precariously held together by institutional arrangements. Apart from institutions, social order is impossible. We agree with Peter Berger when he writes, "If bureaucracy [institutions] vanished from America tomorrow, not only would our lives be thrown into immeasurable chaos, but most of us would literally die." [2] Thus we take a cautious and skeptical view toward the proposition that old institutions must be destroyed before new ones can emerge. This is not to say we stand in opposition to new institutional forms; quite the contrary. However, we most certainly part company with those who stand ready not only to abandon but to encourage the destruction of old institutions before new institutions are even on the horizon.

This component of our value presuppositions is most assuredly conservative. But we feel it important to distinguish between conservatism which is uncritical and protective of existing institutional arrangements, i.e., supportive of the status quo, and

15

conservatism which is grounded in suspicion of the consequences of radical alterations. While the former stands in opposition to change, the latter is deeply concerned about the *process* whereby change can be achieved without causing chaos.

Against our cautiousness toward change must be juxtaposed a belief that the fundamental demographic, technological, and organizational processes of human society are in the midst of a furor of change which is unprecedented in human history. Without endorsing many of the particulars of Alvin Toffler's best seller, *Future Shock*, we believe him to be correct when he wrote, "Western society for the past 300 years has been caught up in a firestorm of change. This storm, far from abating, now appears to be gathering force." [3]

We believe our posture of conservatism is not inconsistent with the advocacy of change, sometimes even radical change. In traditional sociological perspective, we believe social structures to possess imposing realities which mold and shape our individual and collective destinies. It has long been the dominant posture of the church, and in very substantial measure the belief of the leadership of this nation, that the social order can only be changed in proportion to individual change. As a nation we are now becoming more sophisticated about this. How many times have we all heard the statement, "You can't legislate against prejudice"? Perhaps not, yet the experience of the past two decades has provided an abundance of evidence to prove that it is possible to change social structures which are every bit as oppressive as individual prejudice. It remains to be seen whether, in legislating against discriminatory institutional arrangements, we may have de facto "legislated" against prejudice. Our own perspective on this matter is a cautious optimism.

As we become more sophisticated in our knowledge of the importance of social structures, it is important that we also learn to develop strategies and theories to foresee the probable consequences of manipulating social structures. That is, we need to develop ways of foreseeing not only what we intend to happen, when we change a structural arrangement, but also to anticipate that which might otherwise be an unanticipated consequence. Many who should know better have misunderstood Daniel Patrick Moynihan's analysis of the community action component of the

War on Poverty as an angry diatribe by a political turncoat. Moynihan's analysis is sound: the community action structures which the government created to deal with poverty were created in such a way as "to produce a minimum of the social change its sponsors desired, and bring about a maximum increase in the opposition to such change." [4]

Our argument, for all intents and purposes, is the same. During the 1960s, church leaders in every liberal Protestant denomination in America frantically went about the business of creating structures to deal with the many issues of social injustice which bombarded our consciences. The issues were compelling, and they seemed to demand immediate action. In the process of aiding the oppressed, these same church leaders served up to their adversaries the ammunition needed to cripple or obliterate these programs.

There is no point in tallying the assets and liabilities of the churches' efforts in the many social-action programs in which they became involved. The important point is that the very large proportion of their structures, programs, and budgets have been dismantled. Discussions of regrouping, developing new strategies, and decentralizing authority are largely rhetoric. Furthermore, effective new programs and strategies are not likely to emerge until the leadership better understands what happened and why.

While a systematic assessment of the churches' involvement in social action during the 1960s is beyond the scope of this volume, we believe case studies such as we have undertaken here can illumine important issues. We have attempted to be explicit in identifying those aspects of our study which raise policy questions. Critical readers should spot additional issues. The final responsibility to ferret out the policy implications of this study rests with the leadership of America's religious institutions.

How the Study Came About

This study began as a supplementary evaluation of an experimental social-action congregation in Dayton, Ohio. The Congregation for Reconciliation was one of three experimental congregations created in the spring of 1968 in the Ohio Synod of the United Presbyterian Church in the U.S.A. The three congregations were created by separate actions of the Cincinnati, Cleveland, and Miami Presbyteries, but the total effort had been coordinated by members of the Synod staff. All three bore the name Congregation for Reconciliation, were charged with similar goals stemming from the specific issue of fostering racial reconciliation in their respective communities, and were to have a limited life and an absolute commitment to a nonbuilding program.

This was about the extent of their similarities. The National Missions Committees of the three Presbyteries recruited pastors with very different styles and perceptions as to the nature of the experiment, and this proved to have a significant impact on the outcome. The Cleveland Congregation, for a variety of complex reasons, never quite got off the ground. The organizing pastor resigned before the end of the designated experimental period, and the congregation folded without further efforts to hire another. It took half a year for the organizing pastor in Cincinnati to get a group together, but, once formed, the congregation wasted little time in defining and getting on with their business. They saw their goals almost exclusively as working within the structures of the Presbytery. After a three-year life, evaluated as highly successful by themselves, the congregation devoted time to an intense study of death, wrote their own obituary, and passed away.

In Dayton, the organizing pastor spent several weeks getting acquainted with the community before he made any effort to have a meeting of potential recruits. When an organizational meeting was called, the group was off and running. Their style: confrontation politics. Their first target: one of the largest corporations in Dayton. This was followed by a flurry of other action projects which quickly earned them a highly visible and controversial reputation in the city and the Presbytery. Not until strong pressures were brought by the Presbytery did the group slow down long enough to formally organize as a congregation. This formal organization was facilitated by becoming a union church with the United Church of Christ.

In the spring of 1972, four years after the three experimental congregations had been approved, the Ohio Synod and respective presbyteries established study teams to evaluate the three congregations. At that time the Cleveland group was dead and the Cincinnati group was in the process of preparing its last will and testament. The Dayton group, however, had long since decided that it had no intention of yielding to any bureaucratic decision to close the books on the experiment. They had researched their legal status and were prepared, if necessary, to fight those who might resist their plans to remain a congregation.

At this point, the idea of a supplementary evaluation emerged and was envisioned to serve several purposes. First of all, the Congregation felt they deserved a more thorough evaluation than could possibly be accomplished by the Synod and Presbytery evaluation team. Many of the members of the Congregation had invested a major proportion of their time in this experiment over the previous three and a half years, and they genuinely desired the reflections of an independent outside observer. But it also seemed clear that a report from an independent evaluator might be a valuable political document in the event strong opposition emerged to their continuance as a congregation. In the event of a negative report from the Synod-Presbytery evaluation team, a favorable report could offset the "official" evaluation. If both reports were generally favorable, they would have double ammunition against adversaries. Whatever weight may have been given to the supplementary evaluation as a potential political document, some members of the Congregation saw this as added rationale for a second evaluation.

The senior author of this volume was contacted in late April 1972 by the Rev. Richard Righter, pastor of the Congregation, regarding his services as a possible outside independent evaluator. A May meeting with members of the Congregation and the Presbytery's Supplementary Evaluation Committee was scheduled. This meeting revealed significant discrepancies between the committee's list of objectives for the evaluation and our own perceptions of what was possible. Our reservations were twofold. First, we questioned the possibility of *scientifically measuring* the impact of the Congregation on the community with the kind of precision which seemed implicit in their articulation of the objective. Second, we questioned whether it was useful for an outsider, especially a sociologist, to attempt to evaluate the *style* of the Congregation's social action from the perspective of its faithfulness to the mission of the church as revealed in biblical and theological heritage. This objective implied a desire for an affirmative answer. The Congregation obviously believed itself to be faithful to a theological rationale. If there was any doubt about this, the task was one for the members of the Congregation themselves. Moreover, an outsider who happened to agree with them would carry little weight in persuading others who questioned their legitimacy and faithfulness to theological tradition. Finally, we indicated that such a task was not within the scope of our competency.

In general, the committee members present at the May meeting accepted the legitimacy of our reservations about pursuing an evaluation with objectives which were either impossible to evaluate or of limited value to the Congregation and its sponsoring agencies. It was therefore necessary to reconceptualize the goals of the outside evaluator. We recommended, and after considerable discussion and negotiation the evaluation committee concurred, that greater benefit would accrue from an investigation of the sociological dynamics of the Congregation, with emphasis upon assessing its strengths and weaknesses vis-à-vis its own stated objectives, structure, constitution, and bylaws. Aside from the possible political benefits of an outside evaluation report, the Congregation was principally interested in strengthening its organizational structure, preserving and/or strengthening the commitment of its members, developing strategies for social action, and increasing the effectiveness of these programs. The interests of denominational officials lay in examining the Congregation as a potential model for future new congregations; thus they would want to learn all they could about what was done "right" and what might be done better in any subsequent experiments.

The initial fieldwork was conducted during June 1972. The senior author was assisted by Myer S. Reed, Jr., then a graduate student in sociology at Tulane University and presently an assistant professor at Radford College. We were also assisted by Scott Patterson, a student at Princeton Theological Seminary who was employed for the summer by the Oak Creek United Church of Christ in Kettering, Ohio, a Dayton suburb. Mr. Patterson interviewed a randomly selected sample of half of the Presbyterian and United Church of Christ pastors in the Dayton metropolitan area. His interviewing extended into July and August. In total, we conducted about one hundred interviews with present and former members of the Congregation, clergy, business and civic leaders, and representatives of the media who had been involved in covering social-action projects of the Congregation. Our interviews with business and civic leaders on this first field trip were arranged by Ms. Joy Bickerstaff, a member of the Congregation. Our misgivings about having a member of the Congregation arrange interviews, for fear of subtle bias in selecting persons with favorable views toward the Congregation, were quickly dispelled. Conscious of this possibility, Ms. Bickerstaff had bent over backward to arrange for us to talk with people with negative views of the Congregation. Many of these interviews raised hard questions which we brought back to Righter and members of the Congregation. Not once did Righter even hesitate to open his files. Indeed, he offered us far more than we were able to read while in the field. We ended up carrying home more than a file drawer of documents, which we were then able to digest at a more leisurely pace.

Our supplementary evaluation report came slowly for two reasons. First, the senior author's move during that summer from Tulane University to the University of Virginia created the seemingly unending obligations and new duties which inevitably arise from moving and taking on a new job. Second, as we attempted to digest and integrate our data, we found ourselves asking far more questions, important ones, than we had data to answer. We made liberal use of the telephone to follow up on interviews and to seek clarification of materials from the files we had carried home. In time this sufficed to permit us to write a report for the Supplementary Evaluation Committee and the National Missions Committee of the Miami Presbytery, but it did not satisfy the desire to return and explore other issues in more depth. The idea of returning to Dayton for more field research thus emerged early.

During the academic year 1972–73, the coauthors of this

volume began a collaborative analysis of clergy data gathered some years earlier. This working relationship placed the junior author in the role of a captive audience to talk about the Dayton study. Over the year his own background and academic interests drew him closer to the project. When it came time to return to Dayton, he had been coopted into a co-investigator role and subsequently shared fully in analyzing and interpreting our body of data and in preparing this manuscript.

When we returned to Dayton in the summer of 1973, we had had a year to digest the data from the previous summer's research. Whereas our first field trip had been a whirlwind, shotgun happening, we were now in a position to follow the leads of our first trip in more depth. Interviews during the first field trip usually lasted about an hour. On the return trip, the typical interview tended to run two to four hours. All but a few of these were taped, and approximately thirty-five hours of interviews were selected for transcription and further study. This second field trip again raised new questions and opened new vistas for investigation. Perhaps most significant was the opportunity to go to Cincinnati and learn about another Congregation for Reconciliation. While our information on this Congregation is much more limited, we believe it provides invaluable comparative data. Other leads, for reasons of time and financial resources, could not be followed.

Acknowledgments

Studies of this nature create indebtedness which can be neither repaid nor adequately acknowledged. Failure to mention those to whom we are obliged, however, would be unpardonable. Without Richard Righter's tireless responses to our requests for lengthy interviews and access to materials in his files, this study could not have been completed. Without Willie Righter's devotion to her husband and the Congregation, there quite probably would have been no story for us to write. The Righters' roles as informants and principals in the study often placed them in a perturbable position of role conflict. They obviously had a vested interest in presenting themselves and the Congregation in a favorable light.

Such a context would tempt most people, on occasion at least, to consciously distort events or withhold information not explicitly requested. We feel confident that the Righters did neither.

We wish also to thank the members of the Congregation for opening their lives to us with unusual candor. Scott Patterson's interviewing was conducted without compensation. For this, as well as for his sharing with us a report on his interviewing experience for an independent studies course at Princeton, we express our sincere thanks. Robert Edwards, Stated Clerk of the Miami Presbytery, gave generously of his time and offered valuable insights about the life of the Congregation and its relationship to the Presbytery. We are especially indebted to Theodore Erickson of the Board of Homeland Missions of the United Church of Christ, both for encouraging us to return to Dayton and for providing critical financial assistance to make this possible. For financial assistance, we are also indebted to the Miami Presbytery, the Ohio Synod of the United Church of Christ, and the University of Virginia Faculty Small Grants Committee.

The editorial skills of Elaine Hadden have unquestionably made this a far more readable manuscript, but our debt to her goes beyond this. From the onset of the study she has served as a skeptical reactor to our interpretations of the data. Anyone who has attempted to do social science knows there are instances when one's perspective is clouded by being too close or too far from the data. On numerous occasions her critical eye and sociological imagination have served as an important corrective of our tendencies toward myopia, hyperopia, and amblyopia.

Also, a special word of thanks to our immediate families, Elaine, Loyce, Donna, Laura, and Chip, for living with broken promises and postponed family activities during the summer of 1973.

Finally, a few concluding comments regarding the Congregation for Reconciliation and its pastor. First, on September 11, 1973, the Miami Presbytery unanimously voted continuance of the Congregation, thus formally ending their temporary experimental status. Second, those interested in exploring details of the Congregation not covered in this manuscript or in following the continuing life of the group may directly contact the Rev. Richard

Righter, Congregation for Reconciliation, Box 123, D.V. Station, Dayton, Ohio 45406. Third, we would like to be explicit in noting what should be apparent in the text: the title of the book is meant to be analogously descriptive of the accomplishments of this small group of Christian social activists and not prophetic. It is our sincere hope that the Congregation's pastor will not experience the hard times which beset the Old Testament warrior whose name we have borrowed for our title.

Jeffrey K. Hadden

Charles F. Longino, Jr.

Department of Sociology
University of Virginia
Charlottesville, Virginia

24

CHAPTER 1

"A Groovy Trip While It Lasted"

INTERVIEWER: "How do you feel about the church's response to social issues in the 1970s?"

PASTOR: "Well, I think the churches have largely been withdrawing. There is much more internal preoccupation in the church. Some of the activists are now into organizational development patterns in which the church, as organization, becomes a focus for mission. . . . There is an attempt to make its structure what you would want society to be. From a radical perspective one might see this as 'power to the people' in microcosm. The attempt is to open up the decision-making processes of the church in a way that seldom happens in other institutional contexts. In this way the church can set an example for society. I have social activist friends who are very much into matters like transactional analysis, sensitivity groups, and liturgical creativity with their congregations now. There is no doubt that there is a great deal more of this internal preoccupation in congregations recently. But it seems to me that it just represents a whole lot of retreat from social issues which continue. There has not been a great social change. I think the injustice and the polarization between institutional establishments and those who are exploited by them has not lessened. . . .

"I think there has been [among liberal clergy] a lot of disillusionment with the effectiveness of mass movements and a recognition of the entrenchment of social injustice and a real confusion as to where the handles are, and even what are the appropriate social goals. I think a lot of social goals that were assumed to be appropriate ten, or even seven, years ago are now open to question. For instance, how do black and white communities appropriately work together? Are there really convergent goals? Certainly in education the labeling of busing as a bad thing is coming not only from the white but the black communities as well. I feel overwhelmed by the confusion of goals, myself, here as pastor of an interracial church in an integrated neighborhood. Five years ago, I suppose, it seemed like a place to really dig in and stabilize the neighborhood. 'We'll stabilize the neighborhood!' Now what does that really mean when whites say stabilize a neighborhood? 'Organize a community.' Well, what does it really mean when the organization of the community is white primarily? It is to keep the whites sticking around longer and the blacks from coming in. It has become a very confused time as far as the social witness of the church is concerned. I'm sure you've heard that everywhere you've gone.

"Another side of it is the recognition in the whole culture, and the grudging recognition by some of us who really were turned on by the civil rights movement and the peace movement, that there has been a lot of emptiness in the institutional church when throughout society there have been so many manifestations—such as parapsychology, astrology, Jesus freaks, satanism, transcendental meditation—of a tremendous search by people to find personal meaning and transcendence for their lives. I think liberal clergy must acknowledge that we have assumed the so-called spiritual dimension too easily. Ten years or so ago with *The Secular City* and *Honest to God* we were trying to say, 'Hey, world! We're not weird! We are concerned for human beings and human issues and human pain.' But our answers in terms of social involvement did not distinguish us from good liberal humanist people in general. There has been a response to the theological emptiness of social action by middle-American clergy and laity emerging within the churches. It is a conservative reaction [in the form of] a new evangelism and fundamentalism. Liberal clergy and laity are extremely vulnerable to this reaction. We have nothing concrete to offer as an alternative since we have, in the Nixon years, become so goalless and rudderless on social concerns. There may have been an external storm gathering a few years ago, but now the storm is internal, inside the church, and social action is losing out. . . ."

26

INTERVIEWER: "How have liberal clergy responded to this new privatism in the churches?"

PASTOR: "There is now a crisis of confidence. Those who were out there on the picket lines, going south to march, going to city council meetings, have now capitulated in many ways. Some have started playing internal games in their churches, some of which I think have value but tend to ignore the social content of the Christian gospel and thus, in my view, are inadequate in themselves. Some have gotten out of the ministry and gone into social work and planning jobs. Then there are some others, and I think I count myself among them, who are saying, 'Oh, my God! Where is the lever? How can I rally some troops to really take something on? And how can I tap into a transcendent dimension without just staying in the church building, withdrawn from the world?' That is, how can we continue to be on the move and involved in the suffering of the world and at the same time say that we are experiencing what it means to be a Christian?"

INTERVIEWER: "Are you saying that some clergymen who saw the church as a viable institution from which to mount social action campaigns in the 1960s no longer see it that way?"

PASTOR: "I still read *The Christian Century* every once in a while. Andrew D. Templeton wrote in a recent issue that there is still no institution in American society as capable of social transformation and redemption as the church. I don't believe it anymore. I wrote in the margin of the article that I wish that I still believed it as Templeton apparently does. . . .

"I think the church is much more obviously on the fringe now. This is a judgment on the illusion that it was meaningfully involved in the sixties. One of the things that the churches historically specialize in is inspiration and crusades. And, of course, some horrible things have been called by that glorious name. When social involvement and social change were seen primarily in terms of inspiration and crusades, and revivalism, of course then the church was very inclined to be in the center of the arena. But when social change means hard digging and reading through reams and reams of [bureaucratic] reports in order to understand how the system is doing its job, only to discover that you need still more information in order to pin down the concrete, bureaucratic lever which dispenses injustice in certain concrete circumstances—well, you know, that's not very inspiring. This does not call for charismatic leadership so much as dogged persistence. It is not going to light the fires of crusades or revival and it does raise some rather serious questions of staying power. . . .

"The action-oriented clergy are having to go back to where the troops are now that the crusade is over. This may indicate the shallowness of much of what went under the banner of social action and social change in the sixties.

"But wasn't it fun while it lasted? We were turned on by the feeling that we were tilting at windmills and the monsters were really falling. And in a way, I suppose, by creating a social climate in which legislation could take place, we did have some effect. Our cause was so obviously just and the enemy was so dumb as to use knives, sticks, police dogs, and fire hoses. You got some victories then. But the enemy is not so dumb anymore; in fact, the enemy is us. At least we are coopted into the system. Those who are still seriously into social action, who are now doing the hard drudge work of making the system move, they are in the main no longer clergymen, or at least no longer active pastors. But it was such a groovy trip while it lasted. . . ."

During the 1960s liberal Protestant leaders, at every level of church structure, made noble efforts to push, pull, and drag the churches into the twentieth century. But their efforts, having fallen short, instead churned to the surface all the latent conflict and tension simmering deep within. They are now experiencing tremendous pressure to stifle their efforts to enact policies consistent with their understanding of the implications of Christian theology in matters of brotherhood, justice, and peace. They are also discovering that the problem runs deeper than mere resistance to committing the institution to programs of social change; the churches themselves have been and continue to be stalwart agents reinforcing and providing legitimacy not only for the status quo but also for prejudice, intolerance, and hatred.

Our culture has at least momentarily retreated from the central struggles for human justice. And in the respite from battle, liberal church leaders are realizing the folks back home supported the enemy all along. Or, in the immortal words of comic-page philosopher Pogo, "I have seen the enemy and they is us."

Some religious leaders are now advocating that the churches should pay attention to survival and maintenance goals at all costs. What seemed a clearly charted course in the mid-sixties, they argue, was an ill-conceived game plan long overdue for the shredding machine. But for a very large proportion of clergy deeply involved in the struggles for social justice during the sixties, the present is a time of confusion, apprehension, and guilt. They know the problems remain. They also know the unfinished business of creating a just social order involves acting upon the structures which breed injustice.

But how are they to act? They know their personal ministries cannot survive direct confrontation strategies. They know their congregations cannot survive continued polarization. The foregoing excerpt from an interview we conducted in mid-1973 with a former "activist" summarizes well what we sense to be the mood of thousands of clergy whose great expectations now lie shattered. They are discontent with the prospect of returning to a privatized, pietistic faith which knows not and cares not for the problems of our society and world.

Perhaps the most distinctive feature of clergy involvement in social action during the 1960s was their acting in groups. "Where two or three were gathered," commitment to act was reinforced and the brainpower to develop strategies was enhanced. In contrast, the struggle of the seventies to find new handles, new strategies for meaningful ministries, has become a very private affair. Loneliness can breed despair. We hope this volume may in some small measure contribute to dialogue and collective strategies for new vistas of involvement.

Concerning This Book

This is a book about a group of turned-on Christians in a conservative midwestern city who haven't found out that the civil rights movement is dead. No one has told them the churches' hands are tied in doing anything about human injustice. They don't know that confrontation politics are at best unproductive and at worst counterproductive. Nor do they seem to have learned that being a "good liberal" no longer requires one to be against poverty, war, and injustice. Their heads are impervious to the proposition that "little people" are helpless to do anything about the policies of the military-industrial-government establishment which make us all angry and a little less human. A few have tried to tell them that sensitivity training, consciousness expansion, personal growth, mysticism, and other such answers are where it's at now for the churches. They've experimented a bit with these things, but none of them makes the adrenaline flow like a good confrontation with a corporate executive or a politician. They keep plugging away on problems nearly everyone else has become resigned to or about.

This is a book about troublemakers. Their tactics are often abrasive. Their strategies are calculated to anger and frustrate. Nearly everyone in the metropolitan area hates their guts. And to add insult to the injury they have caused the proud town of Dayton, Ohio, they call themselves the "Congregation for Reconciliation." A cartoonist for one of the Dayton daily newspapers delights in portraying their pastor, the Rev. Richard Righter, tiptoeing in bare feet, Bible under arm, across the top of an old porcelain bathtub. And one gets the impression there is little affection implied when the group is referred to in the media as the "Congregation for Wreckonciliation."

But a funny thing is happening in Dayton, Ohio: this tiny band of people is winning. No, the armies of the corporate and political structures have not fallen to their knees, but Gideon's gang is still very much in the battle. Moreover, they can claim some proud victories in the long war.

This is not a book to glorify their heroic endeavors. Perhaps someday, if they stay in business long enough, someone will write that book. And perhaps they will deserve the praise. We see them as a group of people who believe in a radical God who gives a damn, a God who has no hands but ours to do his work. They are ordinary human beings: sometimes ingenious and other times rather thick-headed, sometimes altruistic and compassionate and other times struggling and losing in the battle to suppress their egos for a cheap moral victory, sometimes grasping an opportunity and other times failing to see it staring them in the face. Were they otherwise, we would find them uninteresting or have serious doubts as to our abilities to be, in some measure, objective observers. They are people who have earned our respect the hard way. We were hired to be critical evaluators and we took that assignment seriously. But with our presence they were subjected to double jeopardy, for while we share their concerns, we are not by experience, sentiment, or theory social activists. We rather like these people, but we will not make of them wistful heroes. They deserve better.

This congregation is by no means a model which church leaders all over America should attempt to emulate. To the contrary, such a recommendation would be naïve and irresponsible. As we assess the present mood of this nation and the Protestant churches, very few judicatory units in the country could attempt to create this kind of congregation short of suicide. There are, though, special circumstances wherein a similar congregation might exist without deleterious consequences. We will discuss these in the concluding chapter.

Why, you should be asking, do we bother to write a book about a group holding little promise as a model for the future? We offer three answers.

First, we hope the story of the Congregation for Reconciliation will serve to prick the consciences of Protestant leaders, to remind them that the goals to which they dedicated themselves in the sixties are as yet unfulfilled. We know well the problems which befell liberal Protestant leaders for pushing harder on issues of social justice than their laity and fellow clergy were willing to go. But what of the theology which informed their action? Are church leaders, whose zealousness exceeded their skill, to engage in a cover-up to convince themselves the churches ought not be concerned about social justice except insofar as it is a by-product of changing men's hearts? We hope not.

Our second objective in writing about this experimental social-action congregation is to focus on hope for the involvement of the churches in the struggles for social justice. Those who wallowed in the political process during the sixties learned about the inextricable relationship between social structures and life chances. They now know the unfinished business of creating a just social order involves acting upon the structures which breed injustice. A whole ministry, thus, must serve as more than a first aid or comfort station to the victims of the injustices of institutional arrangements. Nor can the churches continue to pursue schizophrenic policies which legitimize ignorance and indifference to structural injustice while simultaneously attacking that which it has condoned with monies from the same offering plate.

The churches' role in the years ahead must of necessity, we believe, be in substantial measure educational—but education as more than a shibboleth to cover a multitude of sins and failures. The churches cannot be content to label as educational that which fails, by objective criteria of evaluation, to make a difference. Black militant leaders, who in the late sixties told white liberals to help by going home to work in their own communities, were right. The challenge still stands. In fact, we scarcely comprehend the nature of the tasks implicit in the challenge, much less the magnitude of the assignment. But this is the business at hand for liberal Protestants who profess a desire to reduce racism, poverty, injustice, and whatever else they embrace under the banner of liberalism. Until unambiguous evidence confirms that those inside the churches are more vitally committed to the Christian ideal of concern for one's fellowman than the man in the street, liberal Protestantism has fallen short.

We are deeply concerned that liberal Protestants not run away from the task. They must find ways to change people and structures without tearing the church apart, a heavy assignment. There seems to be a growing feeling that the only options are radical social action or retreat to personal pietism, that the comfort and challenge roles are incompatible. We reject such simplistic thinking.

The story of the Congregation for Reconciliation illumines other options in a variety of ways. It is a story of a group of people too put out with traditional forms of congregational life to have anything to do with other churches in the metropolitan area, thereby rejecting one of the two principal goals the congregation's initiators intended. It is a story of other pastors so frightened by social action that they missed a golden opportunity to interpret the activities of the Congregation for Reconciliation, and thus an opportunity to educate and to enhance understanding of the problems the total metropolitan community faced. It is also a story of pastors so threatened by the prospect of losing their own few socially conscious people that they missed an opportunity to multiply the number several fold. In short, the lessons about what didn't happen are every bit as important as the converse. This case study is pregnant with lessons about that which might have been, opportunities which involved neither confrontation nor retreat.

Our third objective in writing this book is to add one small piece to a very large puzzle liberal church leaders must fit together. Liberal Protestantism in America has fallen on hard times, and most church leaders now know this. But they do not agree as to exactly what the present falling barometers purport. To some, present declines in membership, church attendance, benevolences, etc., reflect an inevitable pattern of recession, normal after the long period of growth and development following World War II. A few even see the present trends as healthy and desirable purgation. Most, however, see cause for concern and even anxiety.

Two factors, especially, lend substance for anxiety. First, American society may be "catching up" with the process of secularization which defoliated many European churches decades ago. A very large proportion of the American population, according to this thesis, lacks deep religious commitment, and the cultural options created by our rising level of affluence and leisure entice away marginal participants. The second issue is the saturation and resentment of growing numbers of lay persons with the liberal pronouncements and policies of their professional leadership. Whether these persons in some measure account for the growth of conservative churches or have rather chosen to neither fight nor switch, their disenchantment has led to many empty pews and shrinking bankrolls.

In spite of a very rapid growth in the volume of social scientific studies of religion during the past decade, the field remains undernourished, and critically important issues are not as yet illumined with sufficient scientific data to interpret them confidently.

Social scientists themselves argue about the meaning of the sparse data. Although church records are notoriously unreliable, no one, to our knowledge, argues that the present impression of decline arises from insubstantial data. Consensus does exist that decline, whatever its reasons or meaning, is real. The post-World War II boom in church members, with its accouterments of proliferating building programs, bureaucratic specialization of institutional structures, and rosy optimism about the future, has now ended for liberal Protestantism.

The anxiety felt is heightened by the absence of data and the uncertainty of appropriate theories, models, or analogies for interpreting what has happened or for sketching the morrow. In this age of discontinuity, where knowledge has become the principal asset for dealing with the future, the churches have little reserve capital. Although complex, the reasons for this can be summed up in two interrelated propositions: (1) social scientists have focused little attention on religion and (2) religious institutions have invested preciously few resources in seeking self-knowledge. Further, the churches' limited investments in research, by and large, reflect bad judgment. All too often the principal criterion in engaging a researcher has been the individual's loyalty to the institutional church. Competence to conduct research has received only cursory notice. As a result, much of the existing literature is thinly veiled public relations propaganda to legitimize programs determined before the investigations were ever conducted.

While the churches could, without increasing their knowledge-gaining capacity or their utilization of knowledge, stumble through this critical period of institutional decline and emerge only slightly scarred, those are high gamblers' odds. Whatever else religious institutions may claim, they are voluntary associations competing in a pluralistic society for finite resources. To rely on providence to rescue religious institutions from their present nose dive, without their digging in and utilizing the various knowledge-acquiring capacities of the social-behavioral sciences, stretches credibility.

The claims and hopes for social scientific inquiry have been heralded beyond reality by some. But every exaggerated claim can be paralleled by many instances of premature delimiting of the parameters of social scientific inquiry before the possibilities were understood. Social science offers only one of many legitimate means for gaining significant knowledge about the life of religious institutions. It alone can never be sufficient, but we have entered an age where it is indispensable. Without a solid base of empirical knowledge, no institution can formulate conscientious plans and policies for the future.

CHAPTER 2

Crucible of Crisis:
Background of the Congregation

Understanding the creation of the Congregation for Reconciliation demands recalling the milieu of our society in the spring of 1968. For four years the nation had experienced "long hot summers" of violence and upheaval, and there seemed little reason to believe that the heat would not once again ignite the smoldering nerve ends locked in ghettos across the land. Born in the early 1960s, the hopes and dreams for cracking the barriers to racial justice now seemed crushed by hundreds of outbursts, rebellions, and riots in urban America. The mood of the country was shifting dramatically from sympathy for the causes espoused by the civil rights movement toward determination to legislate against riots and uncover organized conspiracies. The short-lived War on Poverty was already faltering badly, while in Southeast Asia another war, draining the national treasury as well as the collective will to deal with domestic problems, continued to escalate.

There were other moods in the wind as well. As we moved from the mid to the late 1960s, the concepts of power and powerlessness came increasingly into vogue. Such labels as "black power" and "student power" reflected the ambitions of those groups for more control over their own destinies. An anticolonialism term, "liberation," also came to encompass movements such as Women's Liberation and Gay Liberation. During the heyday of the War on Poverty, the phrase "maximum feasible participation" signified an attempt to bring recipients of government spending into the decision-making process. Simultaneously, students on campuses across the nation confronted university administrators with demands for a greater voice in academic affairs under the rationale of "humanizing" the bureaucracy. The goal was the reduction of impersonal formal organizational structures and the attainment of greater accountability from large organizations to their clients or patrons. Ralph Nader's consumer advocacy, arguing that consumers should hold business accountable for its products and by-products, reflected the same mood.

The cry for "power to the people" may have been tainted by its association with the Black Panthers, but nonetheless that sentiment expressed the core of the political ideology this country has had since the eighteenth century, harking back, in essence, to "Taxation without representation is tyranny."

In the 1960s, however, the tyrant role fell not to colonial rulers but to the elites of institutional bureaucracies. Formal organization, like a modern plague, had spread to infest almost every aspect of life. Decision-making moved further and further from those whose lives were affected. And unlike politicians who can be called to account periodically, most of the decision-makers were practically unreachable, nestling in the remote, mysterious, and villainous "power structure."

In this context, the "solution" of *decentralization* sprouted and soon grew to panacea proportions. There are those scholars, of course, who have argued that large organizations, for survival's sake, must decentralize, become more adaptive and responsive to their members, and allow greater participation in decision-making. They see this necessity as created by the need to respond to turbulent environments, by the continued professionalization of lower management, and by the dependence upon technocracy (scientists and engineers) in some large organizations.[1] The "Beyond Bureaucracy" thinkers form the science fiction wing of organizational scholarship, and, like science fiction writers in general, they are prone to moralistic and idealistic flights of fancy about the ability of man to triumph over bureaucracy.[2] More importantly, however, they are welcome prophets reflecting a cultural mood, a national longing.

In the real world, organizational power yields only to counter-power. Dissatisfaction with organizational policy or products, whether from workers, clients, or the public at large, is ignored as long as possible. Only when the dissatisfaction generates its own power base does it merit attention, and the likely response of organizational leadership is a public relations campaign to legitimize standard procedure and discredit opposition.

Studies of debureaucratization are scattered throughout the scholarly literature. Summarizing several of these, Katz and Eisenstadt cite a tendency to relax hierarchical authority in the presence of physical danger and isolation.[3] Both these conditions make superiors more dependent upon their subordinates. And dependency, they argue, forces superiors to rely more upon personal means of motivating compliance than upon authoritarian directives.

In industry, unionization has created a degree of dependency of management upon labor. For clients, customers, and the public at large, however, there is seldom any coordinated process for redress of grievances against corporate irresponsibility. When watchdog and advocacy structures emerge, such as regulatory agencies in government or groups designed to handle public complaints, organizations ordinarily attempt to infiltrate them and neutralize their effectiveness. Thus the emerging public sentiment favoring the enforcement of corporate responsibility has been continually stymied by mechanisms for protecting the incumbent power.

Such was the national cultural milieu in which the Congregation for Reconciliation was established. The traditional conservative environment of Dayton, Ohio, provided no immunity to the tremors which rocked our society. If anything, Dayton's conservative past may have exacerbated the community's difficulties in coming to grips with the problems it faced.

Dayton, at the beginning of this decade, was a city of 243,600 residents. Including its suburbs, the Standard Metropolitan Statistical Area (SMSA) boasted a population of over 850,000, with a median household income of $12,343. Dayton, the historical home of the Wright brothers, is a leader in aviation research and home of Wright-Patterson Air Force Base, one of the largest air installations in the world. Although General Motors is the single largest industrial employer, and National Cash Register has its corporate offices here, the city has a diversified industrial base producing paper, rubber, air conditioners, refrigerators, aircraft instruments, accounting machines, and machine tools.

The city population grew steadily with each census report from the turn of the century until 1970, when it fell to just under the 1950 level. This overall trend, however, masks important racial differences. During the postwar years, the black population increased more rapidly than the total city population. In 1950 blacks constituted 14 percent of Dayton residents; this percentage grew to 22 in 1960 and 31 in 1970. But while blacks were almost a third of the city population in 1970, they were only 11 percent of the SMSA. Their percentage in the surrounding suburbs ranged from .2 to 12, with most clustered at the lower end of the range.

This picture is by no means uncommon to urban America. Dayton, like most industrial centers, has a heavy concentration of black population in the inner city, surrounded by lily-white suburbs.

Racial income differentials also follow the usual pattern. In 1970, the median income of black families was 71 percent of the median for the total SMSA. Seventeen percent of black families earned incomes below the poverty level in 1970, almost triple the percentage for all families in the SMSA.

Nor was Dayton immune to the turbulence which swept through urban ghettos during the mid 1960s. Three times during the summers of 1966 and 1967 Dayton's ghettos erupted in violence serious enough to receive the attention of the McClellan Riot Hearings.[4] The first incident occurred on September 15, 1966, when a black resident was shot and killed by a passing motorist, alleged to be white. This prompted looting and vandalism and three cases of arson. Unprepared, local authorities had to call in the National Guard to restore order. Fifty-four persons were arrested; four civilians were injured. A second incident, again involving looting, vandalism, and six cases of arson, occurred in mid-June of 1967 and resulted in estimated property damage of $200,000. The alleged precipitating event this time was an inflammatory address by militant civil rights leader H. Rap Brown.

Dayton remained tense throughout the summer. Then, on September 19 of the same year, a protest rally following a police shooting of an unarmed black resident resulted in the third civil disturbance within a twelve-month period. For three days there were sporadic incidents of arson and looting. When this outburst ended, 203 persons had been arrested and seven had been injured, including two policemen. In short, Dayton knew the tremors of racial conflict at first hand.

In a *Dayton Daily News* editorial just days before the final eruption, the editor decried the patterns of residential segregation isolating black and white citizens from one another. Pleading for breaking out from educational, social, and residential ghettos, he concluded, "There is a constituency for change in the suburbs, probably wider than most suspect. It is vague now, unformed. It can be brought together and put to work. That requires leadership. Who will provide it? Where, in God's name, are the churches?"

Throughout the 1960s, religious leaders of America had played an increasingly progressive and aggressive role in multiple struggles for social justice. The resolutions of the 1950s had given way to action in the 1960s.[5] This heightened level of involvement would eventually lead to disenchantment with clerical activities and result in significant backlash within the institutional church, but in 1968 the ideals of ministering to social ills still rallied ever greater involvement. The aura of crisis and the spotlights on injustice pushed more and more church leaders toward greater commitment to immerse the institutional church, with its power and pocketbook, in the struggle for brotherhood. In the context of this chaos, the supports for the Congregation for Reconciliation were created.

Where Are the Churches?:
Denominational Response to Crisis

In a very real sense, the Congregation for Reconciliation was the Miami (Ohio) Presbytery's response to the editorial cry of the *Dayton Daily News*. Within a year Richard Righter was in Dayton organizing the mission. Although the city had been bitterly polarized by the series of riots, a renewed sense of urgency to deal with underlying problems pervaded some sectors. Righter sought these pockets of support during his first month in town. The soil and climate of Dayton appeared favorable for rooting a congrega-

41

tion devoted to promoting social change and racial reconciliation.

The Congregation for Reconciliation emerged from cooperative efforts of local, state, and national divisions of the United Presbyterian Church in the United States of America. The context of internal developments within the Presbyterian Church affected the very possibility of a specifically social-action congregation in much the same way as did the activities in the streets. In 1966, Presbyterians approved the first major revision of their confession of faith since the Westminster Confession of Faith had been adopted in 1647. Though *The Confession of 1967* had been on the drawing board for almost a decade, the heightened sense of crisis during the 1960s most assuredly gave it new direction and urgency.

The Confession served two important and interrelated functions. First, it provided unambiguous legitimacy for involvement in the struggle for social justice. It is explicit in stating that the churches' role goes beyond ministering to the victims of injustice and changing the hearts and minds of individuals responsible for injustice. Rather, *The Confession* makes clear the responsibility of the corporate church to act against the social structures of society which perpetuate injustice and inequality. *Duty* to act thus becomes the second consequence of *The Confession*. The church and its leadership not only have the right to be involved but, if true to their faith, they are also obligated to be involved.[6] The following passages (with our emphasis added) underscore the merging of the legitimacy to act upon the perceived social crisis of the 1960s with the duties of faith:

The members of the church are emissaries of peace and seek the good of man in cooperation with powers and authorities in politics, culture, and economics. *But they have to fight against pretensions and injustices when these same powers endanger human welfare.* . . .

In each time and place there are particular problems and crises through which God calls the church to act. The church . . . seeks to discern the will of God and learn how to obey in these *concrete situations.* . . .

God has created the peoples of the earth to be one universal family. In his reconciling love he overcomes the barriers between brothers and breaks down every form of discrimination based on racial or ethnic differences, real or imaginary. . . . *Therefore the church labors for the abolition of all racial discrimination and ministers to those injured by it. Congregations, individuals, or groups of Christians who exclude, dominate, or patronize their fellowmen, however subtly, resist the Spirit of God and bring contempt on the faith they profess.* . . .

The reconciliation of man through Jesus makes it plain that *enslaving poverty in a world of abundance is an intolerable violation of God's good creation.* Because Jesus identified himself with the needy and exploited, the cause of the world's poor is the cause of his disciples. *The church cannot condone poverty*, whether it is *the product of unjust social structures*, exploitation of the defenseless, lack of national resources, absence of technological understanding, or rapid expansions of populations. . . . *A church that is indifferent to poverty*, or evades responsibility in economic affairs, or is open to one social class only, or expects gratitude for its beneficence *makes a mockery of reconciliation and offers no acceptable worship to God.* . . .

The church responds to the message of reconciliation in praise and prayer. In that response it *commits itself afresh to its mission*, experiences a deepening of faith and obedience, and bears open testimony to the gospel.[7]

In 1967 a task force organized by the Board of National Missions and entrusted with the goal of devising new church development policies issued a pamphlet entitled "Strategies for the Development of New Congregations." [8] This publication proposed the testing of the thesis that the congregation can be an "effective organizational form for the ministry of the church in the face of tremendous social change." [9] It encouraged the development of experimental missions of a goal-oriented, flexible, and ecumenical nature, and oriented toward interest and involvement.

The thrust of this document is clearly toward challenge rather than comfort. It urged avoidance of the excessive concern with survival which characterizes most new missions: "Size and safety are not the basic issues. To follow Christ in the life-structures of this society, to probe the foundations of Christian service, to build a witnessing community responsive to God's reconciling work—these should be the goals of the 'new' congregations." [10]

Even more important than discouraging emphasis upon survival goals, the document called for active concern in what *The Confession of 1967* had identified as the central task of the church—the process of reconciliation, defined by the task force as "the breaking down of those barriers which separate God and man." [11] But it expressed equal concern with the "forces of evil that divide men from each other and produce enslavement, hostility, and alienation in the world." [12] Furthermore, as with *The Confession of 1967*, this document insisted that reconciliation cannot be equated with peace, for "peace for one side rooted in injustice for the other side represents an unjust relationship and not reconciliation according to the Gospel of Jesus Christ." [13] In short, "new" missions would be actively involved in the world even to the extent of "relationships of hostility and conflict." [14] The thesis of the congregation as a potentially viable vehicle for the prophetic work of the church in social action stood to be tested.

Finally, the document charged the judicatory with the responsibility for developing plans for the new congregations so that "their ministries are interrelated with the ministries of other [established] congregations." [15] Although they were to be given flexibility sufficient to respond to changing needs, these task-oriented congregations were to do nothing separately which might be done cooperatively and jointly with the established churches. Interdependence and unity in mission were the stated structural goals.

Don't Just Stand There:
The Miami Presbytery Responds

During the postwar expansion period, the Miami Presbytery, following national denominational strategy, had concentrated on new church development in the suburbs. Many of the new congregations established during the early 1960s, however, were running into hard times. A new congregation was allowed five years to develop its membership base before being asked to shoulder complete responsibilities for the cost of its building and ministry. Not uncommonly, however, these congregations were not growing rapidly enough in five years to handle their financial obligations alone and were thus so engrossed in the task of survival that they lost perspective on their missions.

By 1967, the issue of expansion and development had led the Miami Presbytery to seek new directions in the establishment of congregations. When the local National Missions Committee considered the proposal in the national strategy document, they responded positively. Many of the dilemmas of support and survival for a new congregation could be circumvented by the simple scheme of bringing people together around social problems, investing minimally in property and possessions, and relying on mutual goals and activities to sustain congregational life and spirit. The mood of the moment pointed unwaveringly to the racial crisis as a rallying issue for Christian involvement.

Following the guidelines and recommendations of the Board of National Missions, the Miami Presbytery's National Missions Committee devised a plan for an experimental congregation and urged the Presbytery to support the temporary establishment of such a mission "with a like commitment to strive for racial reconciliation both within the Church and within society." [16]

The strategists developing the design for the new congregation assumed that those members of established congregations oriented toward social action could find few opportunities for action programs within the existing churches. They were likely to have neither the support group nor the freedom of action required to sustain long-term commitment to such missions. An issue-oriented congregation, however, could provide both. The planners also assumed that the right congregational design would attract a sufficient number of action-oriented lay persons from existing churches to create a viable support group. From the more than 10,000 communicants in the Dayton churches, certainly the recruitment of a Gideon's army of two or three dozen would present no problem. One of the strategy goals, therefore, was to develop a congregation attractive to social activists, thereby encouraging and endorsing a program for substantial impact upon the city and its racial crisis.

The committee also incorporated a second goal of the national strategy paper into their proposal. They stressed a need for the interdependence of the new congregation with the established church for two basic reasons. First, by this means a certain amount of financial support must be forthcoming from the Presbytery. Second, and more important, other churches within the Presbytery would thus be forced to face the implications of the maverick congregation. Connected closely, as a brother congregation, the inevitable tension would need to be confronted and reckoned with by the established congregations. The founding of a congregation specifically to deal with the Christian faith in direct relation to social issues expressed the Presbytery's commitment to this as an important objective. Further, it was assumed that such a congregation would take unpopular stands and become embroiled in controversy, thus challenging the other churches within the Presbytery to consider the social problems raised. Being under the Presbytery's auspices, the new congregation would be a thorn which could not be ignored.

The documents developed in February and March of 1968 by the National Missions Committee of the Miami Presbytery reflected their focal goals. If the church were to take a role in healing the wounds of social injustice and in restructuring the system for the benefit of all men, those church members interested in social change needed the structural freedom necessary to be effective, "for at present there are few places in the church where those who recognize the need for such adjustments have the necessary influence to bring them about." Further, they underscored the theme of interdependence and unity in mission by commissioning the congregation to "explore ways of involving other congregations in social action and, as far as possible, establish cooperative action programs with them." [17]

As the proposal of the National Missions Committee began to travel the conversation route within the Presbytery, significant opposition arose. The fire, however, came not from conservative clergy and lay leaders but rather from younger and more liberal clergy who immediately recognized the potential siphoning off of the few kindred spirits in their congregations. In retrospect, this normal response should have been anticipated. The threat of losing those few lay persons who supported a ministry of social witness, and thereby managed the Herculean task of maintaining the precarious symbolic universes of their clergy, rallied the more liberal ministers to defend their position. Without these lay persons to support them on the battlefronts of their own congregational ground, even mild attempts to introduce social concerns would lose legitimacy and plausibility. To surrender their soldiers would be tantamount to losing the war of Christian relevancy. And certainly no congregation even approached having an abundance of action-oriented laity.

In a direct maneuver to counter the opposition from liberal clergy, a second document of the National Missions Committee, dated April 16, 1968, elevated the language of cooperation. As envisioned, the new mission would "provide for the Presbytery and established congregations a 'training ground' for members of committees and congregations to learn the methods of direct social action, or to explore the possibilities of supportive ministries in the racial crisis." [18] The final description of the proposed congregation even further escalated the significance of service goals. The Congregation for Reconciliation would "develop a group of skilled communicators, educators, technicians, and planners *for use by local churches,* Presbytery, ecumenical, or secular organizations" [19] (italics added). Conceived as a temporary experiment with a life expectancy of three or four years, the new congregation would have an absolute commitment to a nonbuilding program. Presumably this would leave members, unencumbered by the strong financial pressures of building debts, freer to move in and out, back to their 'home' churches. In addition, "the Presbytery [would] encourage the sessions of established congregations to recruit members with careful attention to the fact that they should plan to relate back to the congregation from which they came if at all possible." [20]

By carefully structuring the proposal, the National Missions Committee tried to avert the possibility of their plan passing in the Presbytery but receiving no cooperation from the liberal clergy or their sympathetic laity. This, they realized, would be most unfair to the organizing pastor, and therefore they presented a palatable package to assure a favorable vote and support afterward.

On April 16, 1968, they got the favorable vote, but not only because of their straining so hard to win approval. The larger world also encroached on the Presbytery and pricked consciences.

Martin Luther King, Jr., had been killed; the *Report of the National Advisory Commission on Civil Disorders* (the Kerner Report) had been issued. Racism was the headline of the day. As one supporter of the proposal put it, "In this context, we could have gotten anything approved. There was so much guilt in the churches, so much feeling that we had to do something."

This desperate sense of the need to act, to do something, may have provided the final push needed to give birth to the Congregation for Reconciliation. But as we shall see, this mood resulted in creating an experimental group without clearly coming to grips with what this meant. The several working papers left much ambiguity as to the goals and expectations for the new church. This ambiguity would provide the organizing pastor and his people the flexibility to "do their thing." It would also prove a source of conflict as the Congregation moved in directions that some did not anticipate, nor think they had approved, when they voted to create the experimental group.

Summary

We have seen that the three historical roots of the experimental social-action congregation were the racial crisis of the 1960s, the Confession of 1967, and the emergence of an official denominational strategy for the development of new nonresidential, issue-centered congregations. Dayton, suffering from the same racial inequities characteristic of most other American cities, and having experienced urban disorders in 1966 and 1967, was a logical setting for the establishment of such an experimental congregation designed to concentrate its energy on the complex problem of racial reconciliation.

The rush to action by the Miami Presbytery, however, produced ambiguities in design and left insufficient time to lay the groundwork to ensure orderly development in keeping with the formally accepted goals of the mission.

CHAPTER 3

In the Beginning:
The Genesis of the Congregation

Creating an experimental congregation is a project fraught with perils. The process from drawing board to formal establishment looms heavy with pitfalls, each threatening abortion. The blueprint of the designers with its expression of their ambition, their choice of an organizing pastor with his own particular vision, talent, and interpretation of goals, and the charter members' individual expectations of the functioning and value of such a group offer a wide diversity of potential directions. Each of these contributors to the creation—the designers, the organizer, the participants—seminally influences what can or will happen. Early patterns narrow alternatives and establish a momentum which will dictate future developments. The character, personality, and mission of the congregation will be molded by the priorities, skills, and style of its three parents interacting within the limitations of environment and happenstance.

What develops through this process of interaction may or may not be as initially designed. A reality must be defined by those who operate within it. The social construction of such a reality is a dynamic process quite antithetical to the analogy of a builder following a blueprint. The construction of a reality capable of generating both life purpose for individuals and task-focused mission and meaning for the collectivity is a far more complex operation.

Calling a Pastor

In the spring of 1968, the Miami Presbytery received approval from the denomination's Board of National Missions for the new congregation. They also got a promise of financial support on a declining basis for the proposed three-year life of the congregation. To express its central concern and raison d'être, the Presbytery named the newly approved mission the Congregation for Reconciliation.

During the next months the New Church Development Subcommittee of the National Missions Committee interviewed several prospective organizing pastors. In late June, after considering several others, the committee invited the Rev. Richard Righter, a pastor in Philadelphia, for an interview. Reared in the San Francisco area, Righter had attended the University of California at Berkeley for his undergraduate degree and had continued for a Master's in Business Administration. After seminary he had interned in an inner-city church in San Francisco before accepting the call to a racially transitional inner-city church in Philadelphia. Righter was an appealing candidate. First, he had a strong track record for involvement in social action in previous pastorates and, second, he had an intense concern with the development of lay leadership skills. In discussing this point with the committee, Righter insisted that the pastor should play a low-key role relative to lay leadership.

The committee was impressed. They anticipated that the experiment would attract strong people with diverse ideas and felt an authoritarian pastor would build destruction into the system. As one committeeman told us, they feared that a pastor who insisted on running the show would trigger an explosion when confronted by a membership of hard-nosed activists: "They would just blow each other out of the water almost immediately. Everybody would leave or else the pastor would have to change his style."

Righter had studied the design passed by the Presbytery and had anticipated some hard bargaining. Eagerness to attempt such an experiment never overrode his rational interest and reservations. The proposal, as approved, provided for a three- to four-year experiment. The design called for three years of financial support, decreasing by one third each year, and had deliberately left the impression of a temporary rather than a permanent experiment. The committee had emphasized impermanence so that the congregation, if it failed to take root and become self-supporting, could be ended with little flak. If the congregation did survive, however, the committee was in a position to consider the possibility of continuation at that time. Righter argued the possibility of permanence. He assumed survival and wanted assurance that the congregation would not be arbitrarily immolated after four years. Receiving this commitment, Righter accepted the call and became pastor of the Congregation for Reconciliation.

Passive Resistance to Early Organizational Efforts

The Righters moved to Dayton the first week in September 1968. The Presbytery had publicized the new congregation in its newsletter and had requested pastors to encourage selected members to consider participation on an experimental basis. When Righter arrived, the Presbytery had a list of twenty prospective members. To the best of Righter's recollection, none of these candidates were actually referred by pastors. Our own interviews with a sample of local pastors also failed to reveal any nominees or referrals. Most, if not all, of the list resulted from the initiative of the individuals themselves, and most of these people cited a front-page newspaper article in April as their primary source of information about the proposed congregation.

During his first week in Dayton, both daily newspapers interviewed Righter and wrote feature articles on the new congregation. This coverage produced additional calls from individuals expressing interest. With these two lists in hand, Righter proceeded to call on his prospective members. Also during his initial weeks in Dayton, Righter visited each of the Presbyterian ministers in the metropolitan area. He described the purpose of his calls as "simply to get acquainted, to personally relate to them and possibly see ways we might be able to cooperate." Righter reports that he did not ask any of them for members from their congregations, nor did any of them volunteer any of their people. This also is corroborated by our own interviews with local pastors.[1] The fears of the National Missions Committee were thus early confirmed. Although the antagonism to the establishment of an experimental congregation had been overcome by the rhetoric of cooperation in the planning documents, the support of local clergymen in the organization of the congregation did not emerge. Passive resistance had replaced active opposition.

In September and early October, Righter organized three meetings in separate areas of the city for those interested in the new congregation. Approximately ten people attended each of these informal meetings, planned only to provide people with an opportunity to meet other prospective members and to share their views as to the nature of the congregation they would like to see emerge. Righter reports the main interest expressed in these meetings was the desire to meet participants in other areas of the city. So, on the third Sunday evening in October, the three groups met together. This meeting further served the function of getting acquainted. No organizational matters were discussed beyond the agreement to hold monthly meetings.

During these initial weeks in Dayton, Righter also made a concerted effort to familiarize himself with the metropolitan area and its problems. He obtained and studied a wide range of research reports on such subjects as demography, race relations, housing, employment, tax structure, utilities, transportation, and business activities. He attended meetings of the City Commission, the Board of Education, and other public groups. He also attempted to meet community leaders, and he cultivated and nourished his initial contacts with the news media. His contacts with journalists continued to provide publicity for the new mission. Equally important, these contacts proved to be an important source of information on community issues and problems. Later, they offered strategic information on issues with which the Congregation became involved.

In summary, Righter's first weeks as organizer of the Congregation for Reconciliation were busy ones. It is probably unfair to describe them as ordinary first weeks for an organizing pastor. In our assessment, Righter went about his work in a highly systematic, disciplined, and professional manner hardly typical of pastors in a new community. One church administrator told us, "Righter had learned more about metropolitan Dayton in a few weeks' time than I had known after a year. . . . He seemed to know how to get around and get the information he wanted." These research skills later became both vital assets in the development of action projects and a routine part of action leadership training in the Congregation.

. . . And Ask Questions Later:
Instant Action Without Organization

The October meeting, while pursuing little more discussion of organization beyond an agreement to meet again, began the Congregation for Reconciliation. Before the next regularly scheduled meeting, some of the participants had already started planning their first social-action project. This apparent lack of concern with the imperatives of formal organization significantly set the mood and the style which became characteristic of the Congregation.

This congregation's reckless abandon of survival-oriented goals stands in sharp contrast to the "typical" life-style of new congregations. An excellent study of six new congregations conducted in 1964 by sociologist Donald Metz documented what every socially conscious church executive already knew: new congregations typically concentrate on one goal, their own survival.[2] The paramount structure and symbol of their viability is the construction of a church building. Closely related to this is the recruitment of new members, essential for financing the edifice. While new congregations typically have formal charters expressing goals relative to their theological heritage, to the nurture of community and spiritual life of the members, and to mission or service, Metz found all these insignificant compared with survival-oriented imperatives.

The lack of concern with formal organization and other survival-oriented tasks among the first participants in the Congregation for Reconciliation is partially explained by the initial conception of the church by the Miami Presbytery. The strategy paper from the Board of National Missions stated that "from the beginning the entire life of the [new] congregation [is to] be geared to its mission task."[3] And the Presbytery committee had explicitly forbidden the Congregation to build or purchase a building. But these directives cannot adequately account for the almost total lack of concern with basic organizational imperatives among the participants of the group. As we shall see, the Congregation has typically dealt with organizational and financial matters only when they have become so pressing as no longer to permit oversight. Structurally, this conflicts with Righter's strong desire to establish a durable, self-supporting congregation. Yet he has seldom, if ever, portrayed survival and social-action goals as in conflict. This would indeed have been a self-defeating strategy during the initial organizational period.

While clearly not true of everyone, many of those who attended the first meeting were intensely interested in social action. Indeed, for some, Righter's credibility rested on his willingness to engage in immediate social action. The tasks of formal organization could wait. This seems to have presented no problem for Righter, as his instincts and impulses lay in the same direction. The group needed more immediately to prove to themselves and to the community their seriousness about social action. But, we should also add, this sense of urgency to act was not at all out of proportion to the mood of many socially conscious people in America at this time.

Their first social-action project, which Righter and some of the participants had begun planning before their November meeting, was to be a supportive action of a group of black employees, the "Second Family," at the National Cash Register Corporation. This group had been actively working against discriminatory hiring practices at NCR. At the November meeting of the Congregation, a proposal to assist the Second Family was presented and an ad hoc committee was formed to meet with both the leaders of the Second Family and executives of NCR. The NCR officials refused to meet with the committee. In early December, the Congregation printed Christmas cards protesting discrimination against minority groups and, on the morning of December 19, handed out 600 of them to white employees at the gates of the NCR administration building. Their activity received television, radio, and newspaper coverage.

The first foray into social action is very significant for several reasons. First, by choosing a major corporation of Dayton as its target, the Congregation from the beginning set itself in opposition to the powerful business community. For those hesitant about participating out of concern that the Congregation might be "too timid," this gesture offered reassurance the group would tackle "the establishment."

This initial action was equally significant in restricting the range of support and participation in the Congregation. Those constituting the initial informal leadership were not content to pursue action seen as "respectable" by community and business leaders. If they were to work with the establishment, it would be on the terms of the Congregation and not vice versa. Thus, those who were either members of the business leadership or who occupied positions in which they felt threatened by identification with the Congregation were virtually eliminated as prospective members. Three or four middle-range corporate executives had been involved in the early life of the Congregation, but they all dropped out. These people offered reasons other than their fear of reprisal, but the evidence of social science overwhelmingly attests that people seldom become actively involved and identified with activities threatening to their financial security.[4] At least one of these corporate executives has continued to provide modest financial subsidy and another has lent support through the Presbytery, but the controversial style of the Congregation barred their visible association with the group.

Individuals at the core of the Congregation are, consequently, persons with the *structural freedom* to participate; they are either self-employed or hold jobs sufficiently insulated from local politics. This has been particularly true of the leaders of social-action projects, that is, those exposed to publicity. Often they have been women whose husbands hold jobs relatively unthreatened by such social activism.

This initial action against NCR also served notice to business and political leaders that power would not ensure safety from attack by this religious group. So, from the onset, community leaders who defined all confrontation or protest politics as "too radical" characterized the Congregation as a group of extremist reformers and potential adversaries.

Another important aspect of this initial social action was its establishment of a modus operandi for involvement which has since continued largely unchanged. Projects are suggested by one or more members of the Congregation, whereupon interested members are encouraged by Righter to form a committee for research and action. Though a committee seeks approval before undertaking action in the Congregation's name, the green light almost always flashes, and a "do your own thing" ethic combined with an emphasis upon tolerance has generally prevailed.

This ad hoc strategy seems a conscious device for diffusing and hence creating effective lay leadership within the Congregation and for dealing with the diversity of interests and orientations. But it has also been an effective device for furthering the power and influence of the activist core within the mission; those most interested in social action have created for themselves a situation of maximum freedom.

The first action project demonstrated Righter's leadership as it had appealed to the New Church Development Subcommittee which had called him to organize the new congregation. He had at once demonstrated his ability as action strategist and developer of lay leadership. He had thereby legitimated himself in the eyes of the committee, although, no doubt, without design.

. . . And Now You Come at Noon: Organizational Postponement Analyzed

Throughout their first year the Congregation's level of involvement in social action escalated while its organizational activity lagged. In January and February of 1969, committees were set up to organize various aspects of the Congregation's life. Regularly scheduled meetings evolved into three types still being used by the Congregation—*celebrations* (liturgy and communion organized around various social issues), *family festivals* (five-hour get-togethers involving communal meals, games, and fellowship, often in the form of picnics or outings), and *house church* (Bible study and communion). In addition, a group meets periodically to pray and share personal concerns.

In addition to this minimal structure, the Congregation established a temporary budget and a committee to pursue formal organization. However, little progress was made until January of 1970, apparently for at least three reasons. First, as already mentioned, the Congregation and Righter directed their attention to the formal goal of social action and avoided concern with survival goals. They preferred to demonstrate to outsiders that they "meant business." But this avoidance of such survival-oriented activity as recruitment and financial stabilization has continued as a dominant theme in the Congregation's life. The presence of other clearly defined formal goals and the directly expressed concern of the Miami Presbytery that they not become survival-oriented only partially explain the avoidance of this common path. Perhaps more important was the antiorganizational bias of many of the mission members themselves. Having witnessed what they felt was exclusive preoccupation with survival-oriented activity in their former churches, they determined not to follow suit in their new congregation.

A second major reason for delay seems to have been the desire, consciously or unconsciously, to avoid potentially divisive issues. From the onset the Congregation contained two latent groups. The first quite self-consciously viewed themselves within the Christian tradition and, although interested in social action and experimental worship, wished to maintain much of the traditional Christian language. The second group encompassed self-consciously secular humanists who viewed the institutional church as a viable organization for working toward social justice. We do not mean to imply a derogatory using of the church for their own goals. Rather, most of them probably philosophically saw the Christian tradition on the side of social justice, and hence it made every sense to align themselves with it. But their theology, to the extent that they had any, consisted in a loosely formulated Christian agnosticism or atheism, and they adamantly avoided "God-talk." While Righter's own theology leans more toward the conservative, he did not insist on imposing his views or making the affirmation of any specific Christian doctrine a prerequisite for participation in the group. While they were in the minority, secular humanists were among the most vocal and active of the participants.[5]

Recognizing the diversity of religious orientations within the group, the Congregation, by preoccupying themselves with social action, avoided the sensitive task of drawing up a statement of mission and postponed the needed reconciliation within their own ranks. Though social action also elicited some controversy, the division came mainly between the aggressive core and the marginal participants. In contrast, the division over religious orientation cut through the social-action hierarchy of the group and presented more of a threat.

The third reason for delay in formal organization relates to the second. It involved difficulty with the affiliation requirements of the Presbyterian Church. Not only did they insist that members ascribe to various doctrinal truths but they also demanded that the authority of the Congregation be delegated to a "session," or board of elders. The humanists, of course, were not prepared to affirm the minimal statement of faith, nor was the Congregation willing to be ruled by a session. Policy matters had from the beginning been discussed and voted on by the entire congregation; this decision-making style suited the temperament of the group far better than a representative style.

That early divisions within the Congregation made formal organization a difficult task was readily acknowledged in most of our interviews. Since we do not consider folklore adequate documentation, however, we searched for first-hand accounts to chronicle these events.

Many of those involved in the Congregation at the onset have since left and were unavailable for interviews with us. Those who remained confess some ambiguity and uncertainty in recalling their own feelings and their perceptions of the feelings of others at that time. Moreover, we found considerable disagreement in the accounts of present members as to why certain former members dropped out. Fortunately, a brief questionnaire completed by those present at the January 15, 1969, meeting had been saved and has proven a helpful supplement to our interviews.

The questionnaire was designed "to help chart the direction the Congregation wishes to take." The instructions at the top of the questionnaire emphasize this was not to be "the total effort in picking goals" but only a beginning. The questionnaire consisted of twelve items. Nine of these could be answered by checking a box or filling in a one-word answer. The other three questions were open-ended, requiring a written response and asking the participants to express (a) their overriding reasons for interest in this experimental congregation, (b) the sort of congregation meetings envisioned, and (c) the nature of pastoral services expected.

The task of answering open-ended questions in a group meeting is by nature not conducive to eliciting lengthy responses. Nevertheless, these short responses, combined with the responses to the other questions and our interviews with members, provide valuable information regarding the background and expectations of the participants in the newly formed congregation. A total of thirty questionnaires were completed and returned. Though the number present at the meeting was not recorded, checking through congregational records encourages us to believe that all or nearly all those present responded to the questionnaire, since attendance at these early meetings seldom exceeded thirty persons. Not all questions were answered by all respondents, but only three failed to write anything on the open-ended questions. Moreover, the length of responses varied signficantly. Twenty-four persons voluntarily signed their names to the questionnaire, and our interpretation of responses partially draws on other information about these people. While an analysis of these responses is open to some misjudgment and error, we believe it does reflect a reasonably accurate picture of the group at the time.

The early participants are in virtual consensus in expressing concern for the racial crisis. However, it is not at all clear that they are of one mind relative to an action strategy for the Congregation. To the question "Do you think the Congregation should work actively for social change or serve as a discussion and educational group?" 10 opted for action, 1 for education, and 19 for both. But while 29 of 30 reported they were in favor of action, this predominant response is not tantamount to a mandate for confrontation politics. To the contrary, a number of responses to the open-ended questions, as well as marginal comments, indicate that several people conceived of action in more traditional, comfort-oriented terms of Christian service. For example, "efforts to serve community needs" and "neighborhood improvement programs" are typical of these responses.

Perhaps more important for understanding the composition of the group is the issue of "secularists" versus "traditionalists." We attempted to code the open-ended questions in terms of the presence or absence of traditional Christian language (using the term "traditional Christian language" very loosely). Any mention whatsoever of ideas like "Christian fellowship," "Christian concern," "worship," or "theological basis for action" was classified as traditional. We recognize, of course, that very unorthodox Christians may utilize such language. However, our concern is an attempt to discern whether the participants conceived and articulated their involvement in the group as "religiously based." Using these admittedly crude measures, we found that sixteen made such use of traditional language and fourteen, including the three who did not answer the open-ended questions, did not. It cannot, of course, be concluded that the absence of Christian language makes all the others in the group secularists. Many of them may very well think of themselves as Christian. However, given the setting (a congregational meeting) in which they answered the questions, we can conclude that they were not easily given to expressing themselves in terms of traditional Christian concepts. And, as already mentioned, we know that at least some of these people did not consider themselves Christians and were reluctant to have any "God-talk" present in their meetings.

Another interesting insight regarding the feelings of the early participants may be gleaned from the question "Do the services meet your religious needs?" To this point there had been only one brief homily which could have been called a sermon. Although there were some prayers, songs, and liturgies, they were informal and experimental in nature, not at all what one would expect in a normal Sunday morning worship service in an established church. Nineteen responded that the services did meet their religious needs and five responded no. An analysis of the open-ended questions of those who responded "no" indicates their desire to have some form of worship service. Two of those who responded "yes" indicated only partial satisfaction and a desire for more worship. Thus we have from the onset a minority of approximately one third who were quite explicit about their desire to have some form of worship or other expressions of their Christian heritage. These responses, no doubt, had much to do with the creation of the once-a-month Sunday evening house church and Bible study. Equally significant, however, is that approximately two thirds seemed satisfied with having a congregational format free from additional forms of Christian worship.

Examination of responses to the question regarding pastoral services expected is also revealing. The largest category indicated an expectation of the pastor as resource person, strategist, and leader in social-action projects. Eight so indicated. Five described more or less traditional pastoral roles. Two others described their expectations in traditional language, such as "be a Christian friend." Two indicated explicitly that they expected no pastoral services. But perhaps the most interesting aspect of this question is that eleven of thirty respondents wrote nothing, by far the largest number of nonresponses to the items in the questionnaire. Since it was the final question, some may simply not have gotten to it. On the other hand, in part, this no doubt reflects the ambiguity built into the structure of an experimental congregation. Many people really didn't know what they expected. But we believe it also reflects for some the lack of background and experience from which to respond, that is, the concept "pastoral service" was foreign to them.

Whether Righter viewed the response to this question as a green light to eschew traditional pastoral leadership and counseling roles is not known. It is clear, however, that he has seldom functioned in these capacities, nor does he feel the Congregation expected such of him. His perception may have had the impact of a self-fulfilling prophecy. For some who left the Congregation, the lack of traditional pastoral care was a problem. Those who are presently in the Congregation do not expect Righter to begin playing a more traditional role, but among a few there remains a quiet wish it might have been otherwise. One charter member told us he felt the group had suffered for want of someone to play the role of "pastor-healer" of internal tensions. Righter seems not to take this too seriously. He insists that everyone in the Congregation is a pastor, tending to the needs and problems of others. To some degree this is probably true, but it does not erase the evidence of unresolved tension.

Sociologically speaking, Righter's low-key playing of the traditional pastor leadership role (including such activities as preaching, counseling, visiting the sick, and presiding over policy-making) served to undermine his legitimacy as the group's leader for some participants. As social-action leader, his guidance is continually evaluated in terms of the individual member's perceptions of the wisdom of his strategies. Had he accepted the role of pastor in the more conventional sense, a greater measure of authority and legitimacy would no doubt have accrued to the office. On the other hand, in order to have convincingly donned a traditional leadership style he might have had to confront those most resistant to strong one-man leadership, thus igniting explosive conflicts and losing several activist participants. This is not to say that Righter never visits the sick or counsels those with difficulties. He does. Our point is that he has consciously played down the traditional pastoral image both within and outside the Congregation.

The dilemma in which Righter found himself in terms of the pastoral leadership role is expressed in notes he recorded immediately after the February 1969 congregation meeting, just a month after the questionnaire had been filled out.

> Tonight was the congregation meeting. It was really something. . . . The Lees and Jacobsons [the names of congregation members have been changed in order to respect their privacy] were so upset by the stewardship mailing [a brochure the Presbytery had asked all pastors to mail to their members]. They had a picket sign that read, "We love you, Dick," and on the other side it said, "But we don't love MONEY EQUALS COMMITMENT." They were organized to burn the [stewardship] pamphlets. I kidded Gail for being so organized. There was some intimate shoving. . . .
>
> The main issue was a group authority or leadership problem with me. The group had their agenda, and that was to air their concerns. They did and then we all shared who we are and what we are involved in. It was a big leap forward toward real community. There were many complaints about the organization, money, committees, and so forth, but no spite toward me. . . . I think the people have really now decided that they are the decision-makers. This is good; in fact it is great. I have the feeling we are really on the way. We only had twenty here but it was a core group.

It is difficult to speculate at this point which pastoral leadership style would have ultimately produced the least tension. One thing is certain, however. For minimum conflict the leadership and congregational style must be complementary. Had Righter opted for a strong leadership style from the onset, the style of the congregation would have had to adjust to minimize conflict.

In summary, results of the questionnaire underscore and support our analysis of the reasons for delay in the formal organization of the Congregation. The divisions in belief and expectation obviously did not open an immediate schism, but they were undeniably present from the beginning. And the desire to avoid internal conflict does seem clearly related to the long delay in formally organizing.

Getting Their Thing Together:
Internal Dissension over Goals

For a new congregation to be organized officially, the Presbytery required a covenant, statement of mission, and constitution and bylaws. The task of developing these documents did not begin until nearly half a year after Righter's arrival. By this time, he anticipated increasing pressure from the Presbytery. Realizing the inherent difficulties, Righter began encouraging movement toward preparing the documents.

The task did indeed produce some considerable tension within the Congregation, as reflected in the working papers. Written by a lay member and circulated among the participants[6] of the Congregation on February 20, 1969, this preliminary draft served as a basis for discussion of goals in four separate meetings held in homes during the last week in February. The entirety of this working paper is couched in "church language." It begins with a theological statement and then moves to the role of laity, corporate worship, style, and service.

Strong reactions to this theological expression are reflected in a position paper prepared by another lay person. She objected to limiting the theological rationale. With reference to Buddha, she wrote:

> We rejoice in this statement, too. It is an extension of the biblical quote [cited in the initial working paper] and shows clearly that our theological statements must encompass all religions from

Buddha to Christ. The church has for too long been exclusive and limiting. But if we dare to be a reconciling congregation we must embrace all philosophies.

She also objected to the concept of worship expressed in the working paper. Substituting the concept of celebration, she wrote that "anything that pulls us together as one is worship: a sit-in, a leafleting, a communion service, a yoga meditation session."

The initial statement, acknowledging but not dwelling upon working relationships with other congregations, proclaimed:

> The Congregation for Reconciliation regards with gratitude the existence of other churches and regards itself as one among them. The difference with the Congregation for Reconciliation is simply that, as intended, it is freer to experiment, freer to change. The similarity with other churches is that it is free to relate to other congregations in implementing specific goals provided there proves to be a mutual desire for such teamwork.

We see in this statement a conditional openness to other congregations, a willingness for other congregations to accept them (the Congregation for Reconciliation) on their own terms.

But this was far too moderate and generous for the author of the position paper, who responded that "the rustic, ridiculously wealthy, over-structured eternal mother figure, the church, guarantees the pledge-paying participant immunity from the world." Then, in a specific statement on the relationship between the new mission and other churches, she wrote:

> The Congregation for Reconciliation acknowledges that the church has great influence and power in the world even though we condemn them for their isolationist and materialistic goals. Because of the impact of a church involving itself in the community we intend to use the church as a base of power. Perhaps if we as a congregation use the power and prestige of organized religion, we may goad other churches to join us in the world.

In short, the position paper indicates clearly the author's feelings that an adequate statement of mission would explicitly indict mother church for her indifference to the problems of the world and, moreover, extend the Congregation's ideological rationale beyond the Christian heritage.

After the four neighborhood sessions discussing the statement of mission (and presumably its rebuttal), a second draft was circulated on May 20, almost three months later. Without abandoning the Christian theological rationale, it made important concessions to the views articulated in the rebuttal position paper. Most importantly, the second draft included a subsection entitled "Diversity Within Unity," a phrase used in the position paper and an idea which became central to the Congregation's rhetoric. This subsection included the comment: "we agree to disagree and with all through Christ to remain one congregation." Equally significant, this compromise draft did not abandon the Christian vocabulary. Note the statement indicates that unity comes "through Christ."

Clearly, however, this compromise was insufficient for some of the secularists. On May 25, twenty-three participants met to hammer out a common set of goals. They proceeded systematically as though twenty-three mission statements were competing in an elimination tournament until one winner would be declared. Each person wrote down his or her ideas for congregational goals and then sought out a person with congruent thoughts. The pair then met with a dissimilar pair to attempt a reconciliation of their goals through compromise. When this was accomplished, the new statement was read, together with the statement that common ground had been found "in the spirit of Christ and/or for the love of mankind." This permitted the option of God-language. At the end of the exercise, however, the group had clearly not reached consensus. Of the 21 persons remaining, 4 had problems with the mission statement, 14 with membership requirements, 7 with bylaws. Four even had difficulty with the proposition that the Congregation should be publicized as a Christian church. Over three quarters rejected certain requirements necessary to be formally established as a Presbyterian congregation, among them that only professing Christians could be voting members and that a church order be accepted whereby policy decisions would be made by the ruling elders rather than the congregation at large. A four-page mimeographed statement of individual goals, not a corporate statement, emerged from the day-long retreat.

Another statement, undated and unsigned but obviously written about the same time, reveals the difficulty of one person who perceived himself as a Christian working in the same group with those who would have preferred to jettison all "God-talk."

I'm looking for a group of people with whom I can work to effect change in the world. However, since I do adhere to the teachings of Jesus I can only work in this context. I became affiliated with [the Congregation for] Reconciliation because it was, as I understood then, a social-issue-oriented Christian group. Now, a Christian group, by its very nature, cannot exclude non-Christians. However, the latter must recognize the group's motivating force and respect its mission. When the group approaches each situation in a Christian manner, guided by the Jesus ethic, the non-Christian member should be expected to have settled any differences beforehand concerning the group's motivation in relation to their own consciences by finding them in parallel . . . or at least similar enough to afford the group an harmonious atmosphere in which to act. Accepting the above, I see no reason why both Christian and non-Christian members cannot vote and hold . . . office.

In short, this person felt it inappropriate to exclude the secularists from the group but thought, by the same token, that the secularists ought, as a criterion of participation, to have accepted the group as organized and motivated by a sense of Christian ethics. Moreover, this person seems to say: Please don't step on my right to express my motivation in Christian language.

Secularists active in the group seem to have accepted this modest compromise. In time they have even come to accept Christian symbols as expressions of the unity of the Congregation. However, at that time, there were secularists in the group who viewed an appropriate "compromise" as the total abandonment of "God-talk." As a result, the "God-talk" seems to have been largely, although not exclusively, restricted to the once-a-month Sunday evening house church during the Congregation's early years.

In terms of the formal statement of mission, the secularists won. The formal statement of goals adopted in February 1970 was almost entirely stripped of the theological rationale and traditional language expressed in the first two drafts.

Unable to agree on a common set of goals, the Congregation compromised with an eclectic statement:

> We seek to be a gathered community celebrating our given life, loving each other and the world, seeking to act in response to our shared goals and in support of each other in our diverse goals. The following goals—shared and diverse—are open to expansion as our congregation grows:
> - Social action
> - Freedom
> - Experimentation
> - To retain personal individuality while working toward social justice through direct action with the golden rule as our guide
> - To be a community dedicated to the humanizing of life for ourselves and for others
> - To become a servant people led by the Holy Spirit, to be an instrument of healing society as well as one another
> - For the love of mankind and/or in the Spirit of Christ, to fight for the freedom of every person to realize his life's authentic potential
> - To be the people of God responding to Him by loving each other in out-pouring our individual and corporate life for His World through social change and healing acts
> - To influence and involve other congregations in placing increasingly higher priorities on human concerns of society.

Three of the secularists remained adamant to the end. At the congregation meeting in February of 1970, one full year after the circulation of the first working paper on the mission of the church, a covenant, statement of mission, constitution and bylaws were adopted, but not without a fight. Some minor concessions were made to the small group of secular-humanists who remained uncompromising. By the time this meeting took place, however, sufficient consensus had developed among the Christian members and the more compromising secularists so that the remaining handful of hard-liners were no longer capable of intimidating the majority. In a final move, they threatened not to join the

Congregation if the proposed documents were adopted, where-upon one usually soft-spoken and pensive participant spoke the will of the group: "If you don't join this congregation after all we have adapted to *you*, then pooh on you." The documents were immediately adopted. At the same meeting the Congregation agreed on continuance after the experimental period on a self-supporting basis as a major collective goal. At last the pieces were falling into place.

The chickens were counted and the hatching was soon to be. But when the local Presbyterian church executives examined the documents prepared by the Congregation, they could not accept them. The Congregation would not disallow avowed non-Christians membership, nor would it submit to representative government. Rather, it had insisted that no credal statement be required for membership and that it would abide by a congregational polity. But even an experimental mission must yield to the *Book of Church Order* before officially becoming a Presbyterian congregation.

Righter's dream of establishing a permanent congregation appeared headed to end in bitter disillusionment. There was no breaching the impasse. The Congregation would play out its experimental life and then die a silent, uncompromised death and be forgotten with other experimental failures. So much time and energy had been consumed in the struggle for self-definition that even one sustained social-action project was unlikely. The Congregation, it seemed, had been born only to die in its crib. Was there not a merciful God in heaven who would stay the executioner's hand?

The Providential Loophole: Union Church

The strategy paper for the development of new congregations passed in 1967 by the General Assembly of the United Presbyterian Church in the U.S.A. expressed a clear desire for ecumenical witness.

Joint development of new congregations with other denominations shall be explored as united ministries. When new congregations are

to be developed cooperatively a clear and acceptable statement of
the relationship of the proposed congregation to the sponsoring
denominations [shall be stated] so that it can draw on the heritage
and resources of [both] the sponsors.[7]

The Presbytery plan for the Congregation for Reconciliation had
also encouraged such a united ministry.

This loophole finally allowed the Congregation not to compromise its membership and polity statements, a compromise practically impossible to make. The dilemma was resolved when the
United Church of Christ, shopping for a new mission project in
Dayton and having been impressed with the social action
accomplished by the Congregation in its first year, expressed
interest in supporting it as a union church. Even the secularists
must have considered this event providential.

Since the procedure for incorporation as a union church
permitted the Congregation to pick and choose from the requirements of the participating denominations, they were released
from the restrictive requirements of the Presbyterians. Though
formally they chose structural elements from both denominations,
in reality most of the elements were UCC since their constitutional requirements did not call for a statement of faith and
specified that authority should be vested in the congregation
rather than in the elders. As a token gesture toward the
Presbyterians, the constitution called for the pastor to be subject
to their tenure procedure and for a council to be established as an
executive board of elders.

In March of 1970 both denominations approved the constitution, and on May 17 the Congregation for Reconciliation was
formally organized. But this was not until a year and a half after
its first meeting. Their viability as a social-action group had long
since been established.

Summary

We have examined the process whereby a reality came to be
defined by those who operated within it. The pastor brought with
him an idea of what he hoped the Congregation would become.
His particular set of skills and perspectives helped to shape the
incipient congregation. His choice to play a low-key pastoral

leadership role encouraged lay leadership development but at the same time contributed, by default, to the internal tensions which retarded the process of self-definition.

Passive resistance of local Presbyterian clergymen to the early organizational efforts of Mr. Righter severely hampered the recruitment of active churchpeople to the Congregation. Attracted by early media attention and the prompt movement to direct social action, those who gathered to form the charter group were a mixture of active churchgoers, disillusioned church dropouts, and secular humanists. The diversity of this group made the development of consensus on self-definition tedious and difficult. Consequently the Congregation was not formally organized for a year and a half after its first meeting in October of 1968, and then only by virtue of becoming a union church supported jointly by the Presbyterians and the less restrictive United Church of Christ.

The statement of mission finally agreed upon by the members was in sharp contrast with the goals of the Presbytery in the design for the experimental congregation. Whereas the Presbytery expressed a clear desire for the initiation of cooperative programs and the service of the mission as a training ground for other interested lay persons, this received only fleeting mention in the Congregation's statement of mission. As a matter of policy and practice, this goal had died in print.

CHAPTER 4

Parental Disappointment: The Problem of Goals

As we have seen, the Congregation for Reconciliation experienced difficulty in developing consensus on even such basic statements as membership requirements and mission. The pastor chose not to promote the adoption of documents suitable to the Presbytery, but rather allowed the members themselves to hammer out definitions of the meaning and purpose of the Congregation and its governance. The members' views on these matters were so divergent and strongly held that consensus building necessitated postponing the formal organization of the Congregation for more than a year. In this chapter, we shall examine the outcome of this self-definition process vis-à-vis the original goals agreed upon by the Presbytery in authorizing the establishment of the Congregation two years earlier.

One Meeting, Two Agendas: Divergent Definitions of Mission

As indicated earlier, the Congregation for Reconciliation grew from church leaders' desires to relate to the racial crisis of the mid to late 1960s. The Miami Presbytery's 1968 proposal for a new congregation and for a ministry of reconciliation drew heavily from the spirit and content of a task force report on strategies for developing new congregations adopted by the Board of National Missions of the United Presbyterian Church the previous year.

The planning committee had stated the thesis to be tested by the proposed project (with our emphasis added) as follows: "Can a congregation based on a community of special concern develop a ministry of racial reconciliation which *both* contributes to needed social change *and* relates helpfully to the ministries of other congregations?" The clear implication in the thesis is: Must these two areas of ministry be incompatible? The mood of the day was one of frustration over the failures of direct action aimed at social change. Black power advocates were telling whites that if they really were concerned to produce social change they must accomplish it on their own turf, by changing attitudes in their homes, churches, suburbs, and white-dominated governmental, educational, and economic structures. It is not surprising, then, to find mission goals presumed to test the thesis would place emphasis upon ways for the experimental congregation to relate helpfully to the racial ministries of other white congregations.

The Miami Presbytery proposal does not explicitly mention the *Report of the National Advisory Commission on Civil Disorders* (the Kerner Report), released two weeks before the circulation of the design to members of the Presbytery. The spirit of the proposal, however, very much reflects the emphasis of the Kerner Report: white racism is at the core of the crisis facing the nation. The suggested objectives for the new congregation stress the importance of dealing with negative racial attitudes within white churches as well as in the broader society. This emphasis on working within white congregations can be seen in the abbreviated summary of goals adopted by the Miami Presbytery on April 16, 1968:

1. Develop a congregation of action-oriented Christians with a like commitment to strive for racial reconciliation within the church and within society.
2. Provide a base for these Christians upon which to develop a program of worship, education, fellowship, and service that will enable them to carry on their ministry.
3. Develop a group of skilled communicators, educators, technicians, and planners for use by local churches, Presbytery, ecumenical, or secular organizations.
4. Support and supplement programs in the area of race relations currently being conducted or planned by established congregations.

5. Provide a training ground for Presbytery and its congregations where members can learn the methods of social action and where churches can lend support to ministries of reconciliation in the racial crisis.
6. Explore all possible avenues of ecumenical witness and mission to bring about needed social change.
7. Explore and develop all possible courses of action that are designed to change negative attitudes toward racial understanding in all white churches.

Five of the seven goals explicitly involve working within existing congregations toward the aim of increasing racial reconciliation within society, and a sixth involves ecumenical witness, implying working within other church groups. The only goal not directly calling for working for racial reconciliation within existing church structures is goal No. 2, and this involves the development of internal programs in the congregation to carry out its mission vis-à-vis the other objectives.

In sharp contrast, the statement of mission adopted by the Congregation for Reconciliation makes only one brief mention of the desirability of working with other congregations. And, significantly, this is the very last sentence in their statement of goals, giving it the appearance of having been tacked on as a necessary token concession to the Presbytery.

In actual behavior, the Congregation has almost totally disregarded its relationship to other churches; it has made only token efforts toward involving others in its projects. Righter sent a letter to each of the Presbyterian pastors in Dayton early in his first year, listing some of the areas he considered likely as social-action projects for the Congregation. He asked if they had lay people whom they would like to see involved in such projects, and offered the Congregation's willingness to work cooperatively with them if mutual concern existed. There were no responses to the letter. But having made this one gesture, neither Righter nor the Congregation ever did follow up.

In fact, the relationship between the Congregation and other area churches has generally been cool, occasionally even hostile. From the viewpoint of several Dayton pastors, the Congregation has made belligerent demands followed by immediate picketing and leafleting of churches, without allowing the congregations an opportunity to consider their claims.

For a variety of reasons, most of the early participants in the Congregation held negative attitudes toward conventional churches. The secular humanists had withdrawn physically and emotionally from traditional religious organizations and, consequently, neither had nor desired contacts with other churches. Similarly, many who had been active in other congregations before joining the mission also felt little incentive or desire to maintain contact with conventional religious bodies. As a rule, they had been labeled as troublemakers by many members of their parent churches and had been frustrated in attempts to initiate social-action projects. Having experienced social isolation for their "deviant" religious perspectives, they had become alienated from their former churches and were not anxious to renew contact. Moreover, they were skeptical of the prospects for involving their parent churches in cooperative programs of social change.

In contrast to the Presbytery's original plan that active church members participate in the mission while maintaining ties to their traditional congregation, only a few participants in the life of the Congregation have maintained dual membership. In June of 1972, only two members were doing so. One was an elderly lady who sought companionship with people her own age in an established church. The other was an official in another denomination who is required to maintain membership in one of its congregations. One year later only the latter remained.

Thus, by the time they had achieved formal organization, the Congregation's profile differed considerably from that planned by the Miami Presbytery in 1968. The Congregation was neither serving as a training ground for individuals expecting to return to conventional churches nor was it engaging in efforts to involve other congregations in cooperative social action.

One Man's Meat . . . :
Initial Recruitment and Goal Definition

On the surface, it would be easy to lay blame for this squarely on the shoulders of Richard Righter. However, we believe the situation to be considerably more complex. As has been mentioned, when Righter arrived in Dayton the Presbytery had a list of only twenty referrals. Moreover, to the best of our knowledge, none of these people expressed interest at the urging of a pastor. Of these twenty, also, only six were to remain in the Congregation for any period of time. Of the thirty-five adults active in the church in 1969, twenty-two were of Presbyterian background but only about half of these had been active in a Presbyterian church prior to becoming involved with the Congregation for Reconciliation.

The failure to recruit active Presbyterian laity into the new congregation is *the* pivotal reason for the subversion of the goals established by the Miami Presbytery. Given the structural realities of the situation, it is hard to see how the Congregation for Reconciliation could have developed in any other manner. This point may now be obvious to those responsible for creating the mission congregation, but we believe it needs to be underscored and analyzed. It seems to us that the most important policy implication to be gleaned from this experiment emerges from understanding the critical importance of initial organizational imperatives.

With the benefit of hindsight, it should be clear that the denomination's efforts to recruit people into the Congregation were inadequate. Consider the following realities:

(1) The emphasis on budgets and warm bodies in American church life is so strong that it is unrealistic to expect pastors to encourage their own members to leave their congregation and join another.

(2) Socially conscious pastors typically have a difficult time encouraging and supporting social action within their own congregations. Socially conscious lay persons not only provide support for social concern, they also provide a "buffer zone" between the pastor and those members who feel the church has no business being involved in social issues. Since socially conscious lay people are typically a small minority in any congregation, it is understandable that pastors are extremely reluctant to see them leave their congregations. The feared loss of activist laity, it must be remembered, signaled stiff opposition to the establishment of the Congregation initially.

(3) A significant proportion of pastors are not persuaded that the churches should be directly involved in social action. The route to social reform, to those who see reform as desirable, is through helping laity understand the "meaning of the gospel." The Christian community manifests itself in the day-to-day business and professional activities of its membership. Such an orientation is at best ambivalent toward the concept of an experimental social-action congregation. Clergy of this persuasion would be unlikely to encourage their laity to participate. Indeed, it is quite probable that they would discourage the flow of information about the social-action group to their congregation by failing either to read announcements or to place them on the bulletin board or in their Sunday morning worship programs.

The cooperation of local pastors was absolutely central to the goal of recruiting active Presbyterian laity. Yet, as we have seen, the obstacles to enlisting their cooperation were considerable. Moreover, there was little or no advance effort to overcome these obstacles. Without careful advance planning, prior to the arrival of an organizing pastor, it was virtually inevitable that the Congregation for Reconciliation would develop in the manner in which it did—attracting dissident and renegade Presbyterians with a supporting cast of humanists who saw the church as an appealing institution through which to work for social justice.

What Might Have Been: A Post Hoc Scenario

In retrospect, questions of the viability of the Congregation for Reconciliation as conceived by its designers keep coming to mind. How might the concept have been handled so as to increase the probability of achieving the stated goals? Post hoc scenarios implicitly seem to carry an indictment absent from future-oriented scenarios, that is, *if* the group in question had done such and such, *then* the desired goals would have obtained. We wish to disavow any such implicit judgment. At the same time, the question of why the specific group in question strayed from the goals set for it looms large. If one concludes the goals were ill-conceived and unrealistic, no further analysis is required. Still, if one considers these original goals worthwhile, the question remains as to whether they might have in some measure been reached. To conclude this requires some image or model of how the organizational task might have proceeded.

In outline form, the following suggests what could have happened. Let us again emphasize that this is not intended in any way as an indictment. Nor do we view it as an exercise in Monday morning quarterbacking. If there is value to be derived from post hoc analysis, it must come from the application of learning to new situations. If, and only if, the lessons of the Congregation for Reconciliation are applied, can the experiment be judged a success vis-à-vis the originally stated goals.

Let us assume that those responsible for the experimental congregation understood that the accomplishment of their goals required the recruitment of active Presbyterian laity. Let us further assume they understood the delicate and precarious nature of this task. What was to be done?

First, local pastors would have needed assurance that they would not lose any laity to the experimental congregation. This guarantee demands a structure for the Congregation that is different from what emerged. Several organizational criteria seem appropriate. For one, joint memberships would have been required of those already belonging to another congregation, with membership in the experimental congregation clearly specified as secondary. Also, membership in the experimental congregation would have been temporary, with the length of affiliation not to exceed, say, two years. Further, persons unaffiliated with or inactive in other churches would have pledged, as a condition of membership, to seek a permanent home church where they would work to achieve the goals of the experimental church. The program of the experimental congregation would have been geared around the development of leadership skills applicable to the home congregation, and this transferral would have been an ongoing process. The experimental congregation would have served as a forum for evaluating and discussing the effectiveness of members' efforts to achieve specific goals in their home congregations. In short, the total socialization experience of the experimental congregation would have been aimed toward return to the home congregation as more effective leaders. And to encourage maximum participation in the home congregation, the experimental congregation would never have scheduled meetings conflicting with the "prime time" meetings of other congregations, such as on Sunday morning. Finally, the charter of the experimental congregation would have clearly been for a limited time. Extension of the life span of the congregation would have been granted only on the basis of demonstrated ability to train leadership for other congregations. Extension of the charter for the purpose of fellowship among the members would have been explicitly forbidden.

A second major pledge to local pastors would have been a reassurance they would not have suffered financial losses. Such a procedure requires commitments. First, it would have meant a guaranteed operating budget for the experimental congregation, backed by the Presbytery and/or the Board of National Missions. Second, as a condition of membership in the experimental congregation, prospects would have had to pledge not to reduce their benevolences to their home church while participating in the experimental group. This would preclude neither the encouragement of participants to give to the experimental church nor the request for support from local congregations. The guarantee, however, that no pastor's budget would shrink as a result of his laity's participating in the experimental congregation is critical.

A third major consideration would have been to stress the benefits of the experimental program to local pastors. The development of leadership skills for the local congregation would have been emphasized. Moreover, the objective of creating a leadership to support and work with the pastor toward the accomplishment of mutually shared goals would have been stressed. While pastors could not be guaranteed that trainees would never work against them or employ strategies they disapproved of, the commitment to the objective of close collaboration between pastors and lay trainees would have provided much additional reassurance.

This close collaboration would have also required pastors to agree to participate periodically with their laity in seminars sponsored by the experimental congregation. These seminars, while designed to educate and enhance rapport between pastors and their laity, would have focused on establishing goals and developing strategies to achieve these goals.

This strategy scenario not only would have reassured local pastors that an experimental congregation would not undermine their own programs but also would have offered them both the prospect of developing lay leadership and the possibility of developing their own leadership skills. By building local pastors into the structure of the experimental congregation, the probability of the success of the program would have been greatly enhanced.

While many modifications or additions to this plan are possible, we believe it outlines a strategy which could have overcome the great obstacle of recruiting active Presbyterian lay persons. It is a proposal not intrinsically threatening to local pastors interested in change. Moreover, the conditions of participation require commitments on the part of both laity and their pastors. The agreements demanded of the laity imply informal social pressure on their pastors to "stick with it," and vice versa. Obviously, not every Presbyterian congregation in the Dayton area would have sent participants. From our interviews, however, we would judge adequate interest to initiate such a program existed. If something like this had been created, the original goals might have been achieved.

Another obvious consideration in thinking through the viability of this scenario is the wisdom of thinking of the program as a congregation. That is, might it have been better to conceive of the experiment as a lay-clergy training institute rather than as a congregation? Some solid arguments can be made for the training institute structure. Without discussing the pros and cons of the alternate structures, however, we think the congregational structure has superior merit. We believe it has greater potential for binding participants together in a common sense of community with mutually reinforcing commitments. The training institute structure, on the other hand, seems to require less psychological commitment on the part of participants. When the scheduling of people's personal lives gets tight, an institute is more easily dropped, just as so many people drop the adult education courses offered by extension divisions in many American universities.

Failure by Default or Subversion?

Nothing like this scenario happened. The question remains: Would it have been possible for an organizing pastor to have conceived of his task in this or a similar manner? We doubt it. Such a general strategy would have to have been worked out prior to the arrival of an organizing pastor, including negotiation with local pastors for lay candidates. Unless the structural principles were worked out and clearly defined by the Presbytery, it would have been extremely difficult for an organizing pastor to gain the support of local pastors.

When Righter arrived in Dayton and made his rounds to meet other Presbyterian ministers, he found considerable interest and enthusiasm for the experimental congregation. Yet not one pastor volunteered the name of a single lay person as a prospective candidate for participation in the Congregation for Reconciliation. We do not believe Righter can be faulted for failing to ask other pastors about prospective members. The development and retention of rapport with other clergy required his abstention from any activity which might be interpreted as an attempt to raid other congregations for membership. Thus, his potential constituency was effectively delimited to those *not* actively involved in a Presbyterian congregation.

By failing to create a structure appropriate for the accomplishment of the goals established by the Miami Presbytery for the new congregation, the planners subverted those goals prior to the arrival of the organizing pastor. Albeit unintentionally, the very persons creating the goals simultaneously undermined them. By not structurally assuring the recruitment of a supportive cast of active lay persons, the designers defined the membership in direct contradiction with their ambitions for the congregation. Looking at the results, one of the initial strategists told us that "we just overestimated the readiness of pastors and their elders and members to respond to this bright, creative, ingenious idea that we had thought up. How could it fail? It was such a beautiful thing. . . . I remember very clearly being bewildered by the lack of response and cooperation and interest on the part of the pastors and sessions in the area. . . . By hindsight, we were just naïve, I guess."

80

In our interviews with pastors and some denominational administrators in Dayton, we repeatedly heard Righter criticized for failing to fulfill his task. It is our judgment that Righter's instincts or predispositions lie in the direction of confrontation tactics and immediate social action rather than in the realm of education and theory. But whether he possesses the flexibility to adapt his leadership style to requirements of a scenario such as we have developed is a moot question. He simply did what he knew best, followed by a constituency which largely shared his orientation toward the mission of the congregation. Had the structural imperatives been better understood, both Righter and the recruitment committee could better have assessed his credentials for the job.

A Matter of Interpretation

The question still remains, however, as to whether Righter ignored the directive and charge laid out for him by the Miami Presbytery. We view this as problematic. To a considerable extent, the constituency he would have to work with was determined before he arrived. Had he pursued more "establishment" tactics he might well have lost the core of his potential congregation and the whole experiment could have died. Given the structural restraints of the inadequate foreplanning, the possibility of recruiting a more "moderate" constituency was doubtful.

Righter had read the list of Presbytery goals for the proposed experimental congregation when he was interviewed for the position of organizing pastor. He had no difficulty accepting those goals. Indeed, even today Righter affirms the goals as legitimizing the style of ministry which he pursued in leading the Congregation. In his view, the Congregation for Reconciliation has to a large degree accomplished the stated goals of the Presbytery.

We went over the list of goals with Righter in a long probing interview. Portions of this interview are quoted below in order to make clear his understanding of what the Presbytery had set out to accomplish through the experimental congregation.

INTERVIEWER: "How do you interpret the following statements and how has the Congregation, and you as its leader, attempted to accomplish each goal? First goal: Develop a congregation of action-oriented Christians with a like commitment to strive for racial reconciliation within the church and within society."

RIGHTER: "That's what I was interested in [coming to do]."

INTERVIEWER: "Second goal: Provide a base for these Christians upon which to develop a program of worship, education, fellowship, and service that will enable them to carry on their ministry."

RIGHTER: "That's the building of a congregation. We have done that."

INTERVIEWER: "Goal three: Develop a group of skilled communicators, educators, technicians, and planners for use by local churches, Presbytery, ecumenical, or secular organizations."

RIGHTER: "That's very, very broad. I don't remember reading that when I first came. It certainly wasn't stressed when I was interviewed. But I think we have fulfilled that goal. To me, it calls for leadership development and we have done it."

INTERVIEWER: "Goal four: Support and supplement programs in the area of race relations currently being conducted or planned by established congregations."

RIGHTER: "We've always supported anything that's been done by other congregations in this area . . . but I don't think much has been done in the last five years. We have never been asked to help with programs in other congregations, probably because of our image."

INTERVIEWER: "Goal five: Provide a training ground for Presbytery and its congregations where members can learn the methods of social action and where churches can lend support to ministries of reconciliation in the racial crisis."

RIGHTER: "I visited all the pastors [in Dayton] early on, and then about a month or two later I sent a letter to all of them. It contained a list of some of the kinds of areas we were considering working in. I asked if they had people that they would like to see involved cooperatively in those kinds of projects or issue areas. I suggested that maybe our congregations could work together in this way. But I never got any responses to the letter at all. We tried to fulfill the goal, but we didn't have any people to train. . . . [I wasn't really surprised or disappointed because] I don't have a great deal of hope in the training institute concept. . . . I think it's pretty hard for ministers to be change agents as far as their congregations are concerned. If they even have dialogue going on within their congregations between persons in different social positions they are doing pretty well. . . . I guess I don't expect great short-run change in the main-line institutional church."

INTERVIEWER: "Goal six: Explore all possible avenues of ecumenical witness and mission to bring about needed social change."

RIGHTER: "Our congregation is one of the most active in the major ecumenical body here—the Metropolitan Churches United. I don't think anyone can fault us on that."

INTERVIEWER: "Goal seven: Explore and develop all possible courses of action that are designed to change negative attitudes toward racial understanding in all white churches."

RIGHTER: "I'm sure, at least in the way this was intended, we did not come through at this point. After the Christmas card leafleting at NCR, the local churches were very suspicious of us. Church leadership knew that politically it would be difficult to bring us to their congregations for workshops and seminars on racial attitude change. And they didn't. It was an image problem. Whether we have had an impact through the media coverage of our involvement in the community—that is, a positive impact on attitude change—I don't know. I would argue that we've had some effect."

INTERVIEWER: "One thing I think is obvious is that we read that list of goals and see entirely different things."

RIGHTER: "I guess it is a political document in a sense because the language can be read in different ways."

The language, indeed, can be read in different ways. Many factors bear upon one's perception. The values and experience brought to a situation determine to a large extent how that situation is defined. The cues from the setting in which communication occurs also place the exchange in "a certain light."

Righter was called by the Miami Presbytery, as he saw it, for the explicit purpose of establishing an experimental congregation as a showcase of direct social action in the city. Our interviews with members of the calling committee indicate his perception was accurate. During his recruitment interview with the National

Missions Committee, the educational role of the proposed mission, emphasized so strongly in the statement of goals, was not emphasized to Righter. His past experience as a social action leader *was*, however, a primary focus of interest. Rightly or wrongly, he assumed the Presbytery expected him to relate to established congregations in the role of action specialist, as a resource available to them upon their request. It fulfilled the Presbytery's goals, as he understood them, to provide for other congregations the *option* of involvement in joint projects or leadership training ventures. That this resource remained unused was not, in Righter's view, a failure of the Congregation. Nor did it come as a surprise. In fact, the offer of assistance seemed to him window dressing, a nice thought but an item much lower on his agenda than developing an activist congregation. Yet he has always considered the doors to other congregations open.

In contrast to Righter's openness to the possibility of involving other churches in social action, the participants of his group expressed little interest in establishing educational-training relationships with other congregations. Indeed, some of them were openly contemptuous of other churches.

Unintended Consequences
of Purposive Social Action: A Blunder

Yet another critical ambiguity remains. While the Miami Presbytery proposal for a new congregation focused almost exclusively on relating to other congregations, a more lengthy rationale and strategy paper on the development of a new congregation lacked precise expression of exactly what they expected. The rationale paper is extremely conscious of the difficulty in developing social action programs within existing congregations. The drafters note "there is no reason to believe that general educational programs will overcome the apathy and hostility that kill off real change in church structures or programs." They go on, in essence, to propose a new mission as provision for a structurally free base for those Christians desiring but unable to initiate social action in their own congregations.

The question of how activists in a new mission congregation could engage their former churches in social action when they could not do so "from the inside" seems never to have been asked. It does seem clear from the rationale paper that the drafters anticipated the new congregation's involvement in activities which, if undertaken in established congregations, would be extremely controversial and probably impossible. To the extent the drafters of the new congregation proposal knew or assumed this to be the case, they ignored another serious structural problem. How could a congregation created, sponsored, and supported by the Miami Presbytery engage in controversial social action without alienating those who were paying the bills? To be sure, the discrepancies between the explicitly stated objectives and the content of the rationale paper pointed further to the lack of advance planning and preparation for the new congregation. It further indicates a failure to understand social structures and anticipate the consequences of the experimental group for the broader Presbytery.

But this may not be the entire story. It seems to us altogether possible that those responsible for creating the new congregation were meaning one thing and saying another. Just as Righter could read the list of goals and say, "Yeah, that's what we are doing," we think those who set up the goals had perceptual problems from the other end.

As reported in chapter 2, two initial goals guided the strategy of new church development in the Miami Presbytery. One was to develop a congregation free to engage in direct social action in order to test the thesis that the congregation *could* be an effective organizational form for inducing social change in Dayton. The second was to develop a congregation to prick the consciences of the established churches in the city. Its function was to confront the main-line churches with social issues and to demonstrate that a Christian congregation could indeed do something by the use of direct-action techniques. The strategists planned the element of "tension" between the mission and other congregations by forcing them to relate to one another in the same local denominational structure.

Politically, the designers of the plan faced a problem. They needed to present their proposal in a way which would win support in the Presbytery. In attempting to facilitate this, they translated the second major goal into language of cooperation and service. They hoped thereby not only to garner the necessary votes to pass the proposal but also to generate the active support of liberal clergy in the promotion of the experiment as it developed organizationally.

Albeit well intended, this political maneuver had unfortunate unintended consequences. Not having made the necessary structural preparation to ensure the recruitment of active Presbyterian lay persons to the project, the educational and service-oriented goals served only to place in the hands of established churches a weapon with which to discredit the Congregation when it began encroaching upon their social consciences. The move was thereby self-defeating.

A retrospective insight of one of the plan's designers is that it may have been entirely unrealistic to have expected pastors of established churches to embrace the Congregation regardless of the resources it had to offer. By doing so, they would run the risk of polarizing their own congregations and thereby inviting nothing but trouble. The Congregation for Reconciliation, as it became embroiled in controversy, simply became too hot to handle. In establishing a structure to maximize freedom for active social involvement while expecting cooperative involvement with established congregations, the National Missions Committee may have been wanting to have their cake and eat it too. We feel the incompatibility of goals could have been overcome with proper forethought and planning. However, the committee person whom we interviewed assessed the situation as it did develop correctly.

Live or Let Die: An Administrative Dilemma

The role of the denominational officials responsible for the mission congregation is also important. Clearly, they recognized at an early date that the Congregation had strayed significantly from the objectives approved by the Presbytery. The handling of this problem understandably presented a serious dilemma. To have intervened with a heavy hand would have been to run the risk of smothering the Congregation before it had a chance to breathe. Such actions would no doubt have stifled any future possibilities for experimental congregations in the Miami Presbytery. On the other hand, to let the situation ride meant imminent conflict within the Presbytery. This may not have been clearly foreseen at the onset. Whether deliberately or through indecision, however, denominational officials did not intervene and conflict within the Presbytery did ensue. Faced with the alternative of having no viable social mission program operating in the area, these officials chose to defend what was emerging. They did so by arguing for the necessity of flexibility, especially in an experimental situation where a model from past experience is nonexistent.

Summarizing the feelings of a review team after the mission's first year of operation, the Ministry Consultant for the Synod of Ohio wrote:

> The membership of the project are working out their own goals, and these are certainly not identical with those initially conceived and approved. However, the review team is convinced that this tension is healthy and creative and not to be construed as a betrayal of the project.

Reviewing the past tension and anticipating the future, he continued, "There has been some hot discussion along these lines already and we fully expect more of the same when the depth review is conducted in 1970." Since that time, the tension between the Congregation for Reconciliation and the Presbytery has continued unabated.

This is not to say that the Congregation is totally lacking in support among Presbyterian executives and some Presbyterian lay persons. We sense considerable sympathy. However, the complex and delicate politics of working with laity—and some clergy—adamantly opposed to the Congregation makes continued support of the mission virtually impossible.

But We Thought You Said . . .

On one occasion the Congregation did make a concerted effort to carry out the Presbytery's goal of exploring all courses of action designed to change negative attitudes toward racial understanding. This attempt ended in a mild disaster. We trace those developments here to demonstrate the difficulties for the Congregation in seeking to follow one of the Presbytery's goals.

In 1969 the General Assembly of the United Presbyterian Church in the U.S.A. ordered the establishment of a task force on Southern Africa. Among other things, it was instructed "to examine the corporations and banks from which boards, agencies, and institutions now purchase goods and services or in which they have investments to ascertain what if any connections these firms and banks have in southern Africa." [1] On the basis of resolutions passed in the 1970 General Assembly, the task force undertook a series of studies focusing upon Gulf Oil Corporation's involvement in Portuguese Angola. As a result, they recommended on March 1, 1971, that Presbyterian stockholders support in person, or by proxy, a resolution to be made at the forthcoming stockholders' meeting of Gulf which would "prohibit the corporation from making or maintaining investments in territories under or so long as they are under colonial rule, including the territories of Angola and Mozambique." This request was sent to all Presbyterian churches.

The Congregation for Reconciliation had been studying the Gulf-Angola question and had in March 1971 passed a resolution establishing a committee to take social action aimed at coordinating a boycott of Gulf products "while the business relationship of Gulf Oil Corporation with the Portuguese Government in Angola continues."

On March 31 a letter addressed to "All Pastors and Congregations" was sent by the Task Force of the United Presbyterian Church, U.S.A., encouraging study, interpretation, and favorable vote. The Gulf-Angola Committee of the Congregation for Reconciliation saw this as an opportunity to offer their services to the local Presbyterian churches. They called all the pastors in the area, offering their committee's resources for study and encouraging pastors to inform their congregations. Most pastors stated they would inform their members. One congregation invited the committee to speak briefly at worship and to lead an adult class afterward. Several other pastors requested proxy statements and further materials.

Three of the largest churches in Dayton, for various reasons, were unable to bring the issue before their sessions and then to their congregations for prompt consideration. This lack of urgency was interpreted by the Gulf-Angola Committee as evidence of unwillingness on the part of the pastoral leadership of these churches to confront their congregations with the Gulf issue or to consult with their lay leadership on the matter. The Congregation for Reconciliation felt an obligation to see that the membership of those churches knew of the stand taken by the denomination and to encourage participation in the stockholders' meeting if they owned stock. One more attempt was made to reach the pastors of these churches. When cooperation was not forthcoming, members of the Gulf-Angola Committee placed copies of a letter to the church members on the windshields of their automobiles during the Sunday worship service on April 18. Attached to the letter was a proxy solicitation.

The response from the leadership of these churches was prompt. Four days after the leafleting a letter was sent to the Miami Presbytery Council by the pastor of the largest Presbyterian church in Dayton, one of three whose members had been leafleted. Portions of the letter follow:

> The General Assembly's action is not the issue, nor the subject of this letter. Rather it is the unprincipled action of the Congregation for Reconciliation. The leaflet which was passed out . . . read "Dear Friends. . . . Last week your pastor received a letter addressed to him and his congregation from the Task Force on Southern Africa concerning a proxy statement on Gulf Oil Corporation. We contacted him to offer our services as resources in presenting this material. . . . We received no support from your pastoral leadership in bringing this issue to your attention. As a congregation mandated by Presbytery to support and supplement programs in the area of race relations we feel that it is essential that you receive this information from the national church." . . .
>
> The statement "We received no support from your pastoral leadership" is . . . an arrogant infringement upon the relationship between the pastor and people of a particular church. It is as though we . . . decided that we know what is best for [another] church and proceeded to contact the members of that church directly, to advance our views, with no consideration for the inner workings of that congregation. Such conduct would be, and is, in the case in question, irresponsible.
>
> The actual effect of such affrontery is to prejudice the congrega-

tion . . . against the Gulf Oil issue. . . . I must admit that I was not surprised at these tactics, since in my view, the Congregation for Reconciliation seems to be trying to bring in the Kingdom through a ministry of harassment and conflict.

[This] church has taken the position that our Presbytery Benevolences be diverted away from the National Missions Committee, largely because of the support given the Congregation for Reconciliation by that committee. We urge other churches of Miami Presbytery to follow a similar course.

A second congregation complained in a letter that they had received the offer of service from the Congregation for Reconciliation without sufficient time to send it through the channels before they were leafleted. They too were offended by the disparaging remarks about their pastoral leadership.

The members of the Congregation for Reconciliation felt, and indeed were operating under, great time pressure, since the Gulf stockholders' meeting was scheduled only nine days after the date of their leafleting. Had they waited for the one congregation to process the request through Session and/or had they firmly established that the pastors had refused to cooperate in bringing the request to their congregations, passing out proxy solicitations would have been an exercise in futility since the stockholders' meeting would already be past.

Some members of the Congregation now concede the message in their leaflet had been tactless at points. This they attribute to the combination of haste to get their message out, their sense of frustration, and their belief that the pastors in question were deliberately uncooperative. To the issue of cooperation with the broader structures of the Presbyterian denomination, they felt they were acting responsibly and in keeping with the goals of the General Assembly and Presbytery.

The Presbytery's National Missions Committee formed a sub-committee to investigate the matter. After a rather prolonged discussion with all parties on May 19, the committee agreed the incident represented more than a breakdown in communication between the Congregation and the three offended churches. In their view it resulted from a "series of serious errors in judgment and tactics by the Congregation." The most serious was the personal attack upon what was called in the leaflet "pastoral leadership." The Congregation was asked to mend its ways.

But the onus of responsibility was not placed as clearly on the shoulders of the Congregation for Reconciliation as the complaining churches and some of the members of the National Missions Committee might have liked. Indeed, the complaining churches were also called on the carpet, as is demonstrated by the following passage from the subcommittee minutes:

> The congregations of the area bear a responsibility for opening and keeping open lines of communication between themselves and the new forms of ministry of the Congregation for Reconciliation, and seeing them as a resource in the life of the Miami Presbytery.

The official letter of reprimand to the Congregation contains milder language than the subcommittee minutes. In fact, it almost has the flavor of an apologetic slap on the wrist. By and large, the members of the Congregation did not even interpret the whole affair as a reprimand. Some became incensed with us when we suggested the experience had been "humiliating."

The outcome of the committee's discipline has been more of a standoff than a truce or reconciliation between the Congregation and the large churches of the Presbytery. The sessions of two of the churches agreed to meet with representatives of the Congregation for Reconciliation. A third refused. These meetings provided an opportunity for both sides to present their views, but if further cooperation is viewed as a criterion of a meeting of minds, this has not occurred. At a later date, the Congregation again leafleted these same congregations, although under the aegis of another organization, the United People (see next chapter).

For the most part, the Congregation's relations with other churches now manifest a "once burned, twice shy" attitude. In spite of the insistence of some that they were not really reprimanded, or if they were, they do not accept the legitimacy of the National Missions Committee's action, they have mostly steered away from other churches. There has been no further "ministry of harassment" because there has been no further ministry. On the other hand, we saw no evidence the established congregations have become more open toward the Congregation for Reconciliation. They have simply stayed out of each other's way.

Summary

The goals of the mission congregation were subverted very early in its life. We have tried to suggest several reasons for this.

First, and most significantly, the achievement of the goals stated and approved by the Miami Presbytery required the recruitment of active lay people. Failure to plan adequately for this structural prerequisite virtually excluded at the onset the possibility of achieving these goals. In our discussion we have attempted to outline a scenario whereby the recruitment of active Presbyterians might have been achieved.

Second, the failure to provide an adequate structure to recruit active lay people meant the only potential recruits into the new congregation were persons alienated from traditional church life, with little interest in cooperating with other congregations. The immediate informal leaders of the mission congregation saw social action as their only legitimate reason for being. Indeed, their remaining in the group seems to have been conditional upon the organizing pastor's consent to move quickly into social-action projects.

Third, there is serious ambiguity regarding the intentions of those most intimately responsible for the creation of the new congregation. While formally stated goals place paramount emphasis on an educational-training relationship with other congregations, a strategy statement leaves open the door for the development of a direct social-action group. This strategy statement provided Righter legitimacy for what did emerge.

Fourth, the development of social-action projects employing confrontation strategies served to create very considerable strain between the mission congregation and other congregations in the Presbytery. At this point, it would be unrealistic to think further financial support for the mission congregation could be approved by the Presbytery. Furthermore, it would be equally unrealistic to think that the Congregation for Reconciliation might be redirected toward the achievement of the original goals.

Finally, given that the structural realities virtually precluded from the onset the achievement of the original goals, a fair assessment of the Congregation must focus on what they have achieved. In the next two chapters we shall examine two of their more important social-action projects. Other projects might have been selected. One, in particular, provides evidence of their ability to work effectively behind the scenes with nonconflict strategies. We have chosen not to examine this project because it is not possible to do so without (a) divulging information gained in confidence from sympathetic business and political leaders and (b) risking the Congregation's future effectiveness in this arena. After examining two action projects, in chapter 7 we shall discuss some broader issues of their conflict strategy.

CHAPTER 5

At War with the Angels:
The United People Campaign

It is not our aim to derive conclusions concerning the effectiveness of the Congregation or their impact on the community. Rather, our principal objective is to examine the *style* of social action pursued by the Congregation and to consider the reactions of various sectors of the community to this style. In this manner we hope to provide church leaders with some additional basis for measuring the viability of the life-style of the Congregation for Reconciliation as a model for other communities.

The Congregation for Reconciliation has been involved in at least forty-one different social-action projects.[1] These range from one-time protests to a campaign sustained since early in the life of the group. Some projects have involved only two or three members and others have included nearly the entire active membership of the Congregation.[2]

The initial projects created media visibility for the mission but had limited possibilities for generating a major victory. The Christmas card leafleting of National Cash Register employees gained public attention but produced no measurable results. The issue, in fact, belonged to the Second Family, a group of black NCR employees; the Congregation only supplied support. Their second project attempted to deal with prison reform. On Good Friday in 1969, several members of the Congregation participated in a pilgrimage in Columbus from the capitol building to the state penitentiary, with cross in tow, simulating the procession of Christ from Pilate's court to Golgotha. At each "station of the cross," press releases were distributed condemning different aspects of the prevailing system for dispensing criminal justice. The symbolism is biting. At the County Courthouse, Christ is condemned; at the Board of Elections, Christ falls. At the State Office Building, Christ falls again, and again at the Federal Office Building. At the Ohio Council of Churches offices, a woman wipes Christ's face, and finally he is crucified at the Ohio Penitentiary. The march was well staged and received extensive coverage by the media. But here again, the Congregation provided support personnel for a project not entirely their own.

By the spring of 1969, Righter recognized the Congregation's need for a long-term project of some magnitude to provide stability and continuity for congregational action outreach and, more importantly, to inspire the hope of a significant victory. Righter had more than his instincts to point him toward the United Fund as a serious subject of direct action.

Physician Heal Thyself:
The United Fund Comes Under Attack

During the 1960s, United Fund and Community Chest organizations across the nation faced increasing criticism. Most of the objections pivoted around the need to reevaluate the allocation of charity funds collected by these groups. There was a growing feeling, in many cases supported by evidence, that funds were being disproportionately allocated to organizations with predominantly middle-class clients. Most visible, for example, were groups such as Boy Scouts, Girl Scouts, and Camp Fire Girls.

The rising awareness of poverty in the country left the United Fund organizations vulnerable. While much of this criticism came from the outside, many within the organizations also desired change and openly denounced some United Fund operations. United Fund boards, however, were generally not representative of the interests of minorities or the poor and hence were seldom receptive to the proposals for change. Rather, their self-perpetuating memberships, selected from the ranks of community corporate structures and the boards of recipient agencies, huddled to protect their own interests.

At the national level, though, pressures did mount for reform from within. At the 1968 annual meeting of the United Community Fund and Council of America (UCFCA), it was proposed that "United Fund dollars be used principally to make services available to those who cannot pay for them and to enable agencies to use fee systems which make possible the extension of services to the largest possible numbers." [3] An even more aggressive role was advocated by William Aramony, executive vice-president of the United Way of America:

> United Funds and Community Health and Welfare Councils should be in the forefront of each community's efforts to meet the special problems of the current central city crisis [and] their leadership should be the first to identify problems and their causes and to speak out against injustice.[4]

In response to these growing expressions of discontent, the UCFCA in 1968 appointed a task force to study community fund organizations and to make recommendations for new priorities. In February 1970 they announced the adoption of a new set of priorities resulting from the task force study. These priorities included the following:

- To support new and innovative services aimed at helping families and individuals break out of the poverty cycle and achieve fuller lives.
- To extend services to blighted areas in cooperation with the residents of such areas.
- To strengthen or develop approaches aimed at reducing crime, delinquency, drug addiction, alcoholism and other manifestations of antisocial behavior.
- To maintain services that build character and self-reliance, promote physical and mental health and preserve individual dignity and family solidarity.
- To enable established agencies to achieve more nearly their full service potential by narrowing the gap between their validated need and present contribution level.
- To increase the participation of citizens in planning and overseeing both voluntary and government social welfare programs.

- To make more funds available by shifting money from outdated or low priority programs, charging more fees to those able to pay for services and raising annual contributions to one billion just as soon as possible.[5]

The United People Campaign

When the Social Action Committee of the Congregation was formally established in March of 1969, a subcommittee formed to consider the United Fund in the city. Research had already begun on the distribution of United Fund services and on the backgrounds of United Fund board members. By May of that year the subcommittee concluded that some within the local organization were committed to such goals as those cited above, and thus the possibility for change was real. In September, one of the two major local newspapers expressed interest in the study of the subcommittee and, in early December, gave the report front-page coverage. The criticisms of the United Fund, now documented, became a public issue.

The United People organization emerged the following summer. A coalition of seven groups organized earlier that year had by then dissolved because of disagreement over boycott strategies. United People actually included the Congregation and the Social Welfare Workers Movement, but press coverage identified the Congregation for Reconciliation as the prime mover and the Rev. Richard Righter as its spokesman. In formulating goals for United People, all had agreed that a shift in UF priorities in response to protest, without an accompanying shift in leadership, would be a pyrrhic victory. The 1968 UCFCA task force had called for the local United Fund organizations to increase the participation of citizens in planning and overseeing programs. The United People expanded the charge somewhat by insisting that the decision-making of the United Fund be open to public surveillance, that the composition of its Board of Directors reflect the backgrounds and interests of a broader spectrum of the citizens of the community, and that member agencies (which received UF monies) not be allowed on the organization's governing board. The United People opted for the long-term strategy of pushing for the creation of countervailing power within the organization rather than only for the alternative of short-term organizational outcomes. They assumed the latter would follow the former and agreed not to be bought off by a temporary shift in funding priorities.

Threatening its fund-raising goal by attracting attention to inconsistencies between the ideals of voluntarism and community service and the fund-raising and funding practices of the organization seemed the surest way to attract the attention of the United Fund organizers. Although a direct menace to the vital fund-raising function of UF seemed to promise real leverage for bargaining, this strategy involved some serious risks. In the first place, the United Fund had over the years cultivated a large reservoir of goodwill in the community. It was seen by most people as a good organization, unselfishly tending to many human needs, providing community services through the voluntary sacrifices of many citizens. For most, to attack the United Fund would be tantamount to attacking goodness and mercy. To threaten the life of the United Fund through a boycott would likewise be an unfair and cruel act, jeopardizing community services to many persons. Who can win a war with the angels? The United Fund would be defended by some for whom it otherwise would have had a low saliency.

The risk, however, was taken. In the fall of 1970, coincident with the campaign of United Appeal, the fund-raising arm of the United Fund, United People distributed 35,000 leaflets to employees of several major corporations in the city. The leaflets called attention to the composition of United Fund leadership, to the underrepresentation of the poor among service recipients, and to several community needs not addressed by the Fund. Arguing that pleas for change through regular channels had been fruitless, the leaflet asked that contributions be withheld from the United Appeal. The United People received immediate television and newspaper coverage. The United Fund responded by inviting their spokesperson to address its executive staff, showing a willingness to hear criticisms and react responsibly to protest. At this encounter the UP spokesman addressed the Board with praise for their dedication to community service, saying the complaint was not with the good the United Fund was doing but with the good it was not doing. The indirectness of this approach made it difficult for the United Fund to attack credibly the motives of United People.

The counter strategy was threefold. First, while building the image of the United People as well-meaning but misguided wreckers of society, the UF organizers simultaneously presented themselves as reasonable in the face of opposition. They further took advantage of the conflict situation to motivate their volunteers to greater efforts, thus using the opposition of the United People to help achieve the Appeal's campaign goal. A letter sent on October 2, 1970, to "All Campaign Volunteers" makes this counter strategy plain:

> A handful of people are trying to destroy your United Appeal. Are you going to let them tear down a part of your society that assisted last year over 300,000 people in the three-county area—people who really needed help? Are you going to "turn the other cheek" and let a handful of people destroy an idea that worked for the good of all of us for more than 50 years? Are you going to swallow the idea that just because the United Appeal has been around those years that it is automatically bad and should be destroyed? Are you going to stand still and put up with factions bent on destruction just for the sake of destruction? . . . The United Appeal, which is made up of people just like you, is continually trying to find better ways to help the citizens of our community. Your United Appeal now invites this handful of people to reconsider their motives, and again invites all people to work together to build an even better United Appeal.

In an attempt to counter the initial leafleting at the gates of local industrial plants, the AFL-CIO Council distributed 10,000 rebuttal flyers to the employees. By mid-October the controversy had escalated into a major social issue in the community.

Calling upon the fairness doctrine of the Federal Communications Commission, the United People pressed the local television stations to give them equal time to state their case opposite TV ads for the United Appeal.[6] Upon receipt of evidence of controversy, the FCC ruled favorably upon the request. Citing cases of alleged coercion by campaign volunteers to solicit pledges from factory workers, the United People attacked the claim of voluntarism on which the Appeal rested much of its asserted legitimation. Over fifty calls came from citizens giving examples of arm-twisting in the campaign. These examples were fed back into the media to broaden the attack.

When the United Appeal campaign ended, pledges totaled $5,601,208, more than $250,000 short of the campaign goal. This marked the first time its goal had not been achieved since the late 1950s. The final act of the 1970 drama came in the public dispute over the symbolic victory of the United People. The United Fund officials publicly denied that the United People boycott accounted in any way for their failure to achieve the predetermined goal. Rather, they pointed to higher unemployment, lower corporate profits, strikes, and inflation as explanations. However, the United People were given implicit credit in press accounts for a symbolic and psychological victory.

Privately, United Fund officials admitted having no reliable appraisal of the impact United People had had on their fund-raising drive. Some suggested that the increased sense of urgency and dedication in many campaign workers may have more than compensated for any loss of funds from those persuaded by the boycott campaign. Having won the psychological victory, however, United People could, at the last curtain call, admit in the press to also not knowing if the boycott had actually affected the United Appeal. After all, 95.6 percent of the goal had been achieved.

During the following year the United Fund made some minor shifts in priorities and installed a few new faces in the leadership circle, but when the 1971 United Appeal campaign was kicked off at a downtown rally, United People members were there leafleting the crowd. As a football was kicked down the street signifying the campaign kickoff, one conspicuous member of United People appeared wearing a sandwich-board sign reading, "The United Appeal Is Carrying the Ball the Wrong Direction."

The 1971 United People boycott campaign basically reran the strategy of the previous year. They did, however, place greater emphasis upon the inconsistency between the national statements of the United Fund organization quoted earlier and the practices of the local organization. United Appeal fell short in its campaign for a second year, despite a decrease in the goal's amount by

$163,000, itself a symbolic victory for United People. Pledges fell $119,000, or 5.1 percent, short of the lowered goal. Again, the United People tallied a victory.

Next, a new executive officer of the United Fund came aboard. Priority changes were more drastic than before. Privately, the president of the United Fund contacted United People in June 1972, after the demands of United People had been discussed in a meeting of the Board of Directors, and informed them:

(1) This year, the Budget Committee [has] adopted a policy that no person serving as a board member of a member agency shall participate on the Budget Committee Panel determining allocations for that agency.

(2) The policy of publicizing the community activities of the candidates proposed for the Board of Directors by the Nominating Committee will be continued.

(3) The United Fund bylaws were changed at the 1972 annual meeting to provide for election of three-fourths of the annual Board of Directors vacancies at the annual meeting. Should nominations from the floor be offered, the chairman of the meeting would decide appropriate action.

(4) The functional budgeting program was developed to facilitate the service funding concept from agencies to communities, to families and individuals unable to pay for the services. . . .

(5) The United Appeal will publicize that donations will be confidentially refunded on presented evidence that the donor had to give because of threat against promotion or threatened job loss. The appropriate 1973 campaign literature will carry this message.

The statement concluded with the hope that members of United People could now "position" themselves as members of the United Fund who could make their own pledges and encourage others to do so.

On paper, United People had achieved most of its objectives. In response to the pledge of the United Fund to meet its demands, the 1972 boycott was called off. The Appeal met its 1972 goal.

United People then tested two of the promises made by the Board of Directors of the United Fund to establish their good faith. Leaflets were distributed to employees of several industrial

102

plants, repeating the United Fund's promise to make refunds upon request. The leaflet included a coupon which could be sent directly to the executive officer of the United Fund requesting the refund of a 1972 pledge. The executive was forced to admit to newsmen that it was more difficult to grant refunds than had been indicated in the United People leaflet. The request must come in the form of a letter documenting perceived threats to one's employment or other forms of coercion connected with the pledge. The United Fund publicly lost face over this issue.

In a countermove, the United Fund held open hearings as part of its annual budget meeting. This move won high praise from United Fund critics, including United People. Despite poor attendance at the six-day meetings, the executive director, in press conference, called opening the session worthwhile "because of what it represents." It was, in a sense, another pledge of good faith.

In the spring of 1973, members of United People made contributions to the United Fund and attended its annual meeting. They came with a slate of officers to nominate from the floor, including ministers, social workers, and others interested in the goals of United People. The statement received from the president of United Fund had indicated that "the chairman of the meeting would decide appropriate action" when nominations were made from the floor. The appropriate action, as it turned out, was to state that the constitution of the United Fund denied the possibility of such nominations. The United People members left before the vote and proceeded directly to the courts with a suit demanding the election be voided and that newly elected directors be prohibited from taking any action until the suit was settled. A real change in the locus of power within the organization had been narrowly averted by the United Fund administrators, but in so doing they had opened the possibility of being paralyzed by court order. A hearing was held in June of 1973 but the judge's decision was postponed; he preferred informally to seek a mutually acceptable solution. The United Fund board wasted no time in establishing a committee to study their election procedures. In July it recommended and the board accepted a procedure whereby nominations would be allowed from the community by petitions of 100 names each, to be presented not less than twenty-one days prior to the 1974 annual meeting. The United People, feeling that their faith in the promises of United Fund leaders had once been misplaced, agreed to the new election procedures but planned a boycott of the 1973 United Appeal campaign to keep the pressure on. If the new election procedures result in a redistribution of power on the governing board of the United Fund in the summer of 1974, United People will have achieved its long-term objectives. At that point it is likely that United People will become a low-profile watchdog organization and will fade from the front pages of the local newspapers.

United People Strategy Reconsidered

The boycott approach taken by United People was a long-term, high-risk strategy. As the drama unfolded, the strategy seemed to have accomplished its goals, or nearly so. Not without costs, however.

Could the same goals have been accomplished over a four-year period by working behind the scenes? The United Fund leadership asserts that most of the changes made had been planned before United People entered the scene. Our efforts, from a distance, to assess social-action projects lead us to believe that UP at least succeeded in speeding the change process. Had they chosen other than the boycott strategy, their demands may not have weighed so seriously, nor the United Fund have taken the initiative itself. One corporation executive privately warned the protest group that "many persons are looking for an excuse not to give to United Appeal and you just may be supplying them with that excuse." Clearly, the boycott, although a high-risk strategy, accurately focused on the most vulnerable flank of the organization. All else depends on fund-raising. In establishing a direct (although farfetched) threat to the organization's existence, they guaranteed a hearing for their demands.

Conflict effects and is affected by four variables. They are: relative power, interaction, sentiment, and attrition.[7] Let's take a look at what happened in the United People campaigns in terms of these variables. Interaction between the two groups had occurred continuously, behind the scenes, moving straight toward the approach of a truce. The open hearings of the UF Budget Committee were not only a pledge of good faith but also a significant step toward reduction of insulation from the protest group.

The United Fund, in attempting to utilize the presence of opposition to stimulate greater dedication on the part of campaign volunteers in 1970, had encouraged, within its own ranks, hostile sentiments toward United People. The United People organization, on the other hand, had attempted to keep personalities out of the conflict and had made every effort to praise the good intentions and dedication of the leaders and volunteer workers of United Fund and United Appeal. In so doing they may have neutralized, to some extent, the bitterness which could have prolonged the conflict and hindered the eventual settlement of differences.

Attrition in the conflict was calculable and highly symbolic. Because funding campaigns must set goals, United People could conceivably score successive victories. Because the dollar figure was so visible, the victory appeared as "all or nothing," although the differential was less than 6 percent both in 1970 and 1971. The success of United Appeal in reaching its campaign goal in 1972, in the absence of a boycott, actually served to reinforce the salience of the earlier United People victories. The United People had a strategic advantage with regard to attrition because its only goal was the prevention of its opponent's goal. Had the United Appeal swung the mallet and rung the bell each year, the attrition of the United People would have been visible, but far less so.

The United People may have made some strategic errors in initial calculations of the power of their opponent. This, perhaps, prolonged the conflict. They seem to have underestimated the reservoir of goodwill the United Fund had nurtured and compounded over the years. United People had chosen a formidable opponent. The lifeblood of fund raising is public relations, and in a fight for credibility the United People were dealing with seasoned thespians of the public theater.

Another significant underestimation was the extent of public resistance to the boycott strategy. The city has long seen itself as a quiet place, benevolently overseen by the corporate elite. Some describe the historic role of National Cash Register as not unlike that of Eastman Kodak in Rochester, New York. We are uncertain just how far one could draw this parallel, but, not unlike Rochester, the city has a history pretty much void of controversial issues—with the exception of racial disturbances in the mid-sixties. And, not unlike Rochester also, the community rose in righteous indignation against those who brought controversy.

In the eyes of the public, the United People, Righter, and the Congregation for Reconciliation were closely aligned. This created two crosscurrents. On the one hand, it provided an air of legitimacy otherwise absent from the United People. As the 1971 campaign chairman for United Appeal said in a news interview, "You know, it's not becoming to a man who's a member of the clergy to go around using those sorts of tactics. I've always felt the United Appeal had a very strong religious flavor, and should have, because it's a humanitarian effort and service. I wish he'd help us." Obviously, the religious symbols embodied in United People created a degree of cognitive dissonance in the United Appeal, since this openly challenged their implicit claim to have God on their side.

On the other hand, the involvement of the Congregation for Reconciliation in a venture potentially undermining of a good liberal cause stirred dissonance among church people. As a result, local clergy, especially Presbyterians, experienced a great deal of pressure from their laity. This was particularly so in the larger and wealthier congregations where corporation support for United Appeal was reflected among active lay leaders. The largest Presbyterian church in the city, in its newsletter circulated to a membership of over three thousand, warned:

> We have an outfit in town called "the Congregation for Reconciliation," which from time to time emerges, mothlike, to flutter about, from out of the fabric of our community, making certain intemperate (i.e., excessive, inordinate, ungovernable) remarks, and then proceeds once again to gnaw away at the warp and weft of that fabric. . . . Recently a pseudo organization called "United People" has been proposed by "the Congregation for Reconciliation" and others, to take the place of the United Fund. The Fund is surely one of the basic strands in the fabric of our community. To undermine it is to threaten the existence of 55 member agencies."

While many clergy recalled threats of withdrawal of money and/or membership from their congregations in protest of the activities of the Congregation for Reconciliation, only a few reported directly traceable loss of members or withholding of benevolences to Righter and his congregation. This should not, however, negate or underplay the sense of pressure felt by many clergy during the United People campaigns.

We should note here the discrepancy between the stress felt by Presbyterian and United Church of Christ clergy. The early publicity about the Congregation had indicated its affiliation with the Presbyterians. Several UCC pastors have stated they did not believe their laity were generally aware the Congregation for Reconciliation was also affiliated with the United Church of Christ.

Typically, community leaders and clergy believed it appropriate and important to call attention to the need for reform in the United Fund. But only three or four people we talked with endorsed a boycott initiated by a church group as an appropriate strategy to accomplish this. Several additional clergy indicated that their immediate personal reaction to the boycott was favorable but that their views changed as they began to feel the repercussions from laity. In 1971 a group of seventeen clergy released a statement calling for reform in the United Fund but explicitly rejecting Righter's methods. They expressed confidence in the possibility of achieving reform from within the organization. Certainly, as strategy, this move was welcomed by the United Fund to restore balance to the "God is on our side" dimension of the symbolic battle for credibility.

Summary

In sum, the prolonged struggle between the Congregation for Reconciliation and the United Fund influenced both organizations. It was the Congregation's first major social-action project, encountering a formidable opponent in a credibility drama which has lasted most of the mission's life. The United People campaign provided needed stability and continuity in social action. It also offered the potential for a visible major victory which would generate recognition and influence for the Congregation in

Dayton. In this sense, the United People, more than any other single action project, gained for the Congregation a public image. The image further reinforced the self-view of the Congregation as a local leader in the area of direct social action.

We feel it appropriate to introduce here a personal observation based on a good many years of analyzing public response to social issues. While we have no hard data to verify the validity of this observation in Dayton, we have every reason to believe Dayton to be no different from other communities from which we have gathered information. We are inclined to accept the sincerity of clergy and community leaders who favor reform of the United Fund but object to United People's tactics. On the other hand, it is a mistake to assume that the average citizen favors reform but simply objects to tactics. Average citizens, in all probability, have no quarrel at all with United Fund. They give to United Appeal not because some of their money goes to aid the poor but in spite of this. They give their money because they know it is used to support Boy Scouts, Girl Scouts, Red Cross, and the Y's. These are organizations from which they have benefited, and they view the United Fund as a sensible way to support these programs. Similarly, most persons have experienced mental illness in their extended families, and the feeling that some of their money is going for treatment is desirable. In addition, probably a subtle psychological feeling of "goodness" or pietism creeps in simply from giving. But it also seems safe to assume the large majority of the population could not name many United Fund agencies in addition to the ones we have mentioned.

Probably the most effective way to reduce giving to the United Fund in any community would be to publicize those expenditures channeled to help the poor help themselves. Monies for legal aid and community organizations have had a terribly difficult time surviving the hatchets of conservative congressmen.[8] Widespread publicity of the use of the United Fund money for such activities would probably arouse the same responses and would seriously affect giving.

The United People campaign assumed that upper- and middle-income people, realizing they were giving not to the poor but to those who could afford to pay, would boycott the United Fund and/or demand reform. We believe this to be a misjudgment on the part of United People. If the issues involved in the boycott were an important component in determining public opinion or the final objective of achieving reform, we believe this would have been a serious mistake in strategy. As our theoretical framework would suggest, however, concrete issues of how the money is spent were not very important in the public drama. Nor was it important that public opinion be sympathetic with the boycott. Indeed, had they succeeded in rallying any serious support for the boycott—that is, had a significant proportion of givers actually withheld their funds—they would have succeeded in sabotaging, not reforming, the United Fund. We are unaware of anyone associated with United People who viewed this as a desirable outcome of the boycott.

The success of United People was in gaining support for the principle of reform in United Fund procedures, an objective many community leaders shared. Indeed, one of the daily newspapers had editorialized for reform several years before United People was conceived. The public specter of a boycott dramatized the need for reform and in the process everyone favoring change, including persons within the United Fund organization, gained a little leverage. United People thus helped grease the wheels of change. And that, after all, was their objective.

CHAPTER 6

Gideon's Gang Marches Again: The Gulf Boycott

Three widely separated concerns in American thought came together in the early 1970s to provide a setting in which the Congregation for Reconciliation progressed from the local to the national scene with a social-action project.

First, the Vietnam war was finally winding down. Pressure for immediate withdrawal of troops mounted in Congress. The Cambodian incursion in the spring of 1970, followed by the killings at Kent State and Jackson State, sparked nationwide student protests demanding an immediate end to the war. In this context much concern for avoiding such future conflicts developed, and American national interests abroad became a focus of assessment.

Second, for at least a decade, support for white-minority-ruled states in southern Africa has been on America's agenda of moral issues. This issue gained a great deal of public attention in 1965 when Rhodesia (Zimbabwe), under pressure from Great Britain to decolonize, unilaterally declared independence. The white-dominated regime of President Ian Smith increasingly implemented a system of racial segregation. In 1968, the United Nations enacted mandatory trade sanctions against the regime. Guerrilla attacks shortly before Christmas in 1972 led Rhodesia to close its borders to Zambia, its black-dominated neighbor to the north. Rhodesia's guerrilla skirmishes called attention to the nearby Portuguese colonial territories of Mozambique and Angola, where revolutionary independence movements have been active for many years, recently with increasing intensity.

Third, consumer groups such as the Nader organization gained national attention during the latter 1960s in calling for business concerns to consider more seriously the social and environmental consequences of their actions.

The theme of corporate responsibility coalesced with the growing interest in racist regimes in southern Africa to focus debate in this country on the proper strategy for companies with investments in that area. In the past few years stockholder proposals and all kinds of protests on the ethics of investment by U.S. corporations—not only in South Africa but also in its neighbors Namibia, Rhodesia, Angola, and Mozambique—have abounded. The suggestion that investments be withdrawn has borne little fruit.

American companies in southern Africa have tended to respond to these protests in two ways. First, by refusing to take advantage of customary racial disparities in pay, and thereby upgrading black employees in these countries, some have argued they are establishing a precedent for the white governments. Second, others have argued that their stimulation of the economies of these countries will gradually undermine their racist policies. In 1973, seventeen corporations faced stockholder proposals urging withdrawal, fair employment practices, or disclosure of investments in southern Africa. This protest is coordinated by a coalition of Protestant church groups called the Church Project on U.S. Investments in Southern Africa.[1]

The Gulf Oil Corporation is the largest single American investor in Portuguese Africa. In 1954 it began prospecting in Cabinda, an enclave of Angola located on the Atlantic Ocean between the two Congos. Its first important oil strike was made in 1966. By 1969, it had invested $130 million in developing the field.[2] In 1972, the oil production rate rose to 127,000 barrels per day, representing approximately 3.9 percent of Gulf's total world petroleum output. In the same year, Gulf paid $61 million to Portugal in taxes and rights.

In June of 1970, the Ohio Conference of the United Church of Christ passed a resolution for a boycott of Gulf products. The denomination's missionary ties with Angola had prompted the resolution. In the war of national independence there, Protestant missionaries have often sided with the insurgents. The resolution's supporters claimed that Gulf, through its taxes, contributed financially to the colonial war against independence. Gulf, in response to the call for a selective patronage campaign, threatened to sue the Ohio Conference. The *Washington Post* picked up the story, and it received wide coverage across Ohio.

Outreach or Overreach?

In the fall of 1970, several Congregation for Reconciliation members interested in the issue of colonialism formed a study group to explore the Angola situation more fully.

Early in March 1971 the research committee presented a resolution to the Congregation calling for social action against the Gulf Oil Corporation. Two controversial issues developed around the resolution. First, several members questioned the wisdom of adopting a social-action project of national scope. It seemed to them a matter of overreach rather than outreach. For so small a group to take on the fourth largest oil company in assets in the world appeared absurd. The Congregation had already proved itself skilled in social action on the local level. Some wondered if a move to a national issue, however, might indicate both foolhardiness and an unrealistic assessment of the Congregation's social-action skill and resources. It would surely be interpreted by the Congregation's detractors as arrogant self-aggrandizement.

Second, in response to this action, Gulf could file a slander or defamation suit against the Congregation, just as it had threatened to do against the Ohio Conference of the United Church of Christ. The Congregation was divided. To some, if the Congregation was unwilling to risk its life, it should get out of the social-action business. For others, the possibility of a legal action which could affect the financial resources of each member was clearly intimidating.

The gravity of the issue led to tabling the resolution and scheduling a workshop to explore the legal ramifications with a lawyer. They then learned that only those voting in favor of the action resolution could be sued. This provided a test of social-action commitment unequaled in the life of the Congregation. Many members agonized over their decisions. The workshop had been well attended, but when the Congregation convened in a business

113

session on March 11 and the resolution came to a vote, only thirteen persons were in attendance. Some who voted in favor of the resolution had taken all property out of their own name and placed it in the name of a spouse who, if he was a member of the Congregation, voted against the resolution. The call for social action against Gulf by the Congregation for Reconciliation passed by a vote of eleven to two.

Since the resolution embodies the basic rationale for what later grew to a national movement, it is important to examine the entire document.

> WHEREAS, the Portuguese territories of Angola, Mozambique, Guinea Bissau, remain the last major European colonies of that continent;
>
> WHEREAS, the United Nations General Assembly "reaffirms the inalienable right of the peoples of the Territories under Portuguese domination to achieve freedom and independence, in accordance with General Assembly resolution 1514, and legitimacy of their struggle to achieve this right" (Resolution 2270, November 17, 1967);
>
> WHEREAS, the United Nations General Assembly "strongly condemns the activities of the financial interests operating in the territories under Portuguese domination, which exploit the human and material resources of the territories and impede the progress of their people towards freedom and independence" (Resolution 2270);
>
> WHEREAS, Christian teaching proclaims release to the captives and liberty to the oppressed (Luke 4:18);
>
> WHEREAS, currently, many Angolans, some of whom are members of the Christian community, are imprisoned because of their struggle for freedom and independence;
>
> WHEREAS, the Gulf Oil Corporation, Pittsburgh, Pennsylvania, has been doing business in Angola since 1957 and considers Angola "A vital source of oil" (Gulf statement, September 10, 1970) and thus provides economic support to Portuguese colonialism in Angola; and
>
> WHEREAS, the Ohio Conference of the United Church of Christ has recommended that its members participate in a selective

patronage campaign by discontinuing the use of Gulf products and turning in their Gulf credit cards: therefore [be it]

[Resolved by] the Congregation for Reconciliation, a member of the Ohio Conference, as a matter of conscience and Christian responsibility, [That it] supports the right of the Angolan people to achieve freedom and independence and their struggle toward that end.

SEC. 2. [It] calls for the release of all political prisoners.

SEC. 3. [It] expresses its disapproval of the Gulf Oil Corporation's business involvement with the Portuguese government in Angola.

SEC. 4. [It] recommends to its own members and to American Christians and the American public that they refrain from purchasing any product of the Gulf Oil Corporation while the business relationship of Gulf Oil Corporation with the Portuguese Government in Angola continues.

SEC. 5. [It] commends the Ohio Conference of the United Church of Christ for initiating the said campaign of selective patronage and authorizes its officers and the Angola committee to participate in and support the said campaign by lawful means and in all lawful ways.[3]

By calling for social action under the legitimation of United Nations Resolution 2270 and scripture, the appeal extends to secularists and Christians alike. Further, the phrasing is clearly an extension of the resolution passed by the United Church of Christ. This would provide legal argument for the complicity of the Ohio Conference of that denomination in boycott activities generated by the Congregation. Finally, the Congregation sought to protect itself by specifying authorization only of such activity using "lawful means."

The boycott resolution could probably have passed when first presented in spite of the feeling by some that the enormity of the undertaking was patently absurd. The Congregation has almost never denied an action committee the right to pursue a project in the name of the Congregation. Holding the workshop and seriously considering the legal ramifications prior to the vote promoted an image of responsibility in action to community leaders, pastors, and denomination executives who knew the history of the boycott. This was consistently borne out in our interviews. The process of adopting the Gulf boycott project thus served two functions. It reinforced personal commitment to social action among many members by making the risks personal and significant, and it earned credibility points from interested observers by demonstrating a high degree of responsibility for the ramifications of congregational decisions.

Two years after the resolution's adoption, the support base for the Gulf boycott had mushroomed beyond the point where a lawsuit leveled at the Congregation would have stopped the movement. The legal risks taken on March 11 then ceased to be an issue in the minds of the members of the Congregation for Reconciliation. For two years, however, those who had voted to support the national boycott of one of America's largest corporations had, in their minds at least, run a risk for their commitments far beyond all but a few church people. Even in a social-action-oriented congregation, that some would abstain when personal risk to property was threatened is predictable.

No doubt some abstained not for want of conviction but in protest to a division of the Congregation's attention between local and national issues. We can understand how the proposed action goal must have seemed a totally unrealistic and wasteful squandering of precious resources in time and energy for a congregation of about thirty members.

Climbing Jacob's Ladder: The Gulf Boycott Coalition

In early July 1971, the Gulf-Angola Committee sponsored a workshop for representatives of several national groups to work on a statement of goals and strategy. Members of the American Committee on Africa, the United Church of Christ Council on Christian Action, and CIRUNA, the United Nations student organization, attended the workshop, coming from such scattered places as New York, Chicago, San Francisco, and Indianapolis. At the workshop the Gulf-Angola Committee changed its name to the Gulf Boycott Coalition. Although the name may seem to imply a coalition of organizations, in reality it represents only a coalition of individuals. The base of the Coalition was and has remained solely the Congregation for Reconciliation, although its boycott has received endorsements from many organizations and prominent individuals.

The meeting was concluded with a celebration (worship service) outside a downtown Gulf service station on the fourth of July. To mark the official birth of the Coalition, they released a large helium-filled orange balloon proclaiming the message "Boycott Gulf." Small grants from members of the United Presbyterian Church and the United Church of Christ symbolically established the initial funding of the organization.

The first action of the newly formed Coalition took place on the Congregation's home turf. Dayton had a contract with Gulf to provide gasoline for city vehicles, renewable every six months on a low-bid basis. The Gulf Boycott Coalition (GBC) began laying a strategy to undermine the Gulf bid. Their research had uncovered that Gulf had only a 4 percent minority work force in its Ohio region; the second lowest bidder (only $150 higher) had a 12 percent nonwhite work force. Since the city government had taken a public stand against minority job discrimination, the GBC began politicking with city commissioners to line up opposition to accepting Gulf's low bid. When the issue came to a vote, Gulf lost its contract.

Rejecting the Gulf bid on December 8 cost the city $150; it cost Gulf more than $55,000. More importantly, the Gulf Boycott Coalition catapulted into brief national prominence. The *Wall Street Journal* carried the story, and such visibility bolstered the Coalition's credibility before other protest groups and served notice of their seriousness on Gulf. Success at the local level where social action processes were well understood served as a springboard to the unfamiliar waters of national action, for they had been noticed.

As a result of demonstrated clout in depriving Gulf of a city contract, the Coalition was invited to participate in the National Conference on Southern Africa in Washington, D.C., several months later. Several national church bodies and a loose coalition of Afro-American organizations sponsored the conference. The GBC participated with the specific purpose of seeking out support for the boycott and cultivating the media. Unexpectedly their involvement also earned them the bonus of an advisory board of prominent individuals who lent their names to the support of the boycott. The national conference, in addition, resolved to support the boycott.

Climbing to national prominence was a progression of happy surprises. Righter, then a Dayton representative for Americans for Democratic Action, lobbied at its national convention for adoption of a strong boycott resolution as presented by the Ohio ADA. The resolution passed and the boycott received further publicity through the ADA newsletter. Further, Allard Lowenstein, president of ADA, whose interest in southern Africa dates back to the 1950s, added his name to the advisory board of the boycott, as did Leon Shull, executive director of ADA, Dolores Mitchell, executive committee chairperson of ADA, and John Kenneth Galbraith.

The ADA endorsement not only gave the Coalition broader visibility than before but, perhaps more important, leaders of the organization opened to the GBC an extensive file of individuals across the country who they felt would be willing to become involved in local boycott activity. Mailings to these persons reaped an expanded list of friends and acquaintances for the Coalition's file.

When the 1972 Gulf stockholders' meeting convened in April, the Gulf Boycott Coalition stood ready. They sponsored a liberation celebration outside the meeting hall in Pittsburgh as stockholders were gathering. Several persons, including an Angola missionary, spoke, and a model of the Statue of Liberty, battered by a Gulf sign, provided photogenic novelty for the press. The celebration ended with the release of dozens of orange "Boycott Gulf" balloons to rise above Pittsburgh, the home base of the international oil corporation.

The Coalition leaders, in collaboration with the Church Project on U.S. Investments in Southern Africa, then attempted to bring resolutions to the floor of the stockholders' meeting. Although the resolutions were allowed, discussion from the floor was tightly controlled. Microphones were turned off at mention of Angola. This experience convinced Coalition leadership that their time was better spent elsewhere.

Many boycott sympathizers on the mailing list of the Coalition were assumed to be timid about the use of confrontation tactics. In order to provide for social-action appeal to the broadest audience of supporters, the Coalition developed techniques of "nonconfrontation tactics." After a feasibility study, the first of these tactics was activated between Thanksgiving and Christmas of 1972.

During this period shopping centers are filled with Christmas shoppers. Gulf had recently distributed bumper decals with seals of the various states through their dealers. Automobiles showing such decals on their bumpers were assumed to belong to Gulf customers. Volunteers flocked into parking lots and leafleted decaled cars in several scattered areas of the nation. No direct confrontation between the customer and the volunteer occurred. The message in the leaflets was designed for middle America, making appeals primarily to patriotism in their request to boycott Gulf products.

In January 1973 the Gulf Boycott Coalition received its first substantial grant. The $8,300 stipend came from the DJB Foundation in New York which funds social-action organizations they consider capable and responsible.

During the first half of 1973 Coalition leaders fanned out across the country, organizing local boycott groups. In these encounters they taught crash courses on research, education, media utilization, and action skills. St. Louis, New York, Boston, Philadelphia, Atlanta, and Birmingham were areas of concentration. In their efforts, they met with a black militant group based in Massachusetts, independently organizing groups in several black communities and preparing to launch a Gulf boycott media campaign in a number of black news magazines. A statewide organization in Maryland operating through campus, political, and church groups and gathering its own endorsements from prominent political and activist leaders was established.

In March, the Coalition was surprised by a call from Congressman Charles C. Diggs, Jr., asking if representatives of the Coalition would testify before the House Subcommittee on Africa which was holding hearings on U.S. corporate investments in Southern Africa. Congressman Charles W. Whalen, a member of the Coalition's advisory board, introduced its representative at the hearing. Whalen's Republican status lent the GBC a degree of credibility it would otherwise have lacked. A free-lance journalist who had followed the subcommittee's hearings told Coalition leaders afterward that one of the subcommittee members who had attempted to discredit previous witnesses from social-action organizations as Communist sympathizers refrained from attacking the Gulf Boycott Coalition in the face of Whalen's strong endorsement.

Additionally, the testimony before the House Subcommittee on Africa led to Congressman Diggs's agreeing to serve as an advisory board member. Congressmen Ronald Dellums and Charles Whalen had also previously agreed to serve in this capacity.

In the spring a staff reporter from the Pittsburgh desk of *Business Week* discovered that no proxy resolutions were to be presented at the 1973 Gulf stockholders' meeting—for the first time in three years. After several calls and encouragement from national leaders in the southern Africa protest movement, the GBC decided the stockholders did indeed need a reminder of the Angola issue. Ignoring the normal routine of advanced planning, they managed a protest at the gathering. In this instance, without a push from the media the meeting would have proceeded without dissension.

In 1972 the GBC introduced and distributed gummed mini-posters which read, "Boycott Gulf, Help Angola—Gulf Boycott Coalition." By the summer of 1973, they decided that dealers made aware of the boycott would become concerned and contact those higher up the chain of command. This would serve both as an annoyance and perhaps a small scare to company officials. To assure dealer complaints from scattered parts of the nation, the Coalition sent out "Vacation Idea Kits" to action volunteers. These kits contained the mini-posters and other boycott materials and invited volunteers to stop at Gulf stations and place the labels in conspicuous places in the station rest rooms. Since the volunteer came and went unnoticed, this was another nonconfrontation action. Purposely, no address of the GBC appeared on the sticker. Dealers had to turn to someone higher in the Gulf organization for an explanation. Boycott stickers have since been placed in Gulf rest rooms crisscrossing the nation.

Gulf ships much of its Angolan oil to Canada for refining. Since the Angola Committee of the Netherlands has successfully pressured Gulf to stop imports to Holland from the Portuguese colonies, the Gulf Boycott Coalition has seriously considered the strategy of organizing activist groups in Canada to campaign against the importation of oil from Angola. On several international policy matters Canada has shown itself a step ahead of the United States. With this in mind, GBC strategists considered the Canadian government more likely to pass legislation banning Angolan oil, given enough attention to the issue in the media. In May of 1973 organizers went to Canada to begin building a Boycott Gulf network.

During the Canada trip, one GBC leader joined a Toronto Gulf action group to call upon the chairman of the board of Gulf Canada to inform him of the issues and to prevent future distortion of the cause. A primary purpose of this visit, however, was the nonconfrontation of Gulf Oil Corporation executives in Pittsburgh, since they assumed word would be passed by the Canadian board chairman. The message, of course, said that the small group of activists, once considered a localized group, was now organizing in Canada as well as the United States.

During our last field contact with the Gulf Boycott Coalition they were circulating a $100,000 grant proposal among several funding agencies, talking of a national media campaign, and discussing research on half a dozen institutional contracts which, with careful planning, could be snatched from Gulf bidders. In addition, three national organizations with large mailing lists have a Gulf boycott endorsement now under consideration.

Grumbling among members of the Congregation for Reconciliation about squandering resources on quixotic national protests is no longer heard. Few would have believed in March of 1971 that a thirty-member congregation could launch a viable national movement. But it did.[4]

The Potentially Prodigious Snowball:
Interpreting GBC Strategy

With the Gulf Oil Corporation, the Congregation for Reconciliation for the first time engaged an opponent with potential to affect resources dear to its members. In that sense, the conflict model developed in chapter 5 more closely parallels that of a war game. The power relationship clearly favors Gulf. Although the tactic might have attracted a great deal of unfavorable publicity and thus have been counterproductive, Gulf could have sued the members of the Congregation who voted to support the boycott. A defamation-of-character suit by Gulf at this point, however, would catapult the Coalition into unimaginable national prominence. The Coalition has had two years to build alliances with journalists and national organizations which would promptly pounce upon such a controversy, leaving Gulf in an awkward and embarrassing public relations posture.

The power of the Gulf Boycott Coalition to affect valued resources of the corporation such as sale of products remains speculative. Damage to the public image of Gulf, rather than actual loss of sales, may be a more realistic measure of attrition.

Interaction and sentiment become vague concepts in this conflict. Nonconfrontation tactics have minimized direct interaction between the parties considerably, although behind the scenes contact with some Gulf public relations personnel—who have the unhappy task of undoing Coalition damage to Gulf's image—has remained constant. Assessment of sentiment is impossible.

The only cost to Gulf thus far has been the growing annoyance provided by the Coalition. Public relations personnel have appeared before several student groups in the past year and have required an increasing number of briefings from management in order to counter pointed questions. This demand upon management resources could become a major annoyance with time, putting Gulf on the defensive and ultimately stimulating internal consideration of alternative policy. Should alternatives be seriously entertained by management, the Coalition has shrewdly provided an opportunity for face-saving. The GBC has never insisted that Gulf withdraw from Angola. Rather, it has placed emphasis upon another option. The Coalition has argued that Gulf can satisfy its demands by "saving" the Cabinda oil—that is, by severely cutting back production until after Angola has become self-governing. In the long run, this would facilitate image cleaning without actual investment loss for Gulf.

On Gulf's side currently is the national attention focused upon "the energy crisis." Public sentiment is now unlikely to support the suspension of any important source of petroleum for whatever moral reason. On the other hand, stories are filtering through to the Western press concerning My Lai type actions of Portuguese troops in Mozambique. Portuguese colonialism may thus receive increasing public attention as the guerrilla war continues. The American experience in Vietnam combined with the appeal of a war for national independence will probably lead American public opinion to oppose Portugal in the struggle. It is predictable that the Coalition will do what it can to fan the flames of public reaction. As Watergate resolves itself, Portuguese colonialism may receive far greater media attention in the years ahead.

Should this happen, the Gulf Boycott Coalition will reap the benefits of public sentiment. Further, they will make every effort to link Gulf symbolically with the image of a cruel and oppressive colonial regime, thus creating a public relations nightmare. Should this happen, Gulf may "save" the 3.9 percent of total petroleum output derived from the Cabinda field rather than suffer through the public relations contortions and accompanying management headaches produced by such a situation.

The Gulf Boycott Coalition would undoubtedly interpret this as a major victory and claim the credit. The outcome of the boycott, therefore, depends more on how Portugal's colonial war evolves than it does on Gulf. In this sense, time is on the side of the Coalition. Obviously, a major "victory" over Gulf would strengthen the perceived power of the Congregation for Reconciliation in future social-action projects.

Summary

To summarize and reflect, the making of a national movement requires progressively expanding sponsorship, which then generates broad-based support. The news media play a crucial role in providing wide visibility for any social movement, and in this instance skills developed in working with local media were transferred to developing rapport with the national media. Church publications responded because of Presbyterian and UCC sponsorship. The underground press rallied behind the boycott's sponsorship by the National Conference on Southern Africa and the regular mailings of boycott material to a large number of activist groups across the country. The story in the *Wall Street Journal*, however, provided a media breakthrough. Since then the Coalition has received some notice from other business-oriented periodical publications.

The dialogue between a social-action group and the media is dynamic and progressive. The action group provides news and the media provide exposure and influence. As interaction develops, action is not only covered but also encouraged by the media. In this way, the media can facilitate, if not create, news stories. The protest at the 1973 Gulf stockholders meeting is illustrative. An action group sensitive to the needs of the media, aware of deadlines, careful to stage suitable protests, and prompt to provide news releases, including background research, can anticipate media courtship.

The Congregation for Reconciliation, in fostering a social-action project aspiring to become a national movement, encountered considerable scoffing at such absurd self-aggrandizement. The thought of a small congregation taking on the fourth largest international petroleum group seemed patent fantasy. Yet as the movement has grown it has become conceivable that given certain circumstances the movement could actually succeed in its goal. Gideon's gang, ignoring its detractors, continues to polish its horns and trim its lamps.

CHAPTER 7

The Question of Strategy: Conflict in Context

The Congregation for Reconciliation has, throughout its life, attempted to induce or encourage social change by calling business, service, and governmental organizations to public accountability. A number of features distinguish their manner of action and need to be identified and analyzed. First, they have typically operated in the *public arena*. Seldom have they privately approached individuals and in effect said, "Hey, this is a community problem for which we believe your organization bears some responsibility. Why don't you go talk with your board and see if you can't do thus and so?" Rather, with the skillful use of the media, they have taken on organizations in full view of the total community. This means, secondly, that they have willfully placed themselves in an *adversary* relationship with organizations they consider to be in need of change. This, in turn, has placed representatives of the organizations under attack in a position of (a) attempting to ignore the charges, (b) defending their policies, or (c) launching a counteroffensive against the Congregation. As a result of deliberately generating such adversary relationships, the Congregation has created community *conflict*.

America, perhaps more than other nations, has difficulty in dealing with conflict as a "normal" or "healthy" social process. We tend to view conflict as a breakdown of everyday social relationships, an abnormal interruption of man's normal state of being, cooperation. Conflict thus is a condition demanding quick remedy, lest the social order be threatened and torn asunder. There are some peculiar ironies about this cultural attitude toward conflict. First of all, democratic governments invariably include structures deliberately created to provide legitimate processes for the resolution of conflict. The very nature of democracy assumes the existence of diverse interests struggling for scarce resources and a voice in public policy. Only tyrannical power, squelching all opposition, suppresses conflict.

Our founding fathers not only assumed conflict as normal but also wanted to assure its inevitability. Those gentlemen, in forging the Constitution of this nation, themselves struggled to protect vested interests while at the same time they compromised to assure the institutionalization of the ongoing struggle so as not to give one side an unchallengeable advantage. At stake in the conflict in Philadelphia was the democratic process itself; they assumed that men of divergent interests and origins would make conflicting claims to status, power, and resources, that the existing arrangements of power and authority were not permanent.

Conflict pervades our history. Sometimes it has been a means for forging unity out of discord and disharmony. Sometimes it has erupted into violent attempts to annihilate the opposition, scarring our heritage. But, amazingly, no group has ever managed to gain sufficient advantage to silence the opposition permanently and thereby terminate conflict. This, we believe, results from an ingenious constitutional system which regulates the parameters of conflict. Between the lines, the Bill of Rights protects an individual's right to engage in legitimate conflict in the pursuit of his own interests, without fear of tyrannical exercise of power by government, neighbor, or adversary. Strange, therefore, that we should come to regard conflict as disruptive, dysfunctional, and abnormal, rather than as inherent in social process.

There is another irony in our cultural attitude toward conflict. In contrast to our uneasiness about conflict, competition is a revered cultural value. Competition is the sacred potion which kindles the spirit of free enterprise, capitalism, and the National Football League. Without competition, we are taught to believe, the furnaces in Pittsburgh, the assembly lines in Detroit, and the stockyards in Omaha would grind to a halt. Stifle competition and you strangle initiative, the backbone of our way of life. If anything rivals apple pie as Americana, most assuredly it is the spirit of competition.

126

At base, competition and conflict are both forms of struggle. But, as Kenneth Burke succinctly says, "the names for things and operations smuggle in connotations of good and bad—a noun tends to carry with it a kind of invisible adjective, and a verb an invisible adverb." [1] Competition carries desirable connotations in our society and is sometimes used to launder abuses and distortions of power in business and government; conflict bears innuendos and is used to describe threats to our social stability, as in marital conflict and the Vietnam conflict. The former implies a fair, and perhaps even friendly, struggle; the latter suggests hostility and foul play.

As a nation, we condone and support such maxims as "May the best man win" and "First among equals." But in the reality of any contest, be it for power, prestige, or resources, we reject such an objective, nonpartisan stance. We define good guys and bad guys. And we also define the nature of the struggle along the spectrum from competition to conflict, thus imposing a judgment on the controversy. Obviously, the attachment of such value-laden words can affect our normative response and distort our perception of the struggle itself. Just as "healthy political competition" is a grossly inappropriate description of the activities of the Committee to Re-Elect the President in 1972, so too is "instigating community conflict" a misnomer, as normally understood, for the activities of the Congregation for Reconciliation. They play by the rules, honor their commitments, and genuinely respect, perhaps even love, their adversaries. They just happen also to disagree with some aspects of the status quo and are engaged in competition to effect social change. Persons who rock boats are seldom very popular, but, in being labeled as engaging in conflict, the Congregation has had the job of communicating the justice and legitimacy of its goals made even more difficult.

Conflict, as we have conceptualized it, and not as it has been culturally defined, can be a positive rather than a negative social process. Rather than being itself disruptive and dysfunctional, it may help to resolve dysfunctional, disruptive, and inequitable social arrangements. "Rubbing raw the sores of discontent," as the late Saul Alinsky used to put it, may well heal social wounds which might otherwise fester and eventually produce far greater social ills.

Few in our society today challenge the proposition that significant inequities and injustices exist. The bone of contention usually revolves around the question of means to effect social change. The argument advanced by the Congregation for Reconciliation, as well as by most groups engaged in so-called direct action or confrontation tactics, is that conflict offers an effective means to move otherwise recalcitrant, reluctant, and resistant institutions. Confrontation is the means, they argue, whereby otherwise powerless change-oriented groups can pressure much more powerful groups to initiate change in the public interest.

The strike or threat of strike is the labor union's institutionally legitimized weapon to pressure corporate structures in the ongoing struggle to foster the interests of labor. Governments threaten banks, corporations, and other governments with economic sanctions to achieve their will in the struggle to determine domestic and foreign policy. Parents threaten children by withholding rewards to gain compliance with their will. Members of voluntary associations threaten to withhold financial contributions to convince leaders to pursue policies consonant with rank and file expectations. There are hundreds of ways individuals and organizations struggle with other individuals and organizations to achieve their will. Usually, however, we use words like negotiation, competition, exercise of proper authority, and the like to describe the process of struggle. Individuals and organizations, whether implicitly or explicitly stated, unconsciously or consciously, seek out effective means (strategies) for getting what they want. The Congregation for Reconciliation has chosen conflict in the public arena precisely because they believe it to be an effective means for achieving their goals.

In this chapter we shall examine their conflict strategy within a framework of dramaturgical social theory.[2] Our approach is neither polemical nor intended to attempt to legitimize their approach to social change. Rather, we seek only to provide a theoretical model which both "makes sense" of their action and can explain their measure of success. Having explored their strategy, we will then examine their own perceived link to a theological rationale. Are the Christian goals of love and reconciliation compatible with their conflict strategy? And finally, we will present a verbatim interview with Righter which reveals something about the value presuppositions informing his style of social ministry.

A Dramaturgical Model
for Interpreting Action and Conflict

Social order is a matter of consent; leaders must persuade followers to accept them. Once done, maintaining approval becomes an ongoing activity, varying in degree with the openness of the system involved. A dictator with strong military support is relatively safe in his power position; a congressman in Washington seldom leaves the campaign platform. The legitimacy possessed by any leader is his key to power; without it he loses not only status and prestige but also his ability to achieve goals.

Maintenance of legitimacy is not unlike a drama. When the script is written as comedy, its plot deliberately sanctions doubt. The audience is invited to suspend its presumptions and convictions and to focus on the incongruities and hypocrisies being dramatized by the actors. Unlike tragedy, which envelops its audience on an emotional level, comedy ultimately appeals to reason. The audience must judge the stage action: Does it confirm or deny the unmasking of the heroic figures? That is, are the power- and status-wielding actors deserving of their legitimacy, or ought they to be denuded and dislodged?

Heroes generally appeal for audience support to maintain the existing social order—i.e., their own legitimacy—on grounds of stability, orthodoxy, tradition, and the like. Their challengers, the villains who may be wearing the white hats all along, appeal for change in social order—and hence in heroic figures—on the basis of obstinacy, heresy, and stagnation in power circles.

Real-life drama flowers as comedy in environments where open criticism is considered valuable; in a democratic social order many of the mechanisms for change and development assume the public form of comedies acted before the voters, the financial supporters, the volunteer workers, etc. In the words of Hugh Duncan:

In democratic society the expression of difference in debate, discussion, and argument is not a way to discord but to a superior truth, because opposition, in competition and in rivalry, makes us think harder about the rights of others and leads us to act in more humane ways.[3]

Thus social action often assumes the form of comedy played before significant audiences. It aims to challenge the credibility of the goals espoused by organizational elites in light of their (organizational) behavior. Both the heroes and the villains plot and act to win audience approval and assurance of legitimacy and cooperative support. Although some kinds of dialogue and action can always be predicted by past stage plays and the experiences of the actors and audiences involved, the outcome is seldom inevitable. In the unrehearsed and unscripted drama of social action, the heroes in the last act will be those most able to woo the audience while discrediting their opponents.

Viewed from a dramaturgical perspective, the adversary relationships engendered in the public arena by the Congregation represent a form of competition. Both parties are competing for public support. Both operate within a framework of rules, those of fair play. To do otherwise could be to draw boos from the audience and to strengthen the opponent's appeal.

Yet, differing from competition in one significant respect, such dramas are termed conflict situations. The struggle's reward is not the same for both parties. Unlike an election, where opponents compete for a particular public office, or an athletic event, where teams compete for the higher score, in social conflict situations the parties seek contradictory goals. Ordinarily such struggles in the public arena focus upon issue-relevant behavior or policy. One opponent challenges, the other defends the status quo. Both seek to have their will prevail. From the challenger's position, the goal of conflict is social change.

When a social-action group appeals for social change, the individual or organization from which such change is sought may respond in one of three ways. First, it may ignore the challenge and continue business as usual. This is an appropriate response when the challenger lacks visibility or where the request is so outrageous as to greatly undermine credibility. Second, it may defend present policy or make cosmetic modifications to give the appearance of reasonable flexibility and accommodation. Third, it

130

may counterattack and seek to destroy the credibility of the challenger.

The Congregation for Reconciliation, in its major action projects in Dayton, has enjoyed a great deal of visibility through the news media. This has rendered the first counter-strategy option useless to their opponents. The second option, since its use is only slightly disruptive to normal routine, has been the favored one, while the third possibility has had mostly surreptitious use.

Interestingly, the Congregation has met little public challenge to their credibility and tactics in the form of attacking their label as a *Christian* social-action group. Such assaults have issued, however, within private conversations and meetings, both from those being directly challenged by the group and from others more peripheral to the action. In terms of dramatic action, such gestures are specifically directed only to segments of the public audience and are used to sway important persons' opinions through the device of invitation backstage, or into the inner circle. We learned in our interviews, for instance, of one clergyman (peripheral to the target of Congregation challenge) who endorsed negative reactions among civically influential laity by privately expressing his own disillusionment with Righter. Though he had actually had only minimal acquaintance with him, he made claims of close personal ties now suffering because of Righter's credibility. Such conversations, while outside the rules of fair play, are an effective strategy technique.

In the public drama, elites—i.e., those with legitimacy—tend to make the rules, and they do so to maximize their advantage. Those who would challenge their legitimacy and authority to write the script and determine the action of the drama must do so without resorting to foul play. Surprise, then, can become an important weapon to catch elites off guard, without script or stage directions. Comedy and irony are institutionally sanctioned forms of disrespect which can be disarming to adversaries in political struggle. While no one in Dayton seems to know the actual size of the Congregation, there is a general awareness that they are not a very large group. This itself, a tiny band of activists taking on the most powerful institutions of the city, is a form of comedy and irony which the Congregation has used well.

The Congregation's image as a conflict group is firmly established. Thus, to those opposing any kind of conflict or confrontation to achieve social change, the Congregation is by definition illegitimate. Three important factors tend to offset this disadvantage. First, some people have come to accept social protest as a legitimate means to redress grievances in American society. Second, the drama is seldom played to win the approval or attention of the total community. Third, in any confrontation, the Congregation's primary objective is not preservation of their own legitimacy but the questioning of the legitimacy of their adversaries. They need be concerned with protecting their own legitimacy and credibility only within certain parameters and to certain audiences, especially the media and community leaders who tacitly support their objectives even though they may disapprove of their means. To achieve this entails honesty, avoidance of the double-cross or other forms of betrayal, accuracy in their research, and faithfulness to their theological rationale.

This is not to say the Congregation can abandon concern for image management in the broader community. Indeed, public *perception* of its action tactics is important, and it has usually avoided tactics likely to alienate virtually the entire community. For example, at no point in the life of this group has any member strategically used, or threatened to use, civil disobedience. No member of the Congregation has been arrested during their demonstrations. By any comparable measure, the tactics pursued by the Congregation have been milder than those followed by other social-action groups in Dayton during the late 1960s. This pattern emerged at the onset. In their first social-action project, the Christmas card leafleting of the National Cash Register Company in 1968, the message was so mild as to belie interpretation as threat. After introducing themselves as a Christian action group sponsored by the Presbyterians, their message stated:

> Looking into the social action situation of Dayton, we find unrest at NCR. In 1968, the estimated population of Negroes living in Dayton is 74,000 (28% of the city). Only 659 (3.5%) of over 19,000 of your employees are black and the majority of these hold menial positions. This indicates to us there is racial discrimination in NCR's hiring, placement and advancement practices.

It is most imperative that your organization, a pacesetter in the greater Dayton area, work toward racial justice. The concept of NCR as a family is too fine to be destroyed by discrimination. We recognize the prevailing attitude of powerlessness at every level of our society, but we encourage you to take courage with us in seeking equal opportunity for all.

Since this is a rather typical tone for the group, the question arises as to why others perceive them as "militant" and "radical." Also, we should make explicit that, contrary to the image of Righter as belligerent and uncompromising, we found few who openly view him as so. On the contrary, most people, including his adversaries, find him mild-mannered, soft-spoken, well organized, and persuasive in presenting his views. Why such dramatically different images? There is no simple answer or easy explanation, but let us consider several issues related to the public image of the Congregation and its pastor.

First, the idea of a Christian church for the expressed purpose of pursuing social action is itself incongruent to a very large majority of the American public. Hence, from the onset, the problem of establishing credibility for this experimental congregation loomed large. For many, any social-action project would be "too radical." Had the proposal for an experimental social-action congregation been submitted in the form of a general referendum to the lay people of the Miami Presbytery, approval would have been unlikely.

A social-action project in the name of the church threatens the average person far more than the same project pursued by some secular group. The church-based group creates cognitive dissonance. When a Black Panther, for example, indicts white society as racist, the average individual has a whole multitude of cognitive apparatuses for dismissing the legitimacy of the charge. But when a white middle-class Christian congregation makes the same charge, the process is complicated by their claiming legitimacy in the name of the same faith as those indicted. To dismiss the issue, the average person must find some basis to discredit his accusers. Hence, fault-finding becomes the name of the game. Retaining public legitimacy becomes an extremely difficult and precarious task.

For those most disturbed and threatened by the presence of a social-action congregation, fault-finding leaves few stones unturned. Its pastor emerges as an outside radical, understanding neither the problems of the community nor the tremendous progress already made. Members of the congregation are typified as radical or misguided idealists mesmerized by a Pied Piper, the Presbytery is controlled by kooks, and any pastor expressing the slightest sympathy becomes immediately suspect. That this reservoir of ill will was not more successfully tapped in Dayton by the Congregation's opponents seems remarkable. We can only surmise that perceptions of the particular role of religious belief in the individual and collective psyche lent this option an air of fragility. Thus, such tactics seldom occurred on front and center stage, where the audience might respond defensively and render the counterattack counterproductive.

Symbiosis: The Congregation and the Media

Just as television and motion pictures have occasionally disseminated fine dramatic art beyond the theaters of major cities, so too the mass media extend the audience of social drama. Where newspaper editors and reporters are interested in issues of social change, the presence of an action group gives them opportunity to call such issues to public attention. For some newsmen in Dayton, the Congregation became a convenient vehicle for exposing social issues. In the process, the spotlight unavoidably illuminated the Congregation and contributed to its public visibility.

The dramaturgical model assumes the presence of an audience, and the news media, in a sense, can provide a stage on which the actors advance and retreat before the audience. Of course, the public relations skills of the opponents relate to the media. But in situations where activist challengers provide the initiative and their opponents assume a passive or defensive stance, the former group will attract greater attention. They command the initiative in the conflict. Only if they encounter an unusually aggressive opponent, or if the media are disposed to protect the status quo, will the activists carry less natural affinity for the media. Like bees and flowers, each meets, to some extent, the other's needs. In the following paragraphs, we will attempt to trace this symbiotic relationship between media and activists, illustrating with the case of the Congregation and the Dayton newspapers.

The Congregation needs the media for several reasons. First, in order for social issues to become "issues" rather than private concerns, they must corner public consciousness. The most effective channel for doing this is obviously the news media. The Christmas card distribution directly reached six hundred persons with a message. The media coverage, on the other hand, probably extended the message to more than a hundred times as many.

Second, organizations desirous of the favorable opinion of large numbers of people to vote for their candidates, buy their products, or contribute to their causes fear adverse publicity as a blow to the efficiency and viability of their enterprise. In this way, a small well-prepared group skillfully using the media wields social power far out of proportion to its wealth or numbers. Thus the Congregation can take on opponents to whom it stands in relative power and size as a flea in a kennel.

Third, the media can create both name identification and image; they can reinforce the credibility of an otherwise anonymous group. Support mechanisms thus fan out far beyond the range of personal penetration into a community. If the Congregation champions a cause and through media exposure gains some lever of public support, subsequent issues more easily find favor with the same audience. Ralph Nader, for instance, has used this transference effect quite extensively as Nader's Raiders have moved from one issue to another. The end result is an escalation of influence in the public arena, a mustering of more clout for future confrontations.

Finally, for the Congregation for Reconciliation, lacking the active support of the Presbyterian clergy to recruit members, the media inadvertently serve to "advertise" the Congregation to potential participants. For activists seeking group-based, issue-oriented involvement, each exposure serves as an altar call for the Congregation.

The media, too, derive benefits from their relationship with this activist group. First, with few exceptions, action committees of the Congregation endure the tedium of research and present credible issues. The "facts" presented to reporters prove easy to verify with committee help and are in most cases accurate. This emphasis on their own credibility manifests an activist profession-alism impressive to news people. The Congregation also eschews resorting to vendettas or smear tactics and discourages drawing attention to personalities. They focus on issues, and where attack is important, their bead is drawn on institutions or organizations rather than on individuals. The advantages to reporters are self-evident. It is clear from editorials, as well as from interviews with media people, that many journalists in Dayton disapprove of some of the Congregation's tactics. Nevertheless, they give coverage to the group both because they feel the issues it raises are important and because its activities usually fit the definition of "newsworthy."

Covering congregational activities also helps anticipate contro-versies. News people do compete with one another, and a good working relationship with key members of the Congregation offers an advantage for scooping stories. Journalistic competition, on the other hand, gives action committees bargaining leverage, ensuring fuller and more conspicuous coverage.

But the symbiotic relationship goes even further. The journal-ist's role reaches beyond reporting the news accurately and fairly. Journalists also judge and select community issues which they think deserve attention for editorial and feature story coverage. Sometimes they latch onto a problem and refuse to let go. Other times an equally serious issue absolutely eludes journalistic imagination or indignation. As the Congregation serves as a resource for the media through its research and involvement in action projects, the media also influence the Congregation. Feature stories bring problems to the attention of the Congrega-tion, and at least some have grown into projects. Also, the Congregation's decision to pursue or drop a project may be directly, but certainly subtly, influenced by whether reporters pay attention to their initial efforts.

Finally, in a countervailing circle paradox, we need to recall that the Congregation began its foray into social action with direct confrontation tactics. On the one hand, Righter had already established media contacts, but to assure wide coverage for the Congregation daring action was needed. On the other hand, the attention-getting event led media people both to report the happening objectively and also to brand the Congregation as "controversial." From this initial point, the circle of mutual expectation has grown.

But What of Conflict and Christian Theology?

Branded as radicals and heavily engaged in community conflict, the Congregation has received frequent attacks in church circles for not demonstrating the spirit of reconciliation for which it was ostensibly created. Contributing to this impression, the Congregation seldom interprets social-action projects to outsiders in religious language. They tend not to wave the banner "in God's name." Arguments from political and economic ideology serve as a public rationale for action far more often than does theology. Many churchmen no doubt translate this to mean the Congregation is essentially a secular organization parading beneath the banner of the Cross. In this view, their theology, to the extent they have any, has been gobbled up by the world. Otherwise, how could they justify such divisive confrontations in the name of Christian reconciliation?

Those familiar with the history of conflict within the Congregation may interpret the low profile of theology in justifying action as resulting from the rapprochement between the God-talkers and the secular humanists. This offers only one element in the answer; the fuller answer is more complex.

When pressed, the theological rationale for mission most often cited by members of the Congregation is consistent with *The Confession of 1967* and with the theological justification for the establishment of new congregations, both adopted by the United Presbyterian Church in the U.S.A. In this sense, the Congregation is orthodox. One word most frequently used to signify a complex of interlocking theological statements, both by the Congregation members and by the denominational documents, is reconciliation. "God's reconciling purpose is to make and keep man human according to the revelation of himself in Christ. . . . The Church is committed, through the Spirit, to his ministry of reconciliation in a broken world." [4]

This ministry of reconciliation, as set forth in national Presbyterian documents, is marked by action focused upon specific contemporary issues and crises. It is *both personal and corporate*

137

and lives by risk in relating to the conditions of humanity. In its dialogue with the Miami Presbytery, the Congregation has never strayed far from its charter regarding the theological rationale for its mission. The legitimacy of this rationale has encountered challenges primarily from main-line churches, placing the Congregation in the curious role of defending the orthodox faith, as interpreted in the *Confession*, from those who see themselves as the most orthodox of all.

In June 1973 the National Mission Committee of the Miami Presbytery met to consider the continuance of its affiliation with the Congregation for Reconciliation. During the continuance hearing, an interesting exchange occurred between one of the committee members and Righter. It clearly sets forth the Congregation's theological position.

COMMITTEEMAN: "Dick, I would like to ask a theological question. . . . Is it possible to transform society without first transforming the individuals within it? Can we accomplish a better society by confronting various groups with a set of outward demands, or would it not be better to confront their members with the inward demands of Jesus Christ so that their hearts can be changed? Is it not from the person's heart that flows the transformed life? Didn't Jesus say that it was out of the heart, the inner being, that flowed the evils of society?"

RIGHTER: ". . . in the story of the Tower of Babel there is the idea of 'corporate sin.' In the first chapter of Colossians, Paul talks about all things, visible and invisible, being created through and for God. All things, whether thrones or dominions or principalities—which I would understand to be institutions [like governments, businesses, large organizations]. Now, what I'm getting at is that I don't see it as either/or. I see it as both/and. Proclaiming Jesus Christ is something that is both personal and corporate—personal evangelism and corporate evangelism."

COMMITTEEMAN: "In the work of the Congregation for Reconciliation, have you coordinated the two, the personal evangelism with the corporate evangelism? Maybe I'm not close enough to it, but all I hear is the corporate, the confrontation of society. I don't hear about the confrontation of individuals with the claims of Jesus Christ."

138

RICHTER: ". . . The Presbytery established this congregation with a special mandate to relate to the area of racial reconciliation. Because of that, and because the Congregation attracted people who have a bias toward corporate or action evangelism, that is where our emphasis has been. There has been an abrupt personal conversion experience by one of the members in the past year, however, the kind within the personal evangelical tradition. . . . We see both kinds of evangelism as a response to the Lordship of Jesus Christ."

COMMITTEEMAN: "There's just one more thing I'd like to ask you about. Your church has 'reconciliation' in its name. Do you feel that in your work you have been a reconciling force in the community, or a divisive force?"

RICHTER: "I would argue that we have been a very reconciling congregation. But you have to get your definition of reconciliation straight. That term is used about six times in the New Testament. Generally what we think of when we hear the term is the reconciliation of men to men or men to God as in 2 Corinthians, Ephesians, and Romans. But the other passage we don't talk about very much is the one in Colossians that says all things are to be reconciled to God. . . . Now, how are institutions reconciled to God, to carry out their God-given purposes? . . . What is the church's role in relationship to those powers, those authorities, those institutions? Are we to be part of reconciling all things to God and his purposes for them? I would argue that scripturally we are. To do that, when we call institutions to reconciliation, we're calling them to change, just as we call individuals to reconciliation, to conversion, to change. Reconciliation changes people's lives; it changes institutions' lives, too. Whenever you have change, whether personal or corporate, you have periods of flux, and sometimes crises, and sometimes controversy, and sometimes upheaval and division. . . ."

COMMITTEEMAN: "While Jesus did confront the Pharisees with rather strong and vigorous words, yet at the same time he was seeking to reconcile not only the scribes and Pharisees but also all men to himself and to God, without setting one against the other."

RICHTER: "I can't see that we're trying to set—"

COMMITTEEMAN: "Well, you may not be trying to; I'm talking about the results of what you are doing."

RIGHTER: "I don't believe that that is the result either. You see, for me, I think the church needs both kinds of reconciliation going on. I don't see very much of the institutional reconciliation going on within the church. I think that there is a crying need for it, too. Not every church is going to be able to do action or institutional evangelism. Some will be programmed for the work of serving those Christians who see corporate evangelism as their calling. There are other congregations—perhaps most—who will be programmed for a ministry of personal reconciliation. But we need both at all times, and I feel that when we are attempting to reconcile, for instance, people who live in slum housing with the kind of institution that allows that to happen, that is a positive reconciliation and that is following the life-style of Jesus."

COMMITTEEMAN: "I would differ with your understanding of the life of Jesus."

Although not all members of the Congregation interpret their motivation for social action in theological terms, those who do also share Righter's view of the centrality of reconciliation.

The last comment by Righter in the exchange just quoted merits special attention. He mentions the relationship between the disinherited and the institutional structures of society implicated in their suffering—if only by allowing it "to happen." The goal of social action thus becomes the adjustment of institutional structures to address the needs of those at the lower end of the social hierarchy more effectively and humanely. Participants and members of the Congregation, regardless of theological position, share this goal. It can be justified in humanistic or religious terms. And it is consonant with the definition of social action prevalent in America since the mid-1960s: action directed toward the humanization of social structures.

The ideological basis of the Congregation's mission was perhaps best phrased not by a member of the group but by a local pastor: "I have not been directly involved in the Congregation's work, but I think I see a thread going through all that it does in the community. It insists on the right of persons and communities to participate in those decisions which affect their own destiny . . . they really rub against the organizational grain." He then described several situations in which the Congregation represented the interests of the poor in pressuring local government or businesses to reconsider their courses of action. The Congregation, when viewed in this manner, stands as a public protector of those who lack the power within organizational structures to defend their own interests in the institutional distribution of social benefits.

In taking an advocacy position and setting themselves against powerful organizations, the Congregation appeals less often to theology than to American values for legitimating their right of organized dissent. They affirm the corporate structure of society as existing by the consent of those affected. This appeal to Enlightenment philosophy could not be more ideologically American. Those affected by corporate decisions, they argue, have not only the right but also the duty to make their views known. Ultimately, in a democracy, power does reside in the people. Free enterprise not only calls for "caveat emptor" but "caveat vendor" as well.

The Congregation possesses a theological rationale for action. Their infrequent use of it to justify their social action, however, reflects more than a lack of consensus on God-talk among members. It is better understood in strategic terms.

Political and economic ideology, they feel, simply have greater persuasive appeal than has theology. When challenged by a spokesman of a skeptical public (outside the church), they feel they can generate more support by appealing to concepts of "corporate responsibility," "institutional accountability," and "fair play" than of "corporate evangelism" or "institutional reconciliation." The tailoring of messages to audiences is the primary step, as Madison Avenue knows so well, in the art of persuasion. And persuasion, after all, is the bread and butter of social action.

Another Side of Righter

Throughout the life of the Congregation for Reconciliation, Richard Righter has served as its principal action strategist. His primary technique has been confrontation and conflict. We have attempted to interpret this from the theoretical perspective of symbolic interaction or dramatism. This seems to us a useful model for understanding the Congregation's activities and explaining their measure of success.

Other social scientists might well employ other theoretical models and see Righter and the Congregation in a different light. To be sure, our approach is not without limitations. When pressed for an explanation to the question of *why* confrontation, our model can say little more than "because it works." In the American tradition of pragmatism, this may well be sufficient. In another sense, it begs other important questions: How do you know that other strategies wouldn't be equally effective? What can be said about the motives or value presuppositions which led Righter and the Congregation to pursue confrontation?

The fact of the matter is the Congregation has seldom employed other strategies. Thus, insofar as the community of Dayton and the specific projects of the Congregation are concerned, we cannot be certain that other strategies would not have worked. We have presented Righter's theological rationale for confrontation, but this too may beg the question of motive. Are there not other ways than conflict to seek reconciliation of " 'all things' to God's purpose?"

Conflict theory would argue that institutions are extremely reluctant to change. Only the mustering of countervailing power can pressure for institutional change. For those who are essentially powerless, their main hope for building power is in the street and through the media, that is, in the public arena.

The "power elite" thesis has traditionally been associated with the "radical left" and Marxist ideology. In recent years, however, the growing evidence of massive concentration and abuse of power by certain sectors of society has moved scholars heretofore considered to be only slightly left of center to entertain more seriously the power elite thesis.[5] Perhaps we now need seriously to consider the possibility that the labeling of potentially effective strategies as "leftist" may present a most valuable tool for elites in the public drama.[6]

As already noted, Righter's quiet, low-key style is disarming to his adversaries. It is not easy to dislike him, and even more difficult to pin him with a "leftist" label. As a student of economics, with a master's degree in business administration, he can't be easily snowed with free enterprise rhetoric. He believes in free enterprise and invests in the stock market. His bone of contention is not with the economic system but rather with corporate and individual abuse of power. Theologically, his views are far more conservative than most Presbyterian and United Church of Christ pastors in metropolitan Dayton. Were he theologically liberal in a conservative denomination, he would be vulnerable to the charge that his "radical" theology has led him astray on social issues. But as a theological conservative, he is immune to such attacks.

At the beginning of this book, we indicated that in telling the story of Righter and his congregation we would not make them wistful heroes. It is not our intent to do so now. What we have tried to say in this chapter is that, in terms of strategy and personal style, Righter has some things going for him that help render his actions effective.

To fail to see Righter as a complex man, however, would do him a great disservice and fall short of providing data to those interested in studying leadership style. Of our many conversations with Righter, the one most revealing of his value presuppositions about the nature of the social order and how one effects social change occurred late on a hot summer night in 1972. We want to quote this conversation verbatim, not to malign him or point to weakness in his character. Such a conclusion, in our opinion, would be an unwarranted value judgment. Rather, we want to provide readers an opportunity to see an important dimension of a complex man. Let us further preface this transcript by explicitly acknowledging that this conversation also reveals a good deal about our own presuppositions about change. At the conclusion of the transcript, we will attempt to interpret it further in light of our different presuppositions as well as in the context of the interview itself.

We asked Righter to talk about how the United People campaign emerged as a central project for the Congregation for Reconciliation and why they decided to pursue a boycott strategy.

RIGHTER: "This was kind of an issue that I always had in the back of my mind. In my opinion, United Fund was kind of irrelevant in Philadelphia and I knew it wouldn't take me long to research this issue in Dayton. Also, one of the church executives responsible for starting the experimental congregations in Ohio mentioned the United Fund to me as a possible social issue. I was not in any way directly responsible to him, but his mentioning of the United Fund as a possible issue led me to believe that I had some kind of institutional 'blessing' to pursue the project.

"Shortly after arriving in Dayton, I asked a campus minister if he knew anything about United Fund locally. He gave me the name of a gal who's a social worker whom he knew to be concerned about United Fund. I went to talk with her and she encouraged me to get involved in this area. I can't remember if we talked boycott at that time or not. At any rate, I decided that this was an issue that I ought to pursue and I encouraged five or six people in our congregation to form a study group. I went around and collected several key reports from United Fund agencies and passed them around to the study committee. I also went around and interviewed five or six agency executives.

"At that point in the life of the Congregation I promoted the concept of study committees and action committees. After the study committee had prepared a brief report, some of these people opted out of pursuing any action. The Congregation then voted to try and get other organizations concerned and to develop a coalition. That was along toward the end of 1969 or early 1970. We got seven organizations into this project. . . . We had a couple of community meetings. We had some people come and talk, with different points of view presented. Sam Morris of the United Fund [as throughout this manuscript, the names of individuals other than the Righters have been changed to protect their anonymity] came to one of these meetings. During the spring we met with some of the staff people, but I don't believe we met with any board people. At this point we weren't rattling fences or threatening boycott. We were simply trying to relate to some of these people and recommend changes.

"Sometime during the spring, at a peace demonstration, I talked with a guy named Bob Shifflett who was very active in a group called Social Welfare Workers Movement. We decided to get our two groups together and sit down and talk about this. . . . In late spring, SWWM and the Congregation voted to work together on a boycott."

[Righter then discussed in considerable detail the next six

144

months of planning for the boycott, launched in the fall just prior to the annual United Appeal campaign.]

"After that campaign we moved into some serious work to detail what we wanted to recommend. We didn't do this because anyone was screaming but because we felt we really ought to get ourselves together. We came up with a five-page list of recommendations which we sent to United Fund and released to the press."

INTERVIEWER: "From what you told me, it seems you really decided on a boycott fairly early, and now you tell me that it was not until after the first boycott that you presented United Fund with a series of demands or recommendations. I am of the opinion that a boycott is a pretty serious kind of action which one takes only as a last resort, after everything else has failed. It seems to me that you either proceeded on the assumption that the boycott was only symbolic, or underneath your rhetoric you did not desire reform but sabotage of the United Fund."

RIGHTER: "I don't see those as the only alternatives, but let me respond. First of all, we could not, even with a tremendously effective boycott, hope to touch more than five or ten percent of their funds. . . . A very large percentage of their funds comes from big business and from employees of big businesses who are pressured into signing pledges. On the other matter, there has been a long history of establishment-type efforts at reform and the United Fund was absolutely unresponsive. In 1963 there was a very extensive study done by a professor from the area, under the aegis of the Health and Welfare Planning Body, as to how United Fund was serving the community and who was getting services. That study was ignored. They also ignored editorializing by the newspapers for reform. Then there were the riots in 1967 which failed to produce any response. Furthermore, our attempts to relate to the executive director indicated that he was totally unwilling to sit down and negotiate with us. It was my opinion after not being here too long, and knowing something about the board members, that a boycott was the only way to relate to the situation. They weren't going to make any changes without a power base for change over against some fifty-five agencies who have full-time lobbyists at the United Appeal to get funds.

Moreover, these agencies have interlocking boards that assure the continuation of the status quo. I take it that you were saying that you would have functioned differently?"

INTERVIEWER: "Yes, I think so. . . . You said that your coalition group presented a list of demands to United Fund. Do I have that in my files?"

RIGHTER: "They didn't present a list of solid demands but they raised some of the basic questions of who United Fund is serving and not serving."

INTERVIEWER: "From what you and others have told me, I would say that the boycott tactic was pursued without first pursuing other alternatives, including presenting the United Fund Board with a formal set of demands."

RIGHTER: "Oh, yes, no doubt about it. We did not use proper process. We never used proper process. We never go the proper way."

INTERVIEWER: "Why?"

RIGHTER: "Because the proper way is established by those who control the system. The system has a proper way of functioning. First you go and meet with them. If you have some clout they'll set up a committee to work on it. But they don't want to change anything. Their proper way of dealing with problems never results in any change."

INTERVIEWER: "Now you're telling me something very fundamental about your philosophy."

RIGHTER: "Yeah, maybe so. Our tactics are not the acceptable tactics of the established decision-makers that we attempt to relate to. Most of the people we are dealing with are not really interested in change. We don't have any power to pressure change from within. This is the only way we have of relating to issues."

INTERVIEWER: "What about the activities of your [Poverty Committee]? From what I have learned, your tactics here were quite different and some people I have talked with would say you have had relatively greater success in effecting change here."

RIGHTER: "Yes, our tactics were very different with the [poverty] project. We functioned differently because we felt there were people within with a lot of clout that we could work cooperatively with to bring about change. I think we have had some success with the [poverty] project, but I'd say we've been much more successful with the United Fund, no doubt about that in my mind. You see, most of the people you ended up talking with are pretty much establishment people and they have a different view of our effectiveness. But we don't get too much opportunity to work with those who really have some clout."

INTERVIEWER: "But I'm wondering if you have thoroughly exhausted the possibilities of working with, rather than against, those who are establishment people. What I've picked up from some of your strongest establishment supporters is that they would like to see you doing many more things with them rather than against them. The scenario or model has repeated itself thousands of times in American politics. There are people on the inside who would like to effect change but do not themselves have the authority or power to do so. Then along comes a group from the outside raising hell or threatening to do so. At that point the person on the inside can go to others and say, 'We've got to respond to their demands.' Perhaps the community leaders I have been talking with are giving me a lot of rhetoric or hot air, but I have a sense that they are more willing to pursue issues with you than you may realize."

RIGHTER: "Yeah, maybe so, but I'm not sure."

When confronted with this interview in an interim report several months later, Righter was quite defensive. "When I read it," he said, "I felt that I had been stripped naked." He would not have been so forceful in his statements, he argued, had the interviewer not pushed so hard. The interview and Righter's reaction to it in print seem to us revealing on several counts. We have little doubt that Righter overstated his views, but consider the context. It was late at night and terribly hot. Prior to this encounter, we had shown only sympathy for the cause. Suddenly and without forewarning, the rules changed. Not only did Righter learn we had serious reservations about the particular strategy in question but, in the context of our impending report to the National Missions Committee, our presence seemed suddenly to shift from support to threat. And Righter blew his cool.

But this is insufficient interpretation. Did he lose control in saying more than he normally would to an outsider or, under fire, did he reveal something to himself about his own presuppositions? We cannot, of course, be certain, but we suspect a bit of each. In any event, this raises yet another interesting question. In the course of pursuing confrontation tactics, Righter has most assuredly faced many threatening and unnerving situations. While we met no adversaries who cited specific instances of Righter being backed into a corner and losing his composure, it is hard to imagine this has never happened. After all, what politician or public figure has not made his faux pas? And to one pursuing confrontation strategies while trying to guard an image of reason and credibility against adversaries looking to discredit, blunders can be costly.

Even if we assume Righter substantially overstated his views, the interview seems nonetheless revealing of certain assumptions about the nature of power and the social order. It is a view from the bottom, championing the causes of the powerless against powerful establishments immune to sentiment or pleas to ethical or religious principles. Power only acknowledges power. And the most viable power of the little man is his ability to disrupt normal activities, to embarrass powerful institutions and their representatives, to threaten public relations images; it is the power of the villain to ridicule and upset the hero.

Righter's overreaction to our probing resulted in his articulation of a harder line than he would normally espouse either privately or publicly. But it also permitted us to get a glimpse of the kinds of taken-for-granted assumptions which inform his action strategies. In sum, when we examine this interview from the perspective of what it tells us about Righter's underlying value presuppositions, we see a logical link between his views about power and social change and the types of strategies and tactics the Congregation has employed.

Alvin Gouldner, in *The Coming Crisis of Western Sociology*, attacks the young American radical of the 1960s for viewing the task of developing theory as "a form of escapism, if not of moral cowardice." The following passage might well serve as an epitaph to the student radicalism of the sixties.

The neglect of self-conscious theory by radicals is both dangerous and ironic, for such a posture implies that—although they lay claim to being radical—they have in effect surrendered to one of the most vulgar currents of American culture: to its small-town, Babbitt-like anti-intellectualism and know-nothingism. Moreover, if radicals wish to change their world, they must surely expect to do so only against the resistance of some and with the help of others. Yet those whom they oppose, as well as those with whom they may wish to ally themselves, will in fact often be guided by certain theories. Without self-conscious theory, radicals will be unable to understand, let alone change, either their enemies or their friends. Radicals who believe that they can separate the task of developing theory from that of changing society are not in fact acting without a theory, but *with* one that is tacit and therefore unexaminable and uncorrectable. If they do not learn to use their theory self-consciously, they will be used by it. Unable either to control or to understand their theories, radicals will thus in effect submit to one form of the very alienation that they commonly reject.[7]

We also believe this analysis says a great deal about why Richard Righter and the Congregation for Reconciliation are still in the battle long after social activists, inside and outside the church, have yielded to alienation, frustration, and despair. Our points of disagreement with the Congregation's strategies and tactics are quite irrelevant in this context. What they boil down to, as Righter indicates in the interview, is that we believe we, in a similar situation, would pursue a different strategy informed by different assumptions. Our disagreement, however, cannot take away what we believe to be clear evidence that their action is informed by a theory of social order and change. As analysts charged with the responsibility to evaluate their activities, we see a clear relationship between their success and their adherence to strategies informed by theory. And as human beings who can imagine ourselves in the role of the Congregation's adversaries, their consistency and integrity commands our respect.

Having reviewed in some detail two social-action projects of the Congregation, and now having reflected on the nature and implications of its approach to social action, we will turn in the next chapter to an examination of the internal difficulties experienced by the Congregation and recent attempts to overcome them.

CHAPTER 8

Organizational Imperatives: The Internal Dynamics of the Congregation

To this point our discussion has focused primarily on the life of the Congregation for Reconciliation in the community; we have described the sociocultural context wherein the group was created, the differences between that which emerged and the expectations of the planners, the Congregation's handling of tension with the parent body, the dynamics of arriving at a set of goals, and some concrete case studies of their social-action projects.

For five years the Congregation for Reconciliation has managed to stay alive in a milieu which had largely defined social activism as passé almost before the Congregation's formal organization. Moreover, it has survived in a fundamentally conservative community where almost any kind of opposition to the status quo is "too radical." Simply to sustain life is thus no small accomplishment. Similar experimental groups across the country have folded. Others have survived only by radically redefining their goals. Not so with the Congregation for Reconciliation. While some members in the group would have liked to have redirected the Congregation, they had little success. The viability of the group has remained emphatically tied to their continuing commitment to the social-action objectives present from the onset.

A number of factors explain this continuing commitment. First of all, they have a leader with a driving commitment to social action, but who is not predisposed to do all the work. He masterfully delegates responsibility and is willing to let a project fail if others don't follow through. But more importantly, the

Congregation itself sets high expectations for its members. The initial recruitment was self-selective of activist-prone people. There have always been more projects and more work than there were bodies and hours to complete the tasks. In this setting, a casual participant soon felt he or she was not carrying a fair share of the load. In most cases, people either became deeply involved in the life of the group or they soon had marginal status and became dropouts.

We have also seen how their success, or at least their perception of success, in the political arena has served to reinforce commitment to goals. Had they received less visibility through the media, commitment might have been more difficult to maintain. The continual news coverage of their projects, however, has sustained and reinforced their belief in their own effectiveness. To this we can add an old sociological maxim which holds that external group conflict generates and reinforces internal group solidarity.

The story of the Congregation for Reconciliation would be incomplete, however, if we left our readers with the impression that the formula for a successful social-action group is as simple as finding a good action strategist, gathering a small group of activists who reinforce one another's commitment, and then skillfully utilizing the media. The Congregation, like any other organization, has faced not only the external problems of goal attainment but also the difficulties of internal integration. In a nonauthoritarian environment, these can grow more acute and threatening to group survival than external opposition.

In chapter 3, we gave some indication of the internal tensions over goals and theological rationale. While this conflict arose substantially from the necessity of dealing with the Presbyterian denomination, it indicated more serious ongoing internal tensions. Goal achievement, at least in terms of consensus on social-action projects, has presented relatively small difficulty for the Congregation. The problems of tension management and integration—or, as they say, achieving "a sense of community"—have been mastered only gradually, haltingly, and at some points dubiously. We turn now to the internal dynamics of the Congregation, the story of the process whereby a group of people who share common goals are learning to live with one another.

In our discussion of the group's instant plunge into social-action projects prior to any thought on formal organization, we described their mood as one of reckless abandon of survival-oriented goals. Only when forced to organize or face a suspension of funds from the Presbytery did the group confront this problem. In this chapter we shall see that postponement, delay, temporary compromise, and even denial have been typical postures toward internal problems. Again and again they have refused to deal with difficulties until they have posed a serious threat to the group. Their boldness in facing conflict in the Dayton community, with the Presbyterian denomination, and with other congregations stands in sharp contrast to their shyness in dealing with conflict within their own ranks.

In substantial measure, their awareness of the precariousness of the group may explain this. Their numbers have never been large enough or their finances sufficient to risk wide-open internal conflict. While they have developed theological legitimacy for conflict as a means to reconciliation in the community, they have largely rejected or avoided applying the same principle within their own group. We are aware of one instance, and suspect others, in which an active member of the congregation sought to subvert the goals of the group and undermine Righter's leadership. Rather than face the problem head on, both Righter and the Congregation struggled on as if nothing were really wrong. Cross-pressured by a spouse who envisioned another agenda for the Congregation, the individual finally withdrew from membership and thus resolved the problem.

While conflicts in personalities and agendas have periodically posed real threats to the Congregation, the more serious menace has been an unwillingness to acknowledge the structural imperatives of organizational survival. We refer specifically to numbers and money. Reduction below present size would not only rest the survival of the mission on a very narrow base, it would severely exacerbate an already critical financial situation. On several occasions during our initial visit to Dayton in 1972, we raised the question of the financial viability of the Congregation. Without exception we were informed this was simply not a problem. Indeed, some expressed outright irritation with our concern for such mundane matters. By this point, Righter knew the grim financial situation and had already devised a face-saving means (for the Congregation) of cutting his salary. But even he refused to admit finances were a problem. In June 1972 he told us, "Whenever the treasury begins to look a little bleak, we have a meeting to discuss finances and somehow we come up with the money to keep going."

Such an attitude has precedence in the faith of Old Testament prophets, but it also seems a naïve way of avoiding the imperatives of organizational survival. The Congregation no longer receives mission subsidy from either the Presbyterian or United Church of Christ denominations, nor, given the controversial nature of their activities, is outside support likely to be forthcoming in any substantial quantity. While mostly middle-class, no member of the Congregation has substantial discretionary income to channel into the budget. Indeed, some already make substantial personal sacrifices to support congregational activities. While some might conceivably give more, it is highly problematic the group can afford to lose many additional members and continue to pay Righter a salary.

In the year between our first and second field trips, survival imperatives finally enveloped the group. When we returned in mid-1973 we found several members had not only recognized the necessity of forceful measures to assure survival but also had taken concrete steps to keep the group alive. Righter feels our queries about survival considerations during our first field visit played a significant role in bringing the group to consider its future viability. We tend to see our probing as relatively incidental to more serious structural dilemmas which confronted the group during 1972–73, dilemmas which finally forced the Congregation to face the problem of survival.

But we are getting ahead of ourselves. Let us return in a more sequential narrative to the internal dynamics of the Congregation. We begin with the issue of membership. What kinds of people sought out an experimental congregation? Who stayed? Who left? For both, why? What kinds of problems arose in moving beyond a collectivity of social activists to a community not only caring about social injustice but also dealing with one another's human frailties?

We need to recall, once again, the mood of crisis hanging over this nation in the late 1960s. The tenor of those years affected not only the institutional churches' response in the creation of experimental congregations such as this one, but also the individual lay person's response to participation in the group. The turmoil across the nation had nurtured frustrations. Democratic process, individual freedom, equal opportunity, justice for all—in short, the American Dream—faced indictments of being nothing more than myth. Many who had little or nothing chose to release their anger in search of some semblance of personhood and importance; many numbered among the "haves" sought desperately for ways to pump new hope into the sagging American ideal.

For those who saw the church as a viable vehicle to effect change, experimental congregations offered an opportunity to channel their energies for social betterment. The creation of the Congregation for Reconciliation, designed for "action-oriented Christians," was a move in this direction. It seems of utmost importance in examining the membership of this congregation to stress this broader social context. The early dropout rate from the group must be considered in the light of people feeling driven to "do something" to respond to crisis. That the fervor of the day led some persons to plunge into involvements they could not sustain is hardly surprising. For reasons of basic disagreement, insufficient time, unexamined commitment, and others of this sort, many persons who initially rallied to membership chose later to leave the Congregation.

Likewise, that the Congregation has always eschewed any formal approach to recruitment seems quite natural within this context. Those who initially joined did so because the Congregation stood as a possible solution to their seeking an outlet for constructive involvement in the society and its problems. The demands which the totally functioning congregation, as proposed by the Miami Presbytery, would make upon its members required deep commitment and extensive work. Only those seeking such consuming involvement could possibly become vital participants. Presumably, too, those in the market for such an engrossing activity would be actively seeking and thus would come to the group. Persons with only a fleeting or partial interest in social-change issues would be less likely to initiate contact, though they might join if invited. Obviously, these often would not retain membership for any sustained period.

As the Congregation began to define and characterize itself to the outside world, its very existence was its only recruitment endeavor. Even the suggestion that meetings be announced in the Saturday religious news of local newspapers was resisted. Instead, the general attitude of the Congregation was simply: "If people are interested, they will find us."

The initial sifting of potential membership and leadership determined the Congregation over the years. The quick steps to confrontation tactics and the limitation of worship activity early delineated the "type" of individual who might join the group. And these, as the members expressed, needed no recruitment.

Naturally, then, the publicity received by the Congregation for its various involvements became a prime channel for introducing new members into the mission. A smaller source emerged in interaction with other social-action groups with which the Congregation had formed temporary alliances. This proximity fostered some interest in other aspects of the Congregation's life and has resulted in some new members. The membership itself has almost totally ignored proselytizing among friends and acquaintances as a source of new participants.

The records indicate that, at one time or another, 110 persons have participated in the life of the group. During the first two years of the Congregation's life the participant list was frequently updated and mimeographed copies were distributed. These lists have become infrequent during the past two years, so the total number of participants is undoubtedly somewhat larger than cited. Technically, there were no members until formal organization in the spring of 1970. In that year there were 40 members. The number shrank to 29 in 1972; at the time of our second field trip in 1973, there were 32 members. Checking through a variety of congregation records, we found that attendance at meetings averaged in the vicinity of 30, with a range from 11 to 50.

Two unique features of the Congregation's record keeping deserve note. First of all, the membership roster is wiped clean each year. Those who wish to continue as members must renew their covenant annually. Obviously, then, the membership list carries no dead weight. A second feature is recognition of an informal status of "participant." In one sense, the participant sans membership status probably feels some pressure to become a full-fledged member. On the other hand, the status of participant has been legitimated and no formal pressures or sanctions are utilized to bolster the membership list. Typically, a participant's involvement pivots around some particular project of the Congregation. There are others, however, who participate at those points when the Congregation solicits their professional competence. There is no record of participants. While the number is not large, this is an important dimension of congregational life.

One reason for fluctuating membership, of course, is the experimental nature of the Congregation. Experimental anythings in our society are bound to attract their share of transient, insatiable seekers, and the Congregation for Reconciliation was no exception. However, as mentioned before, most of those who came to the Congregation were dissatisfied with their previous experiences in established congregations. Their sources of dissatisfaction, and consequently their reasons for joining and leaving the mission, are diverse and complex. At least three primary motives, mixed in various degrees, account for membership changes in the Congregation.

The first and most important of these was concern for social action. As mentioned earlier, many of the members of the Congregation had been previously active in social action, and a number had tried without success to express their concern in their former congregations. By joining the mission they were seeking a place within the church where they could act in accordance with their understanding of Christian duty.

But once inside, some individuals found themselves in basic disagreement with the mission's political style. Some disappointedly found the Congregation far too tame while others perceived it as too radical. A number of individuals in the latter group had come expecting a social-service orientation and experienced discomfort with the mission's confrontation style. Others, though in basic agreement with the social policies of the mission, nevertheless found their involvement embarrassing or threatening to themselves or to other members of their families. No known case exists in which involvement with the Congregation has definitely caused a member to lose his job, but instances of veiled threats and harassment from employers or fellow workers sufficient to cause withdrawal from participation in the mission have occurred.

Closely intertwined with this concern for social action was a desire for experimental worship. For most this meant simply exploring ways of expressing their social concerns through worship services and finding new worship forms to express their religious beliefs. Yet a number of participants have dropped from the mission out of dissatisfaction with the group's religious orientation. On the one hand were those intolerant of even minimal references to God or "religion"; on the other hand were those upset by the lack of traditional elements in the mission's worship services. A small number also came seeking mystical or occult elements and, being unable to stir interest, withdrew from the group.

For most who became members of the group, the issue was neither social action nor experimental worship but rather the balance between the two and the content of worship. A few humanists could affirm the value of "celebration," but they resisted "worship" and found any reference to clearly Christian symbols a threat to their integrity. Over the years those most adamantly opposed to any shades of Christian worship have either dropped out or become more tolerant. As we shall see shortly, the gradual filtering out of those with different visions or hopes for the Congregation has led to substantially greater openness about Christian symbols and even reference to the group as a Christian community.

There is a third and perhaps ubiquitous motivation for participation in the Congregation. This is the search for a sense of community and the emotional support provided by a primary group. As we have seen, most of the persons in the Congregation who had had previous involvement in another congregation had felt varying degrees of isolation and estrangement from the predominantly status quo, comfort-oriented view of religion they had found. Also active at an even deeper level was a dominant theme in contemporary America, the sense of modern urban industrial society as estranged from community.

As nearly as we can determine, virtually everyone ever affiliated with the Congregation for Reconciliation has felt this longing for community. Like all intangibles, community is easier to talk about than to find, build, or recognize. Some persons have zealously sought to impose their own sense of community on the group. Most have remained only a short while before moving on. A few have lingered long enough to become quite divisive forces in the Congregation. And, as we have suggested, the Congregation has typically not dealt harshly with these persons but rather has sought to absorb them into the life of the group, albeit on the terms of the core members. This, of course, has seldom worked and most of these persons have eventually drifted away.

For some, the Congregation became an instant community. Their needs were fulfilled by working on action projects with others who shared their values and goals. Worship services ("celebrations") organized around action concerns reinforced their commitment and bolstered their sense of community. For others, the dominant influence of the activists and the nearly total preoccupation with action projects quite literally left them in positions of structural marginality. These were persons who supported social action but were themselves uncomfortable in the role of picketing, leafleting, confronting. In some measure, Righter's conceptualization of research and action as separate activities provided these persons with a niche in the study of issues. But this proved temporary. In time, a hesitancy to research and plan for projects one felt uncomfortable in executing emerged.

Discomfort with being on the firing line created additional problems of marginality. Often the activists who planned projects would need assistance in executing them and would call upon less active members for help. Frequently these calls for help were also consciously motivated by a desire to make marginal members feel needed. Rather than reduce their sense of marginality, however, these last-minute calls made the less active members feel they were being used as mere bodies to hold picket signs or to distribute leaflets. Furthermore, not having been involved in the research stage, these persons tended to feel uninformed on the causes they were asked to advocate and consequently felt even further discomfort on the picket line. Though the group seems to apply little direct pressure to participate in action projects, some persons nevertheless have felt obligated to do so from guilt and a desire to be "responsible" members of the Congregation.

Over the years, some of these persons have "learned the role of activist" and have come to feel more comfortable in their participation. But all the while they have quietly carried an unfulfilled agenda, a desire to see the Congregation be something more than a social-action group. Though the group obviously filled some important needs, the sense of community felt by the activists eluded them.

Gradually that "something more" began to emerge. Over the past two years, several interrelated factors have contributed to intensified feelings of community among all the active members of the Congregation. First of all, so long as the Congregation membership remained heterogeneous and unstable, the activists could ignore the internal problems of the mission. But as the membership stabilized and the number of active members decreased slightly, internal dissension became increasingly difficult to disregard. Intense involvement in the life of the Congregation, often several evenings a week, had the additional consequence of reducing, if not terminating, friendships outside the group. In short, for many the Congregation gradually became their only source of intimate social contacts and friendships. Dissensus had to be faced, if not squarely, at least sufficiently to reduce latent tensions.

Other factors pushed the Congregation toward resolution of problems too long ignored. One unavoidable reality was the impending end of the experimental mission phase of the Congregation's life. The Presbyterians' financial support for the Congregation had been established on a declining basis: 100 percent the first year, two thirds the second year, and one third the third year. The United Church of Christ, in becoming a cosponsor of the Congregation, extended financial support through five years. In 1971, the Congregation received $6,650 in denominational support, approximately 40 percent of their operating budget. That amount declined to $3,500 in 1972 and only $1,500 in 1973. As of January 1974, the group will receive no further subsidy.

As every pastor and church administrator knows, good liberals like to give their time but not their money. It is not surprising, thus, that with each year's decline in denominational support, the members of the Congregation had to do more soul searching and sacrificing in order to pay the pastor's salary and meet other congregational expenses. Since membership over the years has remained about the same or declined slightly, and since the Congregation had no appreciable sources of additional revenue, the declining denominational support had to be countered by increased financial commitment from the membership.

The final steps toward self-sustenance were major ones. As the Congregation approached 1973, their financial situation looked grim. Making up the difference between the $6,650 of denominational support in 1971 and the $3,500 in 1972 was not easy. During 1972, the Congregation sold $2,250 worth of stock, a gift from a family of the Congregation, in order to meet their fiscal obligations. With most members of the Congregation already feeling maximally pledged, and also feeling the pinch of the general economy, they faced 1973 with the prospect of a $5,000 to $6,000 deficit.

Righter removed much of the weight of the impending fiscal crisis in September 1972 by asking for a 20 percent reduction in his time allocated to the Congregation to pursue personal study. Since a large proportion of Righter's normal work schedule has involved study not dissimilar to what he proposed to do with the cut in salary, this gesture seems to us clearly an altruistic solution to the fiscal crunch. This was possible by virtue of Willie Righter's having obtained full-time employment in April 1971. The Righters' sacrifice, thus, was a reaffirmation of their dedication to the continuance of the Congregation. Others, in turn, reaffirmed their commitment by coming up with sufficient funds to meet the Congregation's obligations. Only one month during 1973 did the Congregation fail to pay their pastor a full salary, and this was rectified the following month.

Nineteen seventy-two was also the year the National Missions Committee of the Miami Presbytery had scheduled continuance hearings for the Congregation. While Righter had received assurances that the door would remain open for the Congregation to continue beyond the experimental phase, such continuance could hardly be assumed. Demonstrating fiscal solvency was necessary, but not altogether sufficient for continuance. The schedule called for an evaluation of the Congregation's performance. Pursuant to the continuance hearings, a team of Synod and Presbytery evaluators were to visit the Congregation and make recommendations to the National Missions Committee. Nervous that their controversial activities might give cause for a negative evaluation, the Congregation requested and received supplementary funds from the Presbyterians and UCC's for an outside evaluator.

These evaluation activities, coupled with an impending financial crisis, placed the members in a situation of having to engage in some serious reflection about their future. Thus, from the spring of 1972 through much of 1973, the Congregation had numerous discussions about where they had been and where they wanted to go. The desire for continuance was unanimous and strongly shared by members of the group. Some could not imagine what they would do if the Congregation ceased to exist. Finally the group came to realize that survival required planning.

The strong desire to continue inextricably related to their emerging identity. At the onset, they were a social-action group strongly divided over the issue of whether their relationship to the Presbyterian church made them any different from other action groups. Debate over this issue continued for a long time and finally resolved itself not in words but in fact. In the process of working together they had gradually become a community unafraid to acknowledge a relationship to the Christian faith.

Those we have previously identified as structurally marginal played no small role in the growth of community, although they were not alone responsible for what evolved. Slowly, their concern for personal growth and for more explicit recognition of their status as a Christian congregation began to be shared by others previously content to focus virtually all congregational ritual and worship around social action.

During the fall of 1972, the Congregation moved in several directions to create programs more nearly representative of "traditional" structures of congregational life in a Christian church. First, they revised the monthly celebrations, heretofore focused almost exclusively around social issues, so that alternate months were devoted to liturgical or personal growth themes. Christmas and Easter were celebrated, and two sessions were devoted to the meaning of death and dying. Christian symbols and language are now used, accompanied by an acknowledgment of broader systems of meaning. So, after four years of sensitivity to the possibility of offending some members, the Congregation moved forward by openly acknowledging their Christian heritage. One member of the Congregation commented, "There is still some awkwardness about not wanting to step on one another's toes. But we reached a point where many of us felt a real yearning to be more open with each other about what we're experiencing. Those of us who come out of a Christian heritage felt a need to be more honest in acknowledging our feelings. The Congregation has now lived together long enough that we are beginning to feel comfortable with this. . . . I think it's kind of like an inter-faith marriage. Members of the Congregation are now able, in effect, to say, 'If this day is really important to you, we'll let you have it and share with you in our own terms, and then later we'll celebrate something which is important to us.' . . . In planning liturgical celebrations, we've tried to be open in allowing for all kinds of meanings; we don't want to ram one viewpoint down anybody's throat. . . . But I feel this greater openness has been healthy for all of us. I think it is a sign of our growth and maturity as a congregation."

Such openness would probably have been impossible at the onset of the Congregation's life. Not until they had begun to grow together as a community could they openly acknowledge and appreciate their own diversity. From the beginning, the Congregation had used the rhetoric of "diversity within unity." Now it had meaning. Not one member was lost as a result of this new openness.

The matter of Christian education for the children in the Congregation had long been an issue for bringing ideological division quickly to the surface. Yet in spite of the wide range of views on doctrinal matters, those with preadolescent children have generally agreed on the desirability of some sort of Christian education. For three years a program was attempted. Each year it failed. There seemed no way of designing a curriculum palatable to the whole membership.

Again, in the fall of 1972, the Congregation launched its first successful Christian education program. The rules for Children's Church were simple. A parent had to accompany the children.

They met three Sundays a month. There were, not surprisingly, some concessions to the humanists. Bible stories received no strong doctrinal emphasis, for instance. At Easter, they not only celebrated the resurrection but also planted a rosebush as symbolic of Easter as a rite of spring. Projects and activities were emphasized: puppet theater presentations, building nativity and passiontide scenes, producing a passion play, and making personal talismans bearing Christian symbols.

In spite of the focus on Bible stories and the absence of pressure to attend, Children's Church was well attended and drew from a cross-section of the Congregation. The perceived need for some kind of formalized Christian or ethical education for the children contributed to the success of the program. So, too, did the open format which permitted parents to introduce their children to the Christian heritage without affirming a doctrinal line. Another important dimension of Children's Church was that it opened the door to discuss ethics and the meaning of faith in the home, a task which had been made awkward by the absence of explicit theological content in the life of the Congregation. Humanists were free to emphasize the symbolic meanings of the biblical tradition, while the traditionalists could affirm what they believed.

Children's Church served another function for the entire Congregation: it brought adults together in a context which made it easier to both acknowledge and share their diversity. The diversity, which in the early years of the Congregation had been a key source of divisiveness between the secular humanists and the traditional Christians, in the presence of children became a source of educational strength. Thus, a latent consequence of Children's Church was a considerable subsidence in earlier tensions and another move toward community.

The group took yet another step toward becoming an explicitly Christian community in the fall of 1972 with the formation of a weekly Saturday afternoon prayer group. When we first learned of this development, we were concerned that it might result in a realignment wherein the orthodox became a new core of the Congregation, with the humanists pushed to the edge. As we write, the prayer group is entering its second year and we see no evidence of its having a divisive effect. Again, this suggests the maturation of the Congregation and their growing ability to openly accept diversity without its constituting a threat to the group.

Although the Congregation has made great progress toward stabilizing and becoming a community, there remain several unresolved problems which in the long run threaten its survival. Indeed, some could bring an abrupt end to the Congregation.

The first critical problem is membership. Four factors, in substantial measure interrelated, have led the group to create a membership committee. First of all, the Congregation has periodically lost members as a result of job transfers. Recognizing the highly mobile nature of our society, the Congregation is aware they may lose further members via this route. Indeed, as we write, the Congregation faces the threat of losing one of its most active couples to a transient job market. Without new members, the Congregation is certain to die the slow death of attrition.

A second factor is the ever-present precarious financial situation of the Congregation. The loss of a few members or personal crises which would necessitate curtailing contributions could create an insoluble financial dilemma. While Willie Righter's employment makes it theoretically possible for them to remain on a radically reduced pastor's salary, it is unrealistic to expect them not to look for greener pastures sooner or later if the situation does not change.

A third factor bringing pressure for new members is a growing realization the Congregation is already spread very thin on its social-action projects. As we have seen, United People and the Gulf boycott have become long-range commitments. The Congregation has had to resist the temptation to get involved in new projects because it simply doesn't have the person power. At the same time, new projects are needed to renew commitment and reassure members that they are not stagnating but are addressing vital issues in the Dayton community. Thus, new members are needed not only to expand current activities but also to move forward into new projects.

Finally, the problem of person power has been exacerbated over the past two years by the entrance of several women into the labor force. Whether through financial necessity or the desire for self-fulfillment in the world of work, the employment of several women in the group has cut seriously into the time earlier spent on congregational projects.

All these factors have interacted to underscore the need for new members. The Membership Committee, however, has approached the matter of recruitment warily. There are several reasons for this. One is the uncertainty that others will want to join them. One committee member described the problem thus: "I think the Congregation is not for everybody. It's probably not as easy to recruit for our congregation as it is to recruit for other organizations which do not make as many demands upon their membership. Besides, it is not the 'in' thing to be involved in social action anymore. Furthermore, the kind of social-action projects we are doing are not so groovy because they require long-term commitments and a lot of hard work. We have been into the United People campaign for four years and are just now beginning to make some inroads; we've been working on [poverty] four years and the Gulf boycott two years. Someone who does not understand that it takes five to ten years on such projects is deceiving himself. And that requires quite a commitment. We really don't know how many people there are out there who want to take on those kinds of commitments and that much hard work and all the stomachaches that go with it. . . . We make a big thing of expecting from members a high level of commitment and discipline. Signing the covenant and becoming a member is, therefore, a serious matter."

In one sense, she is quite correct. Lowering the expectations for new members would set in motion a wide range of new problems for the Congregation. But as we spoke with several on the Membership Committee, we sensed that part of their problem is the newness of the role of recruiter. Not only has the Congregation not previously engaged in recruiting, but also traditional models of proselytizing don't fit. Finally, the committee has found some members of the Congregation less than enthusiastic about their plans for recruitment.

A resolution establishing an accountability system for recruitment was voted at a congregational meeting in the fall of 1972. The Membership Committee would assign prospects to members. A committeeperson would then check periodically on the progress the member was making with the prospect. The resolution itself was slickly written, emphasizing "welcoming people into the Congregation." However, the statement reflected a clear expectation that recruitment would be the job of all members, not just the committee. The Congregation accepted the resolution without protest.

As the system began to function, however, protests did arise. The accountability system left nowhere to hide. Those shy about actively cultivating prospects became defensive, guilty, and even a little hostile after a committee member had checked back three or four times and the prospect had still not been contacted.

Three sources of resistance arose. First, the accountability system and the policy of total membership inclusion in the recruitment effort flew in the face of the established value of automotivation—the "do your own thing" ethic. For some, recruitment, though good and needful, was not their thing. Having received encouragement to "volunteer" for committees and to seek "their own level of participation" in the past, they adamantly resisted the new expectation.

Second, the recruitment drive not only grated against the value of voluntarism, it also brought to the surface much resentment of the established church. Old wounds opened as members recalled the kinds of recruitment pressures espoused in their earlier, and to some nightmarish, church experiences. As one committeeperson said, "I think they were laboring under a lot of old junk out of the institutional church. Some people felt that we were asking them to go out and save souls or something . . . or bring in prospects hogtied and delivered with a checkbook in their hands. This is not at all the spirit of what we were asking. We just wanted a kind of concern. Since the old high-pressure recruitment and all the 'bringing in the sheaves' theology that goes along with it was not the direction from which the Membership Committee was coming, we just never dreamed that some of this sort of resentment and interpretation would come up."

While not explicitly mentioned as a problem, we suspect a third source of resistance came from the subtle security of things as they are and the suspicion of the unknown. What might be called the "charter member syndrome" is a common phenomenon in small and recently formed organizations. New members pose a threat to stable status and power arrangements within an organization. They bring with them a host of new definitions and goals which might alter the already established, meaningful, and satisfying patterns of the group. It took the Congregation for Reconciliation five years to become a tightly knit *Gemeinschaft*. Along the way, the thrust toward community was disrupted more than once by newcomers attempting to impose their own agendas. How could this group not feel some uneasiness about the prospect of new members? Yet many of the members now recognize that the survival of the Congregation depends on the success of their efforts to bring in new recruits.

Two measures helped make recruitment more palatable for the congregation as a whole. They first modified the policy statement to restore a value harmony with voluntarism. In essence, it now expresses the hope that everyone will want to participate in welcoming new members but has eliminated the policy to do so. Second, the Membership Committee sponsored a training program aimed at developing recruitment skills, designed brochures, and put together a slide show recounting the history of the Congregation with an emphasis upon its action programs.

Thus far, recruitment has resulted in few new memberships. From the fall of 1972 through the summer of 1973, three new persons joined. One is a teen-age daughter of members. The others are a couple recently moved to the city who found their way to the Congregation through the media.

The time and energy involved in recruitment thus far cannot easily be measured, but the amounts are significant. Without new strategies designed to ferret out and interest potential members, however, more time and effort will be expended without much success. We believe both that there are persons "out there" who are capable of the commitment needed and that the continued existence of the Congregation hinges on finding and recruiting these persons. A year may be minimal for the group to get in gear and tackle this problem with the vigor and ingenuity they've displayed for other projects. Nonetheless, from a system's perspective, the allocation of resources to recruiting results in a net reduction in social-action areas. And this is the raison d'être of the group. Diminishing the flow of its lifeblood or otherwise reducing the Congregation's quality of life for its members over prolonged time could endanger internal rapport.

In sum, the Congregation, having worked hard for five years to achieve independence and community, now faces what may be the greatest challenge to date. They must recruit new members while avoiding the pitfalls of new internal division and loss of direction in their external goals.

At the present moment, neither of these poses an imminent threat to the Congregation, but the danger of new divisions within the group remains ever present. For one, it is probably too early to be certain that the détente between Christians and humanists is permanent. Likewise, the balance between social action and personal growth may yet be precarious. Those who have pushed for personal growth, having achieved some success, could attempt to lead the Congregation further in this direction.

Another problem which has haunted the Congregation from the beginning is the inherent tension a high-demand organization creates for an individual whose spouse is not a member. This is a difficult problem for us to assess, since we have not probed deeply into the personal lives of most of the members. Clearly, however, a few members have experienced marital conflict resulting from time-consuming involvement in the Congregation. One husband, only marginally involved in the group, expressed his frustration thus: "Sometimes I think she is married to that damned congregation." This comment occurred at about 1:30 A.M. in the couple's kitchen. The dinner dishes were still in the sink; she had not returned from a committee meeting. Another distraught person told us her husband was going to have to choose between their marriage and the Congregation; shortly afterward, he dropped out of the Congregation.

The extent to which congregational involvement is the *cause* rather than a symptom of marital discord is unclear. It may well be that a few individuals, failing to find fulfillment in marriage, have turned to the Congregation for support and meaning. This situation, however, places the noninvolved spouse as odd person out in a triadic struggle.

Our concern with marital tensions within the Congregation involves impact on the future of the group. Theoretically, at least, it is possible all those experiencing difficulties would move to ease their marital tensions by dropping out. While this involves few

169

persons, the Congregation is scarcely in a position to lose any members.

More importantly, though, how the Congregation comes to grips with such personal problems may be some indicator of the value and viability of its community. They have not yet resolved this issue, nor for that matter has it become a problem of a magnitude demanding such attention. But reconciliation needs consideration on the level of individual members also; the weighing of questions of marital obligations and role responsibility versus individual fulfillment and self-identity must be worked through responsibly.

Thus far, the Congregation has handled such problems in a way far healthier and closer to the Christian ideal of ministering to one another's needs than have most churches. They have done this simply by moving problems from the secrecy of the pastor's study out into the air of trust and mutual support they have generated within the group. That's a major step. But it alone solves neither marital tension nor any other personal problems wherein involvement in the group is itself a contributing factor.

The Congregation for Reconciliation has no immunity to the problems experienced at every level of our society. Nor does it seem to have a lesser resistance. It is, however, trying to find its own remedies.

One important problem remains in discussing the internal dynamics and the future of the Congregation. That is the issue of leadership. Righter's style, while nondirective, is nonetheless goal- or task-oriented. Many of the Congregation's projects had their genesis in his mind and came to fruition only through his hard work and persistence. In our interviews with members of the Congregation, many spoke of the abundance of leadership within the group. "Our problem," one enthusiastic member told us, "is that everyone in the Congregation is a leader."

Whether they are all leaders we cannot say. Clearly, however, they are a group of strong-willed people, seldom wanting for ideas or the desire to express them. Many pastors with this kind of group would have failed to mold them into either an effective social action cadre or a community. Righter accomplished both.

While the Congregation's "do your own thing" ethic is real, it is not unbridled. Along the way, Righter has managed to harness collective energies to pursue common goals. Without his leadership, the Congregation would probably have gone off in as many directions as there are members, with little legacy and few accomplishments for their five years.

The critical question now facing the Congregation is whether its members are capable of functioning without his leadership. The issue is not academic, for Righter is planning a sabbatical beginning in the fall of 1974 to study in Europe. Righter discussed his plans with us during our visit in 1972. At that time, we thought this was a device to make a break with a group which had just about run its course. Our return in 1973 altered both our perception of the potential viability of the group and of Righter's motive. As we have seen in this chapter, 1972-73 was a critical period in the solidification of the group. They met more than 90 percent of their budget; they made great strides in resolving some persistent internal difficulties; and they began to take some important steps toward meeting the structural imperatives of survival.

We suspect Righter is quite capable of going out and recruiting enough members to assure his job security for the next several years. We doubt, however, he will take this route; not because he lacks the proclivity, which he may, but rather because to do so would make it *his* congregation. From the onset, the Congregation has belonged to the people, and it is this fact, perhaps more than any other, which has kept everyone working toward common goals. If the Congregation means enough to its members, they will find ways to recruit new constituents and keep the ship afloat while the captain is away.

Righter is realistic about the possibility of things falling apart, but he is optimistic that this will not happen. "We may come home," Righter commented, "and find that they don't want us. That would be kinda tough on Willie and me, for we have grown very fond of these people. But that would be good, for it would mean that they had outgrown the need for us. And that's what it's all about, isn't it?"

Time is needed to know if the Congregation for Reconciliation will survive at all. Our skepticism of 1972 regarding the prospects of survival have now given way to at least a flicker of optimism and—if we may depart from the role of objective observers—a hope that Righter is right. They've come a long way, and there's still no rest in sight. They've grown weary from time to time, but there's a strength that has sustained them through all sorts of adversities. They believe in themselves and in what they're doing, stylish or not. The following reflection sums up this affirmation better than our words could; it was written by a Congregation member for their most recent birthday celebration.

A little extrapolation on the Theology of Celebration will tell you that birthday cake is at least as symbolic of the body of Christ as is bread, and that the blood of the Savior ought to be represented by the effervescence of champagne at least now and then.

Communion is not a ritual—it is the Christian way of life. To me, the beauty of the Congregation for Reconciliation has its essence in this difference: we are communing with the Lord all the time.

When the [poverty] committee confronts public officials on behalf of human beings, that is Communion.

When the Gulf Boycott Coalition confronts the conscience of church delegates on behalf of the cause of freedom for our unseen brothers in Angola, that is Communion. . . .

When United People challenges the paternalism or selfishness of the local establishment leaders, that's Communion.

Play with words with me a moment, or, if it pleases you more, call it working with concepts. The Quakers got their name because it is said they trembled in the presence of the Lord. With that in your mind, look at the modern phrase "Movers and Shakers" in society.

When we shake up the consciousness of our community, locally or internationally, on behalf of Christian principles, when we move the bureaucracy toward practical humanism, we are doing it in the presence of the Lord. That's Communion.

That's the blood of the Lamb being spilled in Angola; it's the body of Christ that shivers in rat-infested housing in Dayton; it's the spirit of the Lord that is being dehumanized behind the walls of Ohio prisons.

An essential problem with the established church is symbolized for me in the ritualized solemnity of the "Communion" service . . . every Sunday at a given point in the liturgy, cued by solemn music.

"Get serious, folks," they say, "we are now going to have communion with the Holy Spirit."

The Christians in this house tonight know about the soberness of communion. Our communion through social action is sobering business. It simply isn't very funny, and it's hard to do it very long with a light heart.

It's when we come together like this that we can lighten our burdens, individually and collectively. Together, we find renewal [being nourished by] each other and Christ. Together, we can laugh and love as human beings.

We can feel secure about our ability to love those unseen, unknown human beings for whom we seek social justice, because we have tried and succeeded in loving each other, whom we see and know. Times like this are sort of a practical lab in loving.

Remember our happy times together: working in the garden, watching our children laugh, gaily baptizing our babies, celebrating and family festivaling and house churching.

And remember our funny times together: following Pete Hanson's meandering tour through Hueston Woods, being attacked by all the men and machines of the south suburban police forces en masse, being hurled fully clothed into the Browns' swimming pool, and all the other good times, happy times, funny, human, laughing times.

All that, too, is Communion.

Communion is not just a part of this congregation's life, it *is* our life. Opening gifts, working jigsaw puzzles, washing feet, lighting candles, it is all Communion, for we are not alone.

So let us now eat, drink, and be merry in Christ, because—by God!—we have much to celebrate!

And indeed they do.

CHAPTER 9

Successful in Life: The Cincinnati Experiment

"Can a congregation based on a community of special concern develop a ministry of racial reconciliation which both contributes to needed social change and relates helpfully to the ministries of other congregations?" Such was the thesis to be tested by the experimental congregations within the Ohio Synod of the United Presbyterian Church. The Dayton experiment clearly failed to provide an affirmative answer. In response to this conclusion in an earlier report, church administrators in Dayton urged us to examine the experimental congregation created from the same planning documents in the Cincinnati Presbytery.

On paper, the two congregations appear nearly identical: city-wide, nonresidential, and testing the same thesis. The same name, the Congregation for Reconciliation, was given to reinforce their raison d'être. Yet, as they emerged, the two experimental missions presented striking differences. While the Dayton group succeeded in contributing to social change on the civic level, it failed to relate helpfully to the ministries of other congregations. The Cincinnati mission, contrariwise, functioned as interpreter and endorser of social change to other congregations while dealing in little direct secular social action. It tested the thesis successfully, lived out its experimental time span, and died peacefully.

How can two experimental congregations, developed from the same design, mature in such different ways? In chapter 3 we argued that the planners, the organizing pastor, and the charter members all made important contributions to the evolution of the Dayton organization. The character, personality, and mission of the congregation were molded by the priorities, skills, and style of its three parents interacting within the limitations of environment and happenstance. The two experiments had only one parent in common and adapted to different community environments. In this sense, similarity would have been more surprising than disparity. Yet it is important for church leaders to understand how such totally different realities can and did emerge from the same paper-and-pen plan.

A Pastor Is Called

The Rev. Duane Holm had interviewed for the position of organizing pastor for the mission in Dayton early in June 1968. Although supported by some members of the Miami Presbytery's committee responsible for recruiting a pastor for its experimental mission, he was turned down in favor of Righter. A few weeks later, when the Committee on National Missions in the Cincinnati Presbytery began seeking an organizing pastor for its experimental mission, Holm was again interviewed. This time he was called.

A graduate of Penn State and Yale Divinity School, Holm had grown up in the Southwest, living in Texas and Kansas. While in seminary, he had taken a year's absence and had ministered to the Iona community, a new working-class housing estate near Glasgow, Scotland. He had returned for two more years shortly after seminary graduation to serve a large church in a shipbuilding district. After this he had pastored an inner-city church on the west side of Chicago for seven years.

Holm's experience in Scotland had given him a deep appreciation for liturgical worship as a basis for community. In Chicago, in a church criss-crossed with racial, ethnic, and social class divisions, Holm viewed the congregation as held together despite its diverse membership largely because of the centrality of worship in its life. Likewise, his background informed his view of social action. Holm felt that unity proceeded from worship. On the basis of a supportive community so engendered, social action would follow. Social action, thus seen, is more a result than a focal concern.

Both Righter and Holm retrospectively viewed the recruitment interview as a bargaining session for seeking assurances, reaching special understandings, and laying fears to rest. Both men had come to the committee with their own agendas.

Holm related the experience of his Dayton interview as follows: "I felt that the interest [of the committee] was primarily social action. And I saw myself essentially as a pastor who wanted the church involved in social action, but my primary base was a worshiping, teaching community. And I didn't see that that interest was strong in the group. In fact, it seemed to me that they were expecting to later evaluate the effectiveness of the new congregation in terms of the results it produced in social change. I was more concerned about the kind of group you created, especially in terms of their orientation through worship of God. Maybe my fears colored what I thought they were saying. But I wanted to know, 'Are you guys really serious about wanting an intensive worshiping congregation?' Because I knew full well that to put some of your energy on that meant, in terms of efficiency, in the short run, that we were going to be less effective in dealing with social issues in the community. . . . And I wasn't sure that they understood that." [1]

Holm received the needed assurance in Cincinnati, however, and accepted the position. It is interesting that he did not pursue the potential of permanence for the new congregation but assented to it as an experimental mission with a life of three to four years.

In Scotland, and even more in Chicago, Holm had worked with house churches. The inner-city congregation being scattered by urban renewal, much congregational activity had taken place in members' homes. This had been a positive experience for Holm and had stimulated his interest in the further possibilities for such a ministry. By 1968 he perceived direct civil rights action was waning. Anticipating social action as becoming increasingly tedious and undramatic, he felt a congregation meeting in the homes of members might better structurally integrate work in worship. Further, in cultivating the feeling of "family" among members, it would provide needed support for the drudge work of social action.

Holm's vision of the mission was well grounded in both experience and theory. His mental picture, as noted in the following statement, was reasonably concrete:

My image of the congregation was that of a specialized lay order. Like the specialized monastic orders of the Renaissance that arose to supplement and complement the work of the parish churches in that increasingly complex, urbanized society (the Dominicans with students, the Franciscans with the poor). We were not the church of the future: we were a part of the whole church which had been released from caring for a neighborhood—the young, the sick, the elderly, and the half-committed—in order to work on the problem of racial reconciliation, for the whole church. We would not become a new sect. We would be accountable to the other churches of Presbytery in order to hold them accountable to us.

That meant we must live with open books. We would tell the other churches what we were doing and why we thought we were doing it, because we would not continue to act on behalf of a church that did not trust us.

In the church, there has been as much need to reconcile evangelicals with activists, as whites with blacks. We would try to interpret what we were doing in terms others could accept. And we would try to work on programs we could openly share with the other churches. We would try not just to "do our own thing." [2]

Thus, divergent directions in the two experiments initially stemmed from differences in the expectations of the organizing pastors, although both did perceive the calling committee as primarily interested in social-action potential. Their basic difference seemed to be a question of *where* the action was, or ought to be. Righter allowed his congregation to develop and coalesce around social-action projects, insulated from other churches. Holm, on the other hand, molded his congregation as a worshiping community accountable to other churches in the realm of social action.

We argued earlier that the planners had failed to recognize an essential contradiction in their goals. On the one hand, they viewed experimental missions as havens where action-oriented laymen could work, free of the constraints of traditional congregations. Following this blueprint, however, leads almost inevitably to conflicts with established churches as controversial and unpopular social issues emerge. On the other hand, the goal of providing a helping ministry to other churches requires the kind of mutual accountability envisioned by Holm. By its very nature, this approach disallows the emergence of a "doing one's own thing" ethic and thus hampers independent, direct social action. Righter followed the former route, and Holm the latter. Both were fulfilling goals established by the planners.

Further, Holm's emphasis upon developing a worshiping community appealed to traditional Christians rather than to secular humanists. The desire for accountability to established churches and the vision of reconciling evangelicals and radicals inspired commitment among a nucleus of people vastly different from the core of the Dayton activists. Thus, the filtration process for forming a charter group produced important differences between the Cincinnati and Dayton congregations.

The organizing pastor's vision of the incipient congregation becomes, to some extent, a self-fulfilling prophecy. Holm himself, in reporting to the Presbytery three years after the congregation first met, recognized this. "How [the organizing pastor] sees it determines how he explains it to others; how he explains it to others determines who comes; who comes determines what the congregation does; and what it does determines what the congregation becomes." [3] His statement is correct, but not complete. The development of a specialized congregation is yet more complex.

We Gather Together: Forming a Congregation

Holm arrived in Cincinnati in September, but it took six months before the nucleus of a congregation had gathered and regular meetings had begun. By then, in March of 1969, the Dayton group had already established itself as viable in social action and had begun the struggle of defining its mission goals.

There were several reasons for Holm's difficulty in recruiting a following. Some of them sound familiar (Righter had the same problems); others were unique to the Cincinnati situation.

In Dayton, the two city newspapers had anticipated the establishment of the congregation and had given it almost continuous publicity during the first year. As indicated earlier, this publicity, combined with a lack of cooperation by pastors, contributed heavily to the special characteristics of the charter group.

In Cincinnati, however, the newspapers ignored the proposed congregation. Perhaps a matter as simple as the interests and inclinations of the religion editors of the papers can account for the oversight. A concerted effort on the part of Holm and the Presbytery spokesmen may have altered the situation. As it happened, however, the unchurched and the church dropouts, so heavily represented in the Dayton mission, knew nothing of the Cincinnati experiment.

As in Dayton, the efforts of the Presbytery and early referrals by pastors proved fruitless. Without press support, and finding little serious interest among those on the initial recruitment list, Holm turned to the local pastors for help. The amount of resistance surprised him. As in Dayton, many of the liberal pastors felt threatened by the existence of the congregation. Several had opposed the proposal to establish the mission and, in effect, told Holm, "You're going to take away my most active members and leave me the rest."

As months passed, Holm's clear conception of a worshiping community had failed to take shape. Finally, he unapologetically asked area pastors for permission to proselytize their social-activist members and found several of them cooperative and responsive. Whether motivated by a genuine desire for the well-being of frustrated and unfulfilled activists in their churches or by an inclination toward the maintenance of congregational tranquility, the more conservative clergy more willingly handed over a number of names. From here, the beginnings of a congregation grew. Later, a Presbytery-wide worship program insert promoting the experimental congregation also solicited some fruitful inquiries.

Naturally, this method of recruitment strongly influenced the profile of the congregation. For the most part, members had been active churchmen. Although they held a range of theological positions, very few could be characterized as secular humanists and none opposed God-talk. Over two thirds came from Presbyterian backgrounds. A number were reared in manses or were themselves ex-ministers. A handful were local denominational administrators. Holm characterized them as overcommitted lay persons who felt their commitment underutilized in their former churches.

As the group stabilized at about forty members, most were professional families. They tended to be middle-income ($12,000 to $30,000) and middle-aged (thirty to fifty). In this regard, collectively they paralleled the membership of the Dayton congregation. The Cincinnati members, however, tended to be more highly involved in the social and civic life of the city. Expectedly, then, many were too busy to devote a sizable portion of their time to the work of the Congregation. In Dayton, congregational activities consumed a far greater amount of members' time and attention.

Holm suggests that his congregation members were unusual in two respects. First, most had lived outside the local area for at least part of their lives. This exposure to a variety of community experiences, he felt, had broadened their vision of possibilities for social action. Second, the majority had undergone some deeply memorable experience of death, separation, alienation, or the like. Such personal histories may have given some members of the Cincinnati congregation empathetic capacities beyond what one would predict from their social backgrounds alone. Emotional support among members developed quickly and was readily sustained; growth of community presented no problems. Holm, at last, had gathered around him a ready and receptive following, a group eagerly capable of developing strong emotional ties in a supportive worshiping community.

As Holm had anticipated, the framework of corporate liturgical worship provided a structure both generating of and reinforcing to the growth of community. Families, including children, attended the worship services. Singing was a cappella or accompanied by whatever instruments members played. Each service culminated in the sharing of bread and wine around a table. Interaction and positive sentiments among participants developed, and a pattern of progressively intimate self-revelation and mutual identification ensued.

The Cincinnati congregation thus contrasts sharply with Dayton, where consensus formation was such a long and tedious process. Had Holm's congregation attracted the unchurched and church dropouts in its early stages, his vision of a worshiping community, accountable and helpfully ministering to established churches in the Presbytery, would have received strong challenge. At a minimum, consensus and solidarity would have been far more elusive.

Pastoral leadership style was another important difference in the two congregations. Righter assumed the permanence of his congregation. He thus afforded himself the luxury of time to allow the group to thrash through its problems and define its own goals. Holm, however, saw the Cincinnati experiment as a three- to four-year project. The delay in gathering a congregation made the generation and execution of social-action projects a race against time. Viewed as such, strong pastoral leadership was required. Holm made decisions for his group which Righter would have insisted the members themselves work out. Holm's position as primary decision-maker and spiritual leader of his flock seldom faced serious challenge. This aspect of reality evolved from the onset. Such a position would no doubt have driven away iron-willed activists determined to do their own thing, had they sampled the Cincinnati congregation's organizational climate. Strong leadership thus reinforced consensus formation in the congregation.

By contrast, Righter's low-key leadership style encouraged, by default, internal conflict and dissent. The solidarity developed in the Dayton group no doubt served them well over the long run, for it implies far greater personal commitment of members. The route taken by Holm obviously served best as a short-run strategy for attaining more immediate goals. We in no way mean to suggest a preference. They are different operational modes, suited to different situations.

The Bible Says . . . : Interpreting Social Action

The Congregation in Cincinnati moved from house to house each month, and this mobility soon necessitated a newsletter, including a map locating congregational gatherings. This also kept members abreast of the activities of various committees and contained chatty notes about important events in the lives of members and their families. Although its ostensible public was the congregation membership, the newsletter addressed another audience as well.

Holm reasoned that if his congregation was to provide a helping ministry to the established churches, such a ministry must be built upon a relationship of mutual respect and trust. The essential prerequisite of trust is communication. Once the newsletter was established, it became a facility for communicating with other pastors in the Presbytery. The stated purpose of such distribution was to keep pastors informed of congregation activities. More importantly, however, it served to interpret social action in terms acceptable to even theologically conservative pastors and laity.

Each month, on its cover page, the newsletter carried a devotional message addressing issues relevant to the social-action concerns of the mission. The message was almost always embedded in a biblical narrative followed by a terse and pointed interpretive statement. Speaking from within the tradition of biblical faith, the newsletter carried an air of authority attractive to orthodox Christians. This approach to Presbytery clergy sought legitimation for congregational concerns in those churches where dormant opposition could have been expected. The strategy goal, moreover, reached beyond simply neutralizing the opposition. It sought mutual respect, reduction of threat, and increase in the common ground of identity on which to build a helping ministry.

To illustrate, one such devotional is cited below. It was distributed on the eve of the November 1971 election day.

Jeremiah was the local white liberal in Jerusalem. There are some in almost every community! And Jeremiah was in a hole. He had called on his country to end a war they could not win. He upset the leaders in the community. He had to be toned down a bit. So they lowered him down to the bottom of a mucky, muddy well.

Well. That's where Ebedmelech came in. Ebedmelech was a black man. He was a government official and a politician. People called him an Uncle Tom behind his back—an "Ethiopian eunuch." They considered him impotent and powerless. But Ebedmelech knew the ropes. He had learned how to work the system. He got orders for Jeremiah's release. He got ropes and rags from the government stores. He told Jeremiah to wrap the rags around him so he wouldn't get rubbed raw by the ropes. "Then they drew Jeremiah up with ropes and lifted him out of the cistern."

The moral of all this is that local white liberals need to have a black politician friend who can pull strings. Good black elected public officials may well be the last, best hope of this nation. Fortunately for us, we have another chance to elect some on Tuesday.

The Dayton congregation contrasts sharply in its approach to established churches for several reasons. First, the social-action goals of the Congregation for Reconciliation in Dayton did not depend for their success upon the cooperation of other churches, nor did they, beyond one initial attempt, ever involve other churches. Second, had some members made this a serious goal, the effort would have almost inevitably generated a new round of conflict within the mission. Considering the style of the Congregation's members and pastor, limitations on project selection and action to assuage other churches could have totally unraveled the group. Third, even if the social-action strategy of working through other churches had been adopted and supported, image management would have presented a structural problem. The news media in Dayton seemed prepared to cover the activities of the experimental congregation even before Righter appeared on the scene. He has, however, skillfully cultivated the media as indispensable tools in the public confrontations characteristic of the Congregation's action strategy. Had Righter and his following desired to court the churches convincingly, media attention would probably have proven dysfunctional and would have been avoided. This is what occurred in Cincinnati. Rather than striving for skill and sophistication in the arena of city-wide media, that congregation developed a commensurate skill in relating to the Presbytery to better fulfill its design and goals vis-à-vis social action.

Action in Search of an Issue

The initial members of the Cincinnati Congregation for Reconciliation, like their counterparts in Dayton, were eager to become involved in social action. During the first month, they decided to support a rent strike among slum tenants. This project seems basically to have been chosen simply because "they had to start somewhere." The strike soon collapsed. Although a few got interested in statewide housing legislation from this, within a short time interest had waned. The Congregation's first attempt at social action was thus a critical disappointment.

Ohio law compels voters to periodically reassess their contribution to public education through tax levies. During the 1960s, more than one Ohio school system closed its doors while defiant voters trudged repeatedly to the polls to defeat the latest tax revision. This issue arose in Cincinnati during the early months of the Congregation's life. The mission soon devised a two-pronged strategy of confrontation. First, they launched a voter registration drive in a low-income neighborhood. Simultaneously, they began working through the Presbytery and its twenty-eight churches within the Cincinnati school district to generate support for the levy. They pushed an advocacy resolution through a meeting of the Cincinnati Presbytery and then distributed literature through the churches urging levy passage.

The two tactics met with unequal success. Holm recounted the experience to us as follows: "We had really seen ourselves in 'Secular City' terms, going out there and outpoliticking the politicians, and we found that we could not deliver many new voters [in the neighborhood where we were working]. The registration drive flopped. For a lot of the folks this was their first encounter with record keeping in the inner city. Just trying to find out where people live, what their names are, and if they are voters was a nightmare. It drove people up the wall. But I think the thing we learned from the experience is that since the Congregation does not have a neighborhood identification we would never be very effective in the secular political realm and our power would come primarily by working through the churches. At least we had access and mutual accountability to these people."

We have argued that the initial social-action project in Dayton established their identity as an activist group. It set the tone and style for later confrontations in the city. It reinforced commitment to direct social action as a means of fulfilling their central goal. The Cincinnati Congregation for Reconciliation, by contrast, had from the onset seen itself as an agency to get established churches involved in social action. The failures it encountered in attempting independent social-action projects reinforced its desire to work through other churches.

Having tried its hand at direct social action and having failed, the Congregation continued to search for an issue around which they could build a ministry of racial reconciliation which would contribute to needed social change and through which they could relate helpfully to the ministries of other congregations. Just such an issue was about to erupt.

The close of the tumultuous decade of the sixties found the nation in a mood of weariness and resignation to racial problems. The War on Poverty had waned, the government had ignored the protest of Resurrection City, Martin Luther King had become a memory, and the Kerner Report had only stirred more words. Conditions for the underprivileged in our society had improved somewhat, but major hurdles yet loomed on every horizon and there seemed little national psychic energy left. Only a genuine shock tactic managed to hurtle the poverty and race issues into the headlines once again.

On May 4, 1969, James Forman, speaking for the Black Economic Development Council, interrupted Sunday services in New York's Riverside Church and presented demands for financial reparations to the nation's black citizens. Accusing the present capitalism of the United States of being oppressive to blacks, the Black Manifesto Forman presented singled out the community of white religious institutions to begin making restitution for generations of slavery and subsequent oppression. Anything more than marginal participation in the society required a massive infusion of funds for black economic development in fields such as banking, education, and communications.

Support for the Black Manifesto was scattered. Some black leaders, within and without the churches, heralded it; others expressed reservations or disapproval. Nonetheless, the issue defied being ignored and white church leaders had to face it. The powerful language of the document repulsed some, and they found in its verbiage sufficient reason for rejection. To others, the radical wording and ideas appeared as a signal of the urgency and immensity of the problem.

Robert Lecky and Elliott Wright, in their volume analyzing the nature and impact of the Black Manifesto, addressed the vulnerability of white religion:

> Reparation is no new idea in America, but demands for financial restitution from religion were unprecedented before the Black Manifesto. Eugene Carson Blake, the American who is chief executive of the World Council of Churches, was likely right when he said the Manifesto came to the church because of what Christians and Jews have confessed about human dignity. In terms of religion's claim to be equipped to explore the moral dimensions of economics, culture and politics, perhaps the target of the Manifesto had providential direction. Scores of white churchmen were willing to concede that likelihood. Few held out dollars to the BEDC, yet from unexpected quarters came thanksgiving to God that Mr. Forman and the Manifesto had given religion an opportunity to be socially relevant. It was, undoubtedly, also a frightening realization. Somebody *was* listening, or seeming to listen, to modern, mainstream religion's verbal positions on justice, human welfare and a better global future.[4]

Hearing then, in 1969, that their collection plates must echo the sentiments of their pulpits, churches mainly responded in one of two ways. They either rejected the Manifesto and claimed already existing support or they rejected the direct strategy of payments to BEDC but did initiate some new program for black economic development.

Hoping to lead its Presbytery brethren in the latter course, the Cincinnati Congregation for Reconciliation began developing strategies for interpreting the Manifesto and devising practical means to address the subject of black economic development. Several weeks were spent developing action recommendations. Their resultant proposal was a package of collateral loans for black business enterprises, coupled with the recommendation that churches deposit money and buy stock in new black-controlled financial institutions in Cincinnati.

Interpreting the Black Manifesto to other churches, the Congregation kept the biblical themes focal. An example of this approach is cited below. It was distributed as part of the

Congregation's newsletter while the black economic development issue still commanded widespread concern.

> If your brother, a Hebrew man or woman, is sold to you, he shall serve you six years, and in the seventh you shall let him go. And when you let him go free from you, you shall not let him go empty-handed; you shall furnish him liberally out of your flock, out of your threshing floor, and out of your wine press; as the Lord your God has blessed you, you shall give to him.
>
> But, said Jacob to Laban, at the end of the years, you would have sent me away empty-handed! . . . If the God of my father, the God of Abraham, and the fear of Isaac, had not been on my side, surely now you would have sent me away empty-handed. God saw my afflliction and the labor of my hands, and rebuked you last night.[5]

The devotional then interprets this Old Testament story of the confrontation between Jacob and Laban as a biblical precedent for reparations to ex-slaves. "We, too, freed our slaves after years, and sent them out empty-handed. Without land or equipment or capital. Which is why black Americans are where they are today." God therefore commends the payment of reparations, it is argued, and through black economic development the churches can respond to the will of God.

Before church sessions dominated by Cincinnati businessmen, the Congregation occasionally legitimated its cause with economic ideology. In these instances, presentation teams argued that belief in free enterprise necessarily means wanting others to share in the system. Once church lay leadership agreed to the scriptural and ideological principles, the presenters could offer concrete proposals for action.

The summary report on the Congregation presented to the Cincinnati Presbytery in October of 1972, following the Congregation's termination, reflects upon this project.

> We took the issue [of black economic development], studied all the alternative answers, and were able to present a concrete solution that made sense to the churches of a conservative, business-oriented community. Through our work on [this issue] we

were able to: (1) discuss black problems with fifty sessions which would not otherwise have been open. When a church can see itself as part of the solution, it can afford to look at the problem. (2) raise over $100,000 in Presbytery commitments to black economic development programs. (3) show ourselves to sessions as practical, prepared, real people who were willing to work with them. . . . (4) begin creating a cumulative self-understanding of Presbytery as one which responded to concerns like black economic development.

Black economic development cost us more than we had expected. It took months to interview [those initially better acquainted with the issue], prepare flip charts, train ourselves as teams, and make presentations [in the churches]. . . . None of our other programs was as big, as long, or involved as much of the Congregation at the same time.

This underscores the position that, for the Cincinnati Congregation, social action was not an end in itself. Equally important was the aim of helping churches to share in the process. This understanding of social action contrasts sharply with that of the Dayton Congregation.

The second major project of the Cincinnati Congregation involved the development of a church school curriculum. This project emerged as an attempt to address an internal structural problem within the Congregation but later suggested a way of providing another service to established churches.

In Cincinnati, as in Dayton, children attended worship services with their parents. Because its membership was so geographically decentralized, however, the Cincinnati Congregation followed its worship service with a second hour to handle most of the committee work of the mission. The presence of children during this period presented a problem. In this context, church school offered a logical solution, and so a curriculum was developed. The lesson material centered on black-white encounters in the Bible, and each adult member of the Congregation took his turn, for one month, teaching church school.

After the material had been completed, the Congregation began to consider how it might serve to enhance racial understanding in established churches. They concluded that evangelical

189

churches were probably least likely to emphasize the contributions of blacks to the Christian heritage. Since their lessons were based on Bible stories, they might well be most appreciated in these same churches. And so the material was rewritten with evangelicals in mind and turned into a vacation Bible school curriculum. Although, at the time of the Congregation's termination, the lesson package had yet to win approval for publication by either a church press or educational board, this may still be achieved. If so, the defunct Congregation will add one more success to its scorecard of strides toward racial reconciliation within established churches. If the issue is not pursued further, however, the Congregation will have missed a significant opportunity to extend its work and ideals while also enhancing its success as an experiment.

You Scratch My Back and . . . :
Reciprocity and Accountability

"We must be accountable to the other churches of the Presbytery in order to hold them accountable to us." So wrote Duane Holm in outlining the philosophy on which his congregation was established. The mission, indeed, lived its accountability to the other churches, deliberately behaving inoffensively and consistently attempting acceptable interpretations of social issues. In return, the Congregation hoped for reasonable responses to their overtures for social-action involvement. They received them.

The Cincinnati Congregation for Reconciliation had carefully and skillfully built a network of good relationships with Presbytery churches based on the concept of mutual accountability. The Cincinnati Presbytery leadership, likewise, worked easily with the experimental congregation. Unlike the Dayton mission, it maintained a low profile, avoided conflict with other churches, and provided an important service to the Presbytery through its social-action ministry. Goodwill abounded.

The mission, having started late because of recruitment difficulties, requested formalization as a Presbyterian congregation at the same time formalization occurred for the Dayton group. The covenant, statement of mission, constitution and bylaws had been developed routinely under the leadership of the pastor. The documents were routine and orthodox in all important ways, and by the spring of 1970 Holm prepared to ask the Presbytery for formalization. The church executives had already reviewed and approved the documents. Only ratification at the Presbytery meeting remained.

No one suspected that formalization of the Cincinnati Congregation might receive challenge. When the issue came before the body, however, several persons began questioning the wisdom of placing so specialized a ministry within the structure of a regular Presbyterian congregation. Should not such a ministry of education for social action be better served in the form of a task force? The task force proposal mustered favor on the floor of Presbytery. A Congregation representative protested vigorously that theirs was a total congregation, thoroughly grounded in Christian worship. Several sympathetic pastors then came to the rescue, arguing fervently that to deny formalization at this point would be to renege on Presbytery commitments. Further, without a congregational form of organization, the thesis of the experiment could never be tested. Finally, the vote carried and the Congregation for Reconciliation became a Presbyterian church. In the process, its debt to Presbytery leadership was reinforced.

An opportunity for the Congregation to reciprocate came one year later. The Commission on Church and Race of the United Presbyterian Church in the U.S.A., in March of 1971, had contributed $10,000 of its Emergency Fund for Legal Aid to the Angela Davis Defense Fund. Davis, a black militant and Marxist, had taught philosophy at the University of California in Los Angeles until expelled from the faculty for her political views. She was later arrested and charged with kidnapping, murder, and conspiracy in connection with a prison escape and subsequent killings. Specifically, she was alleged to have provided the guns for the escape. To many liberal observers, Davis was being persecuted for her political views. Her case, therefore, took on the aura of an essentially political trial, and in this context the Presbyterian denomination had contributed to her defense.

Many conservative Presbyterian church people across the nation were outraged when they learned of the denomination's action. Money contributed to the church for Christ's cause was being spent defending not only a black militant and an avowed

Communist but one who had apparently provided weapons to jailbreakers! By the early summer of 1971, the Davis defense contribution had mushroomed into a major controversy in Presbyterian circles, in Cincinnati as much as anywhere.

The Congregation for Reconciliation, in its newsletter devotional for July, defended the identification of the church with the Davis defense. Characteristically, the devotional provided a theological and scriptural rationale for social action.

> "But now, let him who has a purse take it, and likewise a bag. And let him who has no sword sell his mantle and buy one. For I tell you that this scripture must be fulfilled in me, *and he was reckoned with transgressors;* for what's written about me has its fulfillment." And they said, "Look, Lord, here are two swords." And he said to them, "It's enough." And when those who were about him saw what would follow they said, "Lord, shall we strike with the sword?" And one of them struck the slave of the high priest and cut off his right ear. But Jesus said, "No more of this!" And he touched his ear and healed him.—Luke 22
>
> We seriously question the propriety of our Lord's addressing rallies, raising funds, and conspiring with others to procure weapons to be used against officers of the court. He said it was to fulfill the scriptures, "He was reckoned with transgressors."
>
> Our Lord lost a lot of support out of this. His closest followers were tempted to slip away. Some ran out on him. Some denied him. It's hard to follow a Lord who insists on being reckoned with transgressors.
>
> Through our Emergency Fund for Legal Aid, Christ's church is again being reckoned with transgressors. It's uncomfortable. And we're tempted. Will we run out on him? Or deny him? Or will we follow our Lord who is reckoned with transgressors, and be reckoned with him?

There were lay persons in Cincinnati who had not only opposed the denomination's action but had threatened to demonstrate their opposition by withholding funds from the church. Economically and politically conservative laymen took special offense to church support for an articulate and devoted Communist. This placed Presbytery executives in a difficult position. They dared not openly and actively support the denomination's position on this issue, yet in good conscience they could not actively oppose denominational action in order to mollify conservative laity. The Congregation, however, was well positioned to say what Presbytery leaders dared not say.

The newsletter devotional in August zeroed in on both the Communist issue and the suggestions of economic protest.

Not one of them claimed any possessions as his own, but everything was common property.

"But that's Communism!"

That's what Ananias told Sapphira when they read in the papers what their church was doing. "Those who owned property would sell and bring the proceeds of the sales and place them at the Apostles' feet. They would distribute to each one according to his need."

Ananias and Sapphira had sold some property themselves. They had been going to give all to the church. But now when they knew where the church was giving their money, they tore up the check. They cut their pledge. Never sent it in. Gave to the building fund. Their own kind of missions. They couldn't quit the church and they couldn't give.

Because no church was going to use their money to support Communism.

They didn't tell the church. They didn't discuss it with anyone who might disagree with them. They talked among themselves . . . cutting themselves off from people from whom the Lord would not cut himself off. That was to cut themselves off from him. And it killed them.

There are many like Ananias and Sapphira today. Who can't quit the church and can't give. They're killing themselves. Only with them it comes as a long, bitter withering of the ability to love, learn and live; to change, forgive and give.

As recorded in Acts 5, Ananias and Sapphira were stricken dead in church for their deceit. Theologically conservative pastors and laity who read this devotional, and who no doubt take the Bible seriously, if not literally, must have been impressed by the forcefulness of the Congregation's rebuke.

The relationship between Congregation and Presbytery provides an interesting contrast with Dayton. Although Righter and a few members of his congregation are active on Presbytery committees and attend meetings regularly, in the final analysis the Dayton Congregation feels accountable only to itself. This is not meant to imply that animosity exists between that congregation and the Miami Presbytery leadership. This is not at all the case. There is a genuinely warm relationship present. The relationship, however, does not include the degree of accountability which the Cincinnati Congregation made a premise of its existence. Accountability and reciprocity are not causally linked. The Cincinnati Congregation practiced accountability, hoped for reciprocity, and achieved both.

On Death and Dying:
Terminating an Experimental Congregation

There seems to be something unjust in the death of a youth. Why must such potential be wasted, unlived? Why, too, should the Cincinnati Congregation for Reconciliation have terminated after less than four years? Holm's answer was simple. It could not have supported itself as a small nonresidential congregation. With Presbytery money no longer coming in, the Congregation would have had to grow in order to pay its debts. If it grew, it could no longer remain a house church. It would have to settle down and become a residential congregation with a building of its own. In Holm's view, if that happened, it would be fast on its way to giving up its specialized ministry. Rather than witness this senility, he preferred to see the Congregation die in its youth.

It should be pointed out that the Dayton Congregation has managed to struggle along supporting itself with even fewer members, maintaining a strong commitment to its initial goals. Nor are the Dayton members better equipped financially than their Cincinnati counterparts. The key difference between the two missions, we believe, lies in the matter of commitment. Holm's following was seldom capable of giving the time, resources, and single-minded dedication demonstrated in Dayton.

As a terminal patient, the Cincinnati Congregation lived in the awareness of its coming death. The theme of death recurred over

194

and over through the devotional writings in congregational newsletters. It first appeared in the fall of 1970, only half a year after formal acceptance as a Presbyterian congregation. The references mounted and finally peaked in July 1971, one year before termination. The Congregation quite literally lived with its own impending death and so structured much of its aspirations and actions. The earliest of these devotional references alluded to the "absurdity of being for these few brief years God's Congregation for Reconciliation." Another cited a stage play, *The Last Sweet Days of Isaac*, and drew a parallel between Isaac, who knew when he would die, and the Congregation. Isaac had set out to heighten and record each precious moment of life that remained. The Congregation must do the same. In the final devotional reference to death, a comparison to Christ's death was drawn.

> He began to teach [his disciples] that the Son of Man was destined to be put to death. He told them, not because he wanted their sympathy. But because he wanted them to have no illusions. He wanted them to live those three years together in the awareness of their dispersal. He wanted them to know that things would not always be the way they are. That they would not always be together like this. That the time would come when they would be dispersed and scattered like sheep. . . . Once we have accepted our death and dispersal, we are given back to each other with new meaning.

The period of time in which these devotional references occurred was less than one year, midway in the Congregation's life. There is little doubt the brooding presence of the reaper hovered near for the duration of the mission.

The newsletter continued for several issues after the Congregation had disbanded. It offered a way for the members to hang onto one another, but, perhaps more importantly, it was a means for Holm to minister to their bereavement. The theme of resurrection, so familiar to Christian bereavement ministry, recurred continuously in these issues.

There is a final irony in all this. The Cincinnati Congregation for Reconciliation was specifically designed to place heavy emphasis upon those structural mechanisms which would create strong solidarity and tight cohesion. Worship, for believers, tends to be a unifying force. We would argue that worship was indeed unifying for the lonely, socially conscious church people who came together experiencing, perhaps many for the first time in a long while, a high level of consensus and emotional support in a congregational setting. The problems of internal division and latent conflict characteristic of the early Dayton Congregation were almost wholly absent in Cincinnati. The organizational problem which commanded their greatest attention was external rather than internal: courting the established churches so that a helping ministry could be provided.

In Dayton a helping ministry was hardly attempted; external goals, such as social-action projects, ran fairly smoothly. Contrary to Cincinnati, its problems were internal rather than external. If it had died early, the Dayton mission would have been just a good idea that never got off the ground, a group that couldn't overcome its problems. But Cincinnati was different. From the beginning, it had worked and worked well, particularly in providing meaning, support, and accomplishments for its members. Reinforced by the weekly cycle of worship, the Cincinnati Congregation for Reconciliation faced dispersal with a special agony. The loss of a social-action outlet and its achievements brought sadness; the loss of the support group brought grief.

The ways in which the Congregation coped with the crisis of termination are best described by its pastor in his final report to the Presbytery.

> I was committed to the ending from the beginning. It would give urgency to our work and a poignancy to our caring. We would face death without illusions.
>
> I did not recognize how many people this would put off. We had said no building. But the building is simply a symbol, a mortgage on the future. People give themselves to what will go on beyond them. The church provides the illusion of vicarious immortality, as do many other corporations in our society. A church which can bring no such illusions, which will die before we do, is more threatening than racial reconciliation.
>
> Such is the theory. But it may be that some people knew how

196

much it was going to hurt at the end, and did not want to go through that again. . . . .

It became apparent that failing to deal with death head-on would undermine our work in the fall of 1971. A session committee worked out how to discuss [the issue]. We hired outside trainers to design and lead the discussions. After three intense sessions, we came out with a request to the Board of National Missions for five more months of funding, through December, 1972, in which to work out an ending and possible new beginnings. . . . When the funding proved elusive, people accepted the end and began to plan what needed to be done.

The Congregation did a good job of planning how to give themselves away. Dispersal task forces were formed, and people worked very hard. A People Resources task force catalogued our people's skills and connections, so that we could call on each other for help afterwards. A Place Resource task force listed organizations through which we might work and churches where we might go. A Last Will and Testament task force worked out the dispersal of our goods and assets. An Evaluation task force worked with other judicatories in planning our own and their evaluations. And we kept working on Presbytery's minority investments and minority representation.

In the spring of 1972 we spent a day looking back at where we had come—with the help of the categories from Elisabeth Kubler-Ross's *On Death and Dying*—and we could see ourselves working through denial, anger, bargaining, depression, and acceptance. It did not tell us whether this particular death had been necessary. But it did help us deal with all the other separations, losses, and deaths we face in life.

The last days in June 1972 could not have been planned better. On a Sunday, the Congregation acted on the task force proposals. The next Sunday, we had a chance to tell a Board of National Missions . . . evaluation team what we thought we had been and done. That Tuesday, we led stirring worship at Presbytery, and late at night pushed through our recommendation to increase Presbytery's minority investment and minority representation. The final Sunday, we shared the Lord's Supper for the last time, looked over our shoulders, and went home.

Summary

The experiment had ended. The thesis had been successfully tested. As a mission based on a community of special concern, the Cincinnati Congregation for Reconciliation had indeed contributed to needed social change and in the process related helpfully to the ministries of other congregations. They had succeeded in involving many churches in contributing to black economic development. They had attempted to interpret social issues to Presbytery churches in terms they could accept, thus providing an educational ministry. And they had demonstrated that worship can be an important ingredient in developing a solid support group to sustain social action.

It must be recognized that, in its journey toward death, the Congregation faced an interesting array of fortunate circumstances, each of which helped assure its eventual success. If the goal of social action was paramount to the planners, and the helping ministry was window-dressing, as we have argued earlier, Holm's steadfast insistence upon emphasizing the latter is a remarkable happenstance, not predictable from structural conditions. Committee approval to develop a worshiping, teaching community, as Holm saw it, was conceded as a special condition of his employment, not a prerequisite.

A second propitious happening came in the selection of social-action projects. Although their initial failures were painful, had the Congregation first selected independent, direct-action projects which proved successful and attracted media coverage, the trust of conservative churches might have been irrevocably lost and mutual accountability sacrificed as a result. Once the media would have begun building an image for the Congregation, self-presentation might have escaped Holm's control. As it was, the Congregation was instead reinforced in its desire to work through other churches in contributing to needed social change. The emergence of the Black Manifesto controversy at a time when the Congregation was seeking an appropriate and exploitable issue gave the mission an important time advantage. Having lost half a year in recruiting a following, Holm could conceivably have flailed away at one illusive, unmanageable, or insignificant issue after another until no time remained for mounting a single

198

successful campaign in behalf of social change.

Finally, had the officials cowered under pressure and had the Presbytery voted to deny formalization to the Congregation, favoring instead the task force designation, the thesis, as stated, could not have been tested.

The Dayton Congregation for Reconciliation in its quest for continuation followed a very different course of development. One factor after another denied to that mission the likelihood of successfully testing the planners' thesis. Yet in its own terms, Dayton has not suffered by comparison. Further, outliving the experimental period, it will probably continue to bear the fruit of social action into the indefinite future.

The real value of the Cincinnati experiment will be determined in its death, in its legacy for Presbytery churches. Proving a thesis is insufficient inheritance. The value of an experiment is its usefulness to policy and planning.[6]

Some things generated by the Congregation survived it. Others did not. First, the mission drew together some lonely, frustrated church people and, through worship, welded them into a solid group. One year after dispersal, some members had established new congregational ties, but approximately half had not. Having experienced Camelot, most of them will probably be slow in readjusting to usual congregational life; many may never return.

Second, the church school curriculum developed initially for the Congregation's own use carries legacy potential. If published, it could continue to advance racial understanding in other churches across the nation. As yet it has not found a means for dissemination. Thus it cannot be counted as inheritance.

Third, the Congregation proved to established churches that they could become involved meaningfully in social action without reaping internal dissension in the process. Having learned the lesson, some may continue to do so. If they do, they must now take the initiative, but this seems unlikely without planning and coordinating services from some agency.

Fourth, the Congregation, just prior to disbanding, pushed through the adoption of minority investment and minority representation proposals at a Presbytery meeting. If the Presbytery has the will, these may continue as memorials to the experiment.

The stewardship of the Congregation's legacy depends upon three groups: ex-members, clergy, and Presbytery leaders. We can only raise questions concerning possible actions of these three groups since the eventual outcomes are unknown.

First, will ex-members continue to provide a leavening function for Presbytery churches, encouraging them toward social action? Will they join established churches, forming cells within those bodies to generate new social action plans, interpret them in reconciling ways, implement them, and involve other members along the way? If this happens, the skills nurtured in the experiment for relating to conservative church people and pastors will continue to serve the cause of social change. The helping ministry would thus continue and action would be forthcoming. Whether many of those who were mission members can assume such a leadership role, however, having depended upon Holm's strong leadership in the mission, seems questionable. It is conceivable that in forming groups within existing churches these ex-members may tend to seek security and warmth of supportiveness above social-action goals. In that case, deprived of Holm's leadership, their continued impact upon the social ministries of Presbytery churches is likely to be slight. Holm may have committed a serious disservice to his members in monopolizing Congregational leadership. The tactic no doubt facilitated efficiency in accomplishing certain goals and reinforced consensus among members. At the same time, it left members without the skills needed to continue the Congregation's ministry after dispersal. Such trained incapacities may considerably reduce potential impact by ex-members.

Second, will Presbytery pastors court ex-members, encouraging them to develop a helping ministry within their churches? The prospect of living cells of these mild-mannered activists within the body of traditional churches may yet be too threatening to some pastors. The risk of polarizing their congregations on social issues may be too great to take. For clergy willing to take the risks, however, it seems that the availability of these potential members should not be ignored.

Finally, has the Presbytery leadership learned anything of

lasting value to their planning? These leaders were supportive to the Congregation while it lived. Congregation members provided concrete benefits for the Presbytery and were encouraged in this endeavor. The ministry of educating, interpreting, planning, and executing designs for social action was appreciated. But it could end there. Proving such accomplishments may be sufficient for these leaders. They may not feel compelled to utilize tested insights, to build them into other programs.

Church leaders have been backpedalling on social action since the turn of the decade. In Cincinnati, the experimental congregation demonstrated approaches to involving even conservative churches in meaningful social action with minimal polarization and backlash. Rather than learning from the experiment and making use of the skills, techniques, and approaches proven successful in test form, the Presbytery has shown a reluctance to move ahead with structural designs aimed at building upon so bold a beginning. One administrator, acquainted with the experiment from the beginning, told us, "The Congregation's post-mortem impact in the Presbytery has been subliminal, demonstrated in posture, insight, and approach rather than in any explicit or formalized manner. It left many church leaders with altered attitudes, impossible to measure, but has generated no specific programs since its death." While we have great respect for this particular individual's track record as a strategist and leader in pushing the Presbyterians toward social concerns, we are inclined in this case to translate his assessment as "the experiment made lots of people feel good." Hard-nosed evaluation demands demonstrated results. If all that remains for the Presbytery is a good feeling and nice memories, the transitory Congregation for Reconciliation has left no living legacy at all. It will have been just another "groovy trip."

CHAPTER 10

Toughing Out the Storm

In the spring of 1966, the late J. Howard Pew, oil magnate and powerful conservative church layman, wrote an article for *Reader's Digest* entitled "Should the Church 'Meddle' in Civil Affairs?" To those familiar with Pew's long and hard-fought battles to squelch liberal programs of the National Council of Churches through his role as chairman of that organization's National Lay Committee, it came as no surprise to learn his answer to the question was an emphatic *No!*[1]

The Christian Century responded to the "uncomfortable Pew" with a blistering editorial accusing him of producing "more mischief with one blow than the God-is-Dead fury produced with several."[2] For some time we were perplexed by the ease with which *Christian Century* could so readily make bedfellows of Thomas J. J. Altizer and J. Howard Pew. But with recent revelations of the extensiveness of the public relations ploys of the boys at the White House and the Committee to Re-Elect the President to make "Newspeak"[3] the official language of the Republic, the *Christian Century* linkage now makes sense.

Both Altizer and Pew were disturbing the liberal Protestant establishment's connivances to extend their power and influence in the political arena. The Altizers and Hamiltons symbolized the politicized component of the radical student counterculture. They were dangerous not because their ideas were so radical but precisely because they were not. When the sensational rhetoric is stripped away, it becomes clear that they were wrestling with essentially the same difficult questions many Christian theologians have been agonizing over for a long time. But "ordinary Christians," laity and most clergy, should not know the details of the serious, sensitive, and secret talks and negotiations to bring forth credible reinterpretations of "the Word" which were taking place behind the closed doors of seminaries. The Altizers and Hamiltons were the Ellsbergs and Russos leaking to the press the religious establishment's top-secret documents.

Pew, on the other hand, symbolized the power of a vigilant judge and a fearless press to reveal the extensiveness of the establishment's involvement in domestic affairs. The fifteen million circulation of *Reader's Digest*, along with its popularity among conservative church people within liberal Protestantism, was more than embarrassing. Pew threatened not only to blow the cover wide open but also to set in motion the machinery which could ultimately topple the establishment.

Both Pew and Altizer had to be thoroughly discredited. Altizer and his friends were labeled a "lunatic fringe" with ideas completely foreign to anything else being thought in the seminaries. A fury of vitriolic editorials and articles in liberal Protestant publications in effect booed the Death-of-God boys from the stage. Then followed a shield of silence and the would-be "movement" quickly died. The potential investigations and probes which might have purged seminaries of all but the most orthodox faculty were averted. Only liberals in conservative denominations were hurt by the fallout of the "scandal."

Pew was not so easily discredited and silenced. To be sure, liberal Protestantism's continued efforts to plunge more deeply into the political arena faced an inevitable destiny of discovery and resistance from those within the ranks who had had enough. But looking back, Pew's single shot seems indeed to have accomplished more than his years of efforts working "within the system." This single article now appears to have had considerable influence in drawing the battle lines and calling forth thousands of other influential lay persons to combat. Most of the readers of *The Christian Century* probably agreed that Pew's version of the faith was a compartmentalized, schizophrenic fantasy, but their 40,000 circulation was no match for *Reader's Digest*. The beginning of a decisive battle neared; the curtailment of abuses of power approached.

If and when the full truth of Watergate is known, perhaps the most worthy finding will be a quantum leap forward in our understanding of man's capacity to deceive himself, to become so completely captive of a reality he and his friends have created that they are incapable of seeing the gravity of their thoughts and deeds. Today, thousands of church leaders in liberal Protestantism are participating in a massive cover-up which, in terms of the future of moral leadership for this nation, is every bit as grave as the Watergate scandal. Like Watergate, the religious establishment's cover-up involves the utilization of the most sophisticated public relations techniques: taking the offensive against those who bring bad news, rendering inoperative programs, positions, and convictions which only yesterday were an integral part of the institution's integrity, twisting facts to fit newly emerging "realities," and performing radical surgery to remove internal dissent. As they move to close ranks, they are creating a world as unreal as the world created by the men of Watergate who shut themselves off from all but the creation of their imaginations.

To be sure, the crimes now being committed within the structures of liberal Protestantism are not the kind for which people are sent to prison. They are crimes of commission, omission, impotence, and incompetence, committed by men and women whose motives are pure and honorable and whose loyalty is impeccable. But their misdeeds, if unchecked, may permanently intercept a noble institution's rendezvous with the struggle to promote human dignity and justice.

To Conservatives with Love . . . From 475

One of the loudest voices in the cry to reconstruct reality in liberal Protestantism is Dean M. Kelley. His widely read book *Why Conservative Churches Are Growing* is not about why conservative churches are growing at all, but why liberal churches are declining.[4] As a member of the inner circle of the National Council of Churches and possessing a sterling record on the front lines of the civil rights movement, Kelley has all the requisite credentials for summoning the attention of main-line Protestant denominations. Who, better than an insider who has fought the good fight, can tell us what has gone wrong and whither the morrow?

In an age when science and human resources are rapidly

opening new vistas and unimagined horizons to the potential for individual and cultural fulfillment, Kelley suggests that seeking maturity for the human race is too threatening a business for the churches. Instead of helping the world cope with ambiguity and possibility, the churches should treat men to the security of a warm blanket and the milk of certitude on which to nurse.

At a time when our culture has at least momentarily retreated from the central struggles for human justice, it is not surprising that liberal Protestantism should follow course. Within this mood of retreat, thus, Kelley is making a bid to become the Daniel Patrick Moynihan of 475 Riverside Drive. He is telling his brethren it is time for the churches to treat issues of brotherhood, justice, and peace with a little benign neglect. So benign is this theoretician, however, that he neglects to mention the possibility that the problems the liberal churches now face may in some considerable measure stem from their leadership's aggressive programs in civil rights which moved beyond the wishes and expectations of the laity.

Not once does Kelley ask how we can get back in the battle. He assumes it was all wrong. Like the prodigal son, the church's fling with the world is over. Take no thought of the noble causes left scattered across the battlefield. It is time for repentance. Survival demands our attention now. Maintenance goals must take precedence over mission outreach. Therefore, drastically reduce wasteful and wistful programs and austerely eliminate the frills from bureaucracy. Most importantly, focus attention on the renewal of meaning among communicants. This is one sure thing that will keep them coming. Encounter groups may help members find themselves but, more importantly, seek ways in which religion can be relevant to the private lives of parishioners as they celebrate their joys, seek comfort for their sorrows, and ask for guidance when decisions must be made. As their personal needs are met, their commitment to the church will increase.

Pastors will find Kelley challenging them to take a firmer stand in their sermons, not on social issues, of course, but on doctrinal issues. Parishioners must know what to believe and must believe it absolutely and fervently if the church is to conserve its strength. Doctrinal distinctions between denominations must be emphasized so members have a clear sense of religious identity. Feeling they are right, though they respect the privilege of others to be wrong, will reinforce their own special Christian identity.

Church rolls must be cleared of dead weight, those who never attend or offer financial support, perhaps even uncommitted members who only occasionally attend and give. Such a purging increases per capita religious activity and communicates a greater sense of momentum to those who remain, thus generating some of the excitement of being a member of a religious movement. More careful attention to church rolls and the processes of entrance are similarly essential to weed out less serious applicants who might otherwise endanger group discipline.

These are but a few of the admonitions and suggestions which pastors and religious leaders might infer from Kelley's work. For the weary or weak-headed, all of this may seem to make sense as a game plan for the time frame of the seventies. But before Kelley's advice, direct or implied, is taken very seriously, his arguments and analysis require a more critical examination.

Kelley's entire analysis proceeds from a vision—a vision gleaned dimly from his examination of a set of time series tables of growth trends for several religious groups. While not predisposed toward visions ourselves, we are not opposed to this medium if it leads to insight and understanding of a problem. Unfortunately, what emerges is not insight and understanding but a neatly woven tapestry which blends smoothly from truths to half-truths to blatant distortions of social science theories and data.

Kelley is not the first churchman to discover a statistical table and instantaneously feel the "call" to social science. But the scope and magnitude of the proposals for which he claims legitimacy behind the sacred cloak of social science must certainly be without precedent. The discipline of his mind is revealed in the following comment: "Most of these [hypotheses] can be verified empirically but have not been" (page xi). Presumably, he has some providential assurance of the validity of his holy writ. Such bombastic utterances are not only a flagrant violation of the logic of scientific inquiry but an insult and betrayal of those who have turned to him in trust for guidance. But enough with our anger. Let us now take a careful look at what Kelley has to say.

Kelley's analysis begins with an examination of statistics for liberal Protestant denominations, most of them available in the

Yearbook of American Churches. The chapter title, not surprisingly, is "Are the Churches Dying?" The data are grim. During the latter half of the 1960s, the major Protestant denominations ceased growing and began shrinking. Not only church school and communicant membership but also the contraction of building programs, foreign mission establishments, and denominational bureaucracies indicate this decline. For Kelley, these developments bespeak an obvious loss of social strength in the major liberal Protestant denominations.

We turn to chapter 2 and are asked, "Is Religion Obsolete?" Kelley cites two factors which might account for the organizational deterioration observed in chapter 1: obsolescence or internal failure. In a brief but competent presentation, he summarizes arguments for the obsolescence of religion in the modern secular world and quickly discards them. So now he has nailed the problem down to internal failure and set us up for his next startling discovery: not all churches are declining! Again he whips out his time series tables: notice the continued growth of the Southern Baptists, the Missouri Synod Lutherans, the Seventh-Day Adventists, and the Church of the Nazarene. Indigenous American religions, such as the Jehovah's Witnesses and Mormons, are also continuing to grow rapidly. Decline is not universal in American Protestantism. "Conservative" churches, as evidenced by their continued institutional vitality, are gaining social strength. Why the difference?

The difference for Kelley is simple. Main-line churches are failing to meet the needs of the parishioners. Amidst the carrousel of services, organizations, and projects, the liberal churches have missed the golden ring. Neither bingo tables nor picket lines, nor the panoply in between, have met the one essential of all religious organizations everywhere. The churches are not filling the hole in existence, the meaning in life. Main-line denominations offer ambiguous answers to ultimate questions; the growing denominations proffer certitude. In worrying about religious "relevance," Kelley reasons, the liberal denominations have failed internally to wind the mainspring of religious motivation: meaning. And this he defines as content plus demand. Humans respond with commitment, and in commitment lies social strength for the institution.

From here Kelley proceeds to develop a model for explaining

the difference between strong and weak religion. Organizations handle the problem of meaning for their members by unspecified mechanisms through which shared goals are defined and inculcated, appropriate religious behavior is controlled through rewards and sanctions, and the communication of religious behavior is channeled. In a strong religion, therefore, the preaching of goals solicits commitment, and discipline produces strictly followed attitudinal and behavioral codes resulting in an outpouring of missionary zeal. This is then illustrated by case studies of four social movements: the Anabaptists, the Wesleyan revival, the Mormon migration, and the Jehovah's Witnesses. In each case, the movement members saw themselves at battle with the outside world, strict discipline was maintained, and commitment to movement goals produced zealous, self-sacrificing, and, by inference, "meaningful" behavior. In strong social movements, Kelley asserts, discipline and commitment to goals leads to absolutism of belief, conformity to the will of the group, and fanaticism in the view of outsiders. These characteristics may be called "traits of strictness."

On the other hand, he argues, main-line churches are characterized by "traits of leniency." Goals are relativized. A diverse rather than a conformist response to goals is encouraged. Finally, in communicating the faith to outsiders, dialogue (not conversion) is preferred. Rather than producing zealous, self-sacrificing behavior and deep meaning for the communicant, these traits of leniency nurture lukewarm faith, individualistic behavior patterns, and negligible or nonexistent evangelism goals. Having defined his concepts, Kelley hypothesizes that "A group with evidences of social strength will proportionately show traits of strictness; a group with traits of leniency will proportionately show evidences of social weakness rather than strength." [5] Social strength and leniency are therefore incompatible by Kelley's definitions.

Beginning thus with the empirical observation of the decline of certain Protestant denominations and noting their membership in the National Council of Churches, Kelley proceeds to spin a conceptual web to certain assumed underlying causes in a "follow the bouncing ball" string of inferences. Ecumenism implies social weakness. After all, support for the ecumenical enterprise indicates laxity in beliefs. Viewed from the bench of strictness, those who differ from oneself in doctrine would be perceived as benighted and unworthy of parity in the journey of faith. Those denominations willing to join in such alliances must therefore have a lenient, relativistic view of doctrine and thus a lukewarm commitment among their members. Without commitment, the need for meaning cannot be fulfilled. That, Kelley argues, is the reason why communicants are dropping out and the denominations are suffering such losses.

The reverse holds for the "conservative" churches, in Kelley's view. Those religious groups least attracted to the ecumenical movement, like the Evangelicals, Pentecostals, and Southern Baptists, have an absolutist, strict, and uncompromising view of doctrine. They must be uncompromising since they have organizationally avoided ecumenism. This indicates a strong faith commitment on the part of their communicants. The inescapable conclusion, for Kelley, is that their needs for meaning in life are being met. Their denominations continue to grow. Kelley works the puzzle neatly and easily, but, after all, he did cut his own pieces to fit.

Moving onward, this soldier in the battle for church survival turns his attention to the cause of the weakening. How did main-line Protestantism lose grip on its primary function and degenerate into leniency, social weakness, and the loss of members? Once again, simple: entropy. Religious groups gradually run down. Tightly wound springs unwind with time.

To illustrate the aging process, the decline of strictness, and the loss of commitment and meaning, Kelley resurrects the Church-Sect typology and argues that movement from sect to denomination leads to loss of strictness. He calls this process the "dynamic of diminishing demand." Success defeats a movement, both on the individual and the institutional levels. The poor, seeking meaning in life, adhere to a religious group which meets their need and offers a disciplined approach to life, eventually paying off in worldly success. Secular goals and meaning gradually undermine religious commitment and devotion. Organizations likewise grow large and indolent. They win the war by surrendering; they lose their impetus, their youth, and their vigor.

One survival strategy does offer consolation even in the face of the inevitability of entropy, according to Kelley. Churches can follow the medieval Catholic example in the formation of "orders." Rather than allowing schisms, the churches can contain new social movements within the larger religious body through a process of *ecclesiola en ecclesia* (allowing little churches to develop within the church). As pioneers emerge, mother denominations with foresight and resources can foster new life.

But mother churches pregnant with little churches are insufficient for Kelley; his major prescription for conserving social strength is a restoration of strictness in the main-line churches. Retaining the key to this cage, though, Kelley warns in the next breath that strictness may be almost impossible to recover. "People who have become accustomed to leniency do not find it congenial to contemplate strictness, let alone live under it. Yet . . . strictness is the only way to conserve social strength, whether in *ecclesia* or *ecclesiola*." [6] Kelley recommends that churches serious about their faith must (1) develop sufficient consensus on belief so members can savor their uniqueness, (2) make high demands upon members and expel those not fully committed, and (3) encourage talk about faith and beliefs and vigorous defense against those not inclined to take it seriously.

After stressing a need for firm and consistent demands for admission to and retention of membership, Kelley launches a rambling excursion into the failure of social-action goals in main-line churches. His observations are scattered and at best loosely related to his central arguments. He reminds us that religious institutions have always been repositories of beliefs for the society. Therefore, they are basically conservative organizations. Unfortunately, members' feelings concerning conservation of values do not necessarily coincide with the perceptions of the initial movement but rather stress the culturally dictated (ideological) beliefs of the past. Since social action is more often legitimated in terms of current social movements, the plea for change falls on unresponsive, if not hostile, ears and fails to arouse the enthusiasm of the guardians of received values. Even when social action can be justified in terms of past values, the conservationists of "truth" are unlikely to have the requisite inclination to innovate. In a battle for freedom of the press, the writers, not the librarians, will move to the front lines.

Most church people, Kelley argues, are more interested in

continuity and stability than in change. Nor do the majority of communicants hold any core of belief so meaningful and vital as to mobilize them for social action. Hence, social action, as a top agenda item of liberal religious leaders during the 1960s, was doomed from the onset. Action leaders misread the pew-sitters in calling the churches to the barricades, according to Kelley. Rather, the churches are "conservatories where the hurts of life are healed, where new spiritual strength is nourished and where the virtues and verities of human experience are celebrated." [7] They are the field hospitals, so to speak, not the troop barracks. Not surprisingly, therefore, those seriously interested in social action abandon the churches, or at least remain in only remnant fashion.

The treatise winds down in a gloomy mood of pessimism. Periods of vitality and revival in religion, in which new movements grow and flourish and established institutions are revitalized, do occur. And, intermittently, so do periods of consolidation, introspection, and regrouping, when social strength must be conserved against the tide of decay. Main-line American Protestant denominations are now moving through such an era of "tightening up" and reorganizing the structures fallen into disrepair during the preceding expenditure of a seemingly boundless supply of energy upon ever less central goals (such as justice, freedom, and peace). The church is patching the cracks and pulling the shutters against the winds, waiting out the storm.

To be sure, there is much merit in many of Kelley's arguments. We are on record as having made a number of the same observations. Our point of debate is with his apparent inability to differentiate between empirical observations, plausible theoretical interpretations, faulty logic, and value presuppositions which have no anchor in reality. Were Kelley simply a knuckleheaded academic and were church leaders not groping for understanding of what is happening to the churches, his book would have gone unnoticed. But church leaders are groping, and he is a church executive attempting to influence policy. The indiscriminate mixture of sense and nonsense therefore becomes a dangerous political treatise. Let us turn, thus, to a critical examination of his central arguments.

To begin, Kelley's entropy hypothesis, the principal organizing concept of his work, distorts empirical reality. The major liberal denominations have not gradually wound down with age. They have declined suddenly, in the past half-dozen years, after a period of unprecedented growth. Ecumenism, Kelley's chief exhibit of leniency, coincided with growth, not decline. This suggests something perhaps far more complex than entropy at work.

Further, this period of growth during the postwar period cannot be attributed to unusual religious zeal in the churches. A number of factors, most not ideological in nature, converged in time and fostered expansion. Rapid suburban growth, coupled with a new idealism in family life stressing the sharing of voluntary and leisure activities, made the church an extremely attractive locus of activity. Family weekend camping, now cutting into church attendance, springs basically from the same impulse. The sense of national well-being, economic stability, and the rightness of American life may have contributed to the popularity of the church, which, as Kelley observes, has been a conservatory of traditional values. But the racial and urban crises of the sixties, an unpopular war, an uncontrolled inflationary spiral, the energy crisis, ecological survival, and the loss of confidence in government's ability to police itself make the 1970s a very different world. No doubt the American public is facing a crisis of confidence concerning our abilities and possibilities for coping with these vexing and complex issues. But the extent to which this is reflected in a sense of meaninglessness, as Kelley uses the term, is an open empirical question, one blindly ignored by him and on which his book sheds little light. The only way one can interpret the boom period in American Protestantism in simplistic social movement terms is as Kelley does, with vague ideas and question-begging assumptions which are meaningful arguments only to those so deluged by desperation as to grasp at any passing piece of debris which offers hope.

Kelley's conceptual model applies adequately to some types of social movements, including conversionist sects. However, identifying strictness as the independent variable affecting social strength is to get the cart before the horse. Strictness spontaneously arises in the process of social interaction when other factors are present. If commonly held beliefs and goals are considered desperately important and efficient, and if concerted effort is required to accomplish the goals, then behavior or attitudes of members seen as undermining goals or morale will be strongly censured by group pressures, formal and otherwise. Imposing artificial codes of strictness will only drive members away. Enforcing external conformity to revitalize motivation is like painting an old automobile which needs a new engine. It may look better, but it still won't run. Nor will walking under open umbrellas make it rain.

Dogged persistence in discipline does not necessarily prevent institutional decline either. Take, for example, the United States Air Force Academy at Colorado Springs. In the past few years it has suffered increasingly high attrition rates in its student body. The present graduating class will represent only about 60 percent of its entrance total. Yet the administration is determined to maintain the rigid codes of discipline it considers an important part of education in the academy. The "social weakness" of the academy, as measured by the attrition of its student body, has developed *in spite of* enforced discipline. If Kelley would argue that the academy remains socially strong because of its strictness, then social strength and institutional decline are not correlated. If he would argue that social weakness is reflected in its high attrition rates, then strictness and strength are not correlated. Kelley's logic falters when tested on real organizations, rather than a superficial historical analysis of social movements.

On closer examination, also, most of the growing "conservative denominations" are not qualitatively different from main-line liberal Protestant churches in either missionary zeal or disciplined conformity. Excommunications among Southern Baptists, for instance, are rare indeed. Nor could the vast majority of this denomination be characterized as fanatical in their missionary zeal. The model which Kelley develops perhaps holds for the two ends of the continuum. Those small, growing social movements holding strong commitment from a high percentage of members, and encouraging and rewarding absolutist faith, a "chosen people" self-definition, and zealous goal-oriented behavior would be considered strong by most social-organizational definitions. On the other extreme, those organizations unable to develop and maintain either a strong sense of commitment to goals or an

214

identification among the members will motivate little goal-oriented behavior, zealous or otherwise, and will be considered weak almost regardless of the taxonomy or evidence of strength employed. However, there are very few religious groupings of any size in this country on *either* end of that continuum. Almost all fall somewhere near the middle, where relative strength or weakness, by Kelley's definition, is a matter of degree and not kind.

On closer examination, Kelley's taxonomy proves neither logically coherent nor capable of generating his hypothesis. He builds a typology on three organizational dimensions: goals, controls, and communication. His intention is to explain the maximum cohesion, vitality, and functional effectiveness of religion in its ideal form. However, he never specifies the unit of analysis and consequently shifts among the three levels of analysis without apparent rationale or consciousness. Strong and weak, strict and lenient, whether dealing with goals, controls, or communication, may refer to individuals at one end of a sentence and congregations or denominations at the other. The result is a massacre of the precision of the language and a muddling of already convoluted argument. The three dimensions, for instance, are introduced in organizational terms, presumably denominations. They are units which set goals and standards and communicate with their members and outsiders. The taxonomy as it develops, however, is illustrated almost exclusively in terms of how individuals respond to goals and controls and how they communicate. All this leads to a hypothesis which again is stated in terms of organizations—this time, presumably, congregations! Do you follow? What may first appear as intricate truth, opaque but meaningful, is actually only more polluted hot air, stifling to the social scientist impatient with untestable theory. From hypothesizing about the relationship of social strength and strictness, Kelley bounces to a wholesale condemnation of ecumenism and leniency in the main-line Protestant denominations. His is at best a leap of faith, politely referred to in the social science community as a problem of internal validity.

Another area of confusion in Kelley's argument focuses upon the central concept of meaning. He early states that content (belief?) plus demand equals meaning. Meaning so defined is difficult to distinguish from his use of the concept commitment, which is what gives religious groups social strength. Later he argues that the church specializes in meaning crisis management. It excels, we are told, in interpreting the meaning of birth, death, tragedy, and decision-making for its clients. He also argues that downtrodden minorities seek in a religious movement meaning for their lives, implying a new status order for discovering self-worth and dignity.

His inconsistency with so central a concept leads one to wonder if Kelley expects anyone to seriously attempt to follow his argument. Note the following juggling act: "Ultimate meaning is essential to human life, and it is effective to the degree that it demands and secures a commitment in men's lives." [8] And, "Nevertheless, most people do not become perpetual devotees of a meaning regiment; their need for ultimate meaning is succeeded by other needs and interests, and their attention to the meaning-system wanes." [9] And again, "Many people today may not be aware of a dearth of religion or meaning in their lives." [10] It sounds as though religion must create the need for meaning before it can satisfy it. And finally, Kelley advises, "Religious groups should not abdicate their unique and essential contribution to healing the world's wounds: meaning." [11] Right on . . . if only we knew what Kelley means by meaning.

The Dayton Congregation
for Reconciliation Under Kelley's Microscope

Case studies never provide sufficient data to prove any thesis. They can, however, provide sufficient evidence to seriously challenge the plausibility of a theory. The Dayton Congregation for Reconciliation provides just such a challenge to the Kelley treatise. Let us therefore turn briefly to examine the Congregation from Kelley's perspective.

Kelley's major prescription for conserving social strength is a restoration of strictness. To review briefly, he recommends that churches serious about their faith must (1) develop consensus on beliefs, (2) expel those not fully committed, and (3) encourage talk about faith and beliefs and vigorously defend them against those not inclined to take them seriously.

Contrary to Kelley's theoretical model, we found that the

Congregation for Reconciliation has maintained a high degree of social strength without doctrinal strictness. There has never been an emphasis upon doctrinal uniformity in the Congregation. Indeed, as a membership requirement it is unnecessary to make even the most rudimentary statement of faith. For Kelley, this would be evidence of leniency and social weakness.

Second, the Congregation for Reconciliation is ecumenical in concept and practice. It is a union church, a member of both the United Presbyterian Church in the U.S.A. and the United Church of Christ. Further, its membership represents several denominational backgrounds, and it is very active in the primary ecumenical organization in Dayton, Metropolitan Churches United. This, also, Kelley would interpret as predictive of social weakness.

Third, the movements illustrative of social strength in Kelley's book manifest a high degree of control over members' behavior. Such control is generally exercised by the group's spiritual leader. Just the reverse is seen in the life of the Congregation for Reconciliation in Dayton. Leadership is unusually decentralized. A "do one's own thing" ethic guides the modus operandi of the group in social action, and conformity in behavior and belief has never been a matter of concern. Kelley would argue that this, too, is evidence of weakness. Yet the social strength of the Congregation cannot be seriously contested. Over the years it has become a solid, supportive group in spite of its diversity. Its accomplishments in social action bespeak its strength.

It is not strictness which gives the Congregation strength, but commitment. On this point Kelley would appear to be correct. But it is not commitment generated from internalizing theological dogma, as Kelley predicts, but through devotion to the goal of producing social change, whether in the name of Christ or of humanity.

The comparison of the Congregation with Kelley's theory could be elaborated at much greater length. Such an effort, we feel, would quickly reach a point of diminishing return. The Congregation seriously challenges virtually every argument in the Kelley model. It is reproduced unedited from his book. The information presented in this volume will provide sufficient data to examine the Congregation for Reconciliation from the perspective of his model.

Kelley's Model of "Strong" and "Weak" Religious Groups

Social Dimensions		GOALS	CONTROLS	COMMUNICATION
"STRONG" GROUPS	**A** — Evidences of Social Strength	1. *Commitment* —willingness to sacrifice status, possessions, safety, life itself, for the cause or the company of the faithful —a total response to a total demand —group solidarity —total identification of individual's goals with group's	2. *Discipline* —willingness to obey the commands of (charismatic) leadership without question —willingness to suffer sanctions for infraction rather than leave the group	3. *Missionary Zeal* —eagerness to tell the "good news" of one's experience of salvation to others —refusal to be silenced (Acts 5:26) —internal communications stylized and highly symbolic: a cryptic language —winsomeness
	B — Traits of Strictness	4. *Absolutism* —belief that "we have the Truth and all others are in error" —closed system of meaning and value which explains everything —uncritical and unreflective attachment to a single set of values	5. *Conformity* —intolerance of deviance or dissent —shunning of outcasts (*Meidung*) —shared stigmata of belonging (Quaker garb and plain talk) —group confessions or criticisms (Oneida) —separatism	6. *Fanaticism* (outflow > inflow) Flood (or) Isolation —"All talk, no listen" —"Keep yourselves unspotted from the world" —cloister
"WEAK" GROUPS	**C** — Traits of Leniency	7. *Relativism* —belief that no one has a monopoly on truth; that all insights are partial —attachment to many values and to various modes of fulfillment (not just the religious) —a critical and circumspect outlook	8. *Diversity* —appreciation of individual differences (everyone should "do his thing") —no heresy trials; no excommunications; no humiliating group confessions of error —leadership is institutionalized, not charismatic	9. *Dialogue* —an exchange of differing insights, an exploration of divergent views —appreciative of outsiders rather than judgmental (inflow > outflow)
	D — Evidences of Social Weakness	10. *Lukewarmness* —"If you have some truth and I have some truth, why should either of us die for his portion?" —reluctance to sacrifice all for any single set of values or area of fulfillment —indecisiveness even when important values are at stake	11. *Individualism* —unwillingness to give unquestioning obedience to anyone —individuality prized above conformity —discipline? for what? —leave group rather than be inconvenienced by its demands	12. *Reserve* —reluctance to expose one's personal beliefs or to impose them on others —consequent decay of the missionary enterprise —no effective sharing of conviction or spiritual insight within the group

218

The most compelling conclusion we reach in examining this chart is not that the Congregation has all the traits and evidences of weakness (although it does tend to fit in these boxes more readily than in those characterizing strength). Rather, what we find is that the model, without serious revision, is inappropriate for describing the Congregation for Reconciliation. For example, the Congregation does evidence commitment, discipline, and zeal, *but not in Kelley's terms!* Hence, if these are indeed manifestations of strength, and we tend to believe they are, Kelley's model needs to be radically revised so these are not seen as embodied and manifested solely in conservative groups. Clearly they are not. And were one to attempt such a revision, the total logic of Kelley's thesis crumbles. As we examine each of the cells in his chart, we find difficulty relating them to the Congregation for Reconciliation. The Congregation either falls on the wrong side of the strong/weak dichotomy or the cell is irrelevant or nondescriptive of the group.

In short, we find the model unhelpful, and at several significant points wrong, when we attempt to apply it to the Congregation. This, coupled with our logical, theoretical, and empirical critique, leads us to seriously question the value of Kelley's treatise. We have, in fact, only highlighted some of the confusing and misleading points of this book. To analyze Kelley's work comprehensively would require a volume of at least equal length. We hope, however, that we have raised sufficient questions here to dissuade church leaders from believing that Kelley has delivered a patent medicine which can quickly restore the health of the ailing patient. To the contrary, we feel that following his prescription would have more deleterious consequences than following those who would drag the churches deeper and deeper into radical social action with a laity-be-damned attitude. If church leaders do choose to swallow Kelley's magic potion, let them know the concoction was not a product of social science.

CHAPTER 11

Quo Vadis:
Whither Liberal Protestantism?

We want now to consider what we think we have learned from this study and reflect on some possible policy implications. Others will have different interpretations and see different implications. If this book simply stimulates serious discussion about the future of liberal Protestantism, then the support and effort it embodies will be recompensed. The members of the Congregation will have opened their lives to public scrutiny in an extension of their ministry of reconciliation. If, on the other hand, this book serves only as a rally focus for those in agreement with us and an annoyance for those in disagreement, little will have been gained. We do not fear nor hide from the conflict this book may generate. We can see from this study, and in a broader sense from the turmoil of our society during the past decade, that conflict can be absolutely devastating to everyone involved or it can be an *opportunity,* a door to reconciliation, a challenge to move beyond the present to a future yet unknown but most certainly a little more human.

The Imperative of Planning

The first lesson of this study is the necessity of learning how to plan. The motives, as we understand them, of those responsible for creating the Congregation for Reconciliation were impeccable. Racism, poverty, and injustice are woven tightly into the fabric of our society. It is not enough to utter pious platitudes which acknowledge responsibility while doing nothing. Reconciliation will come only when the price is paid. As individuals whose relationship to institutional faith is precarious, one foot in and one foot out, we echo the editorial writer of the *Dayton Daily News*, "Where, in God's name, are the churches?"

The churches of America are deeply implicated in the tragedies of our society, past and present. The time has passed, if ever there were an appropriate time, for self-flagellation. The hour is late to be seeking comfort in intentional morality. Where is the evidence that our good intentions are manifest in concrete programs which, by objective criteria, make a difference?

The Miami Presbytery moved, in a moment of great crisis, in a manner they believed responsible and responsive to the racial turmoil straining the seams of our nation. Possibly some on the planning committee now feel the Congregation met their intentions. But, unquestionably, none really foresaw what was to emerge from the experiment. If the product had indeed been anticipated, it is not likely that the necessary votes for authorization of the project would have been tallied. Once the creation began to take shape, however, it was too late to abort. So the National Missions Committee, the Presbytery, and local congregations learned to adjust. Indeed, most people even believed the experiment was creative and useful, if occasionally painful and embarrassing. That we share this conclusion does not alter the fact of unanticipated consequences, and hence the need for more careful planning.

Several conclusions seem inescapable. The opportunity to minister and educate creatively in member churches of the Miami Presbytery was missed. This is partially explained by a lack of consensus that this was the primary goal. But more importantly, the leaders failed to think through the hard questions of how to bring their creation to fruition in the desired manner. They ignored structural prerequisites. They probably hired the wrong man as pastor, if they desired to produce leadership for educating and interpreting racism to other churches. They designed a structure with almost no opportunity for recruiting active Presbyterian lay persons. They planned no channels for the constructive utilization of the potential resources of the experimental group by local pastors and congregations. And finally, they failed to foresee the inevitability of conflict, basically negative in consequence, between the action-oriented experimental congregation and the local congregations footing the bill.

If we assume the formal list of goals drawn up by the National Missions Committee of the Miami Presbytery (see chapter 4) did not reflect the majority sentiment of its membership—that is, that these were consciously concocted to make the experiment palatable to Presbytery—then we must ask the question, Why were the leaders oblivious to the need for precisely the type of experiment they proposed? Why did they not see that the large majority of white Americans, including those in the pews of Presbyterian churches in Dayton, categorically repudiated the indictment of racism and their complicity in the perpetuation of the suffering of Blacks? Why did they not hear the voices of angry black leaders telling us to go home to our lily-white suburbs and churches?

These questions echo far beyond the membership of the Miami Presbytery's National Missions Committee; they haunt all of us who profess to care and yet do so little. These people, after all, did something. Indeed, they had quite an impact on the city of Dayton. But the mission committee deserves no laurels for serendipitous behavior. We must insist that *doing something* is not enough. This results in far more wasted time, energy, and resources, and even in occasional disasters, than we as a society can long afford. Leaders must understand *what* they are doing. They must come to appreciate the necessity of planning for desired results.

The lesson here reaches beyond church leaders engaged in programming to promote social justice. A much more fundamental issue is at stake. Churches, universities, governments, and even businesses too often assume an unobstructed path between the creation of a structure and the solution of a problem. Departments, committees, bureaus and the like, do not inherently produce desired goals. Structures demand structuring to achieve the results for which they are intended. Their goals must be clear. Their resources must be adequate. And there must be an infusion of the will and purpose of those responsible for their creation. With less than these preconditions, the results or consequences of new structures are likely to differ from their creators' intentions. In short, leadership needs always to ask, What are we trying to do? Are our resources adequate? Is the leadership right for the task? What else is occurring in relevant cultural systems which might impede the accomplishment of our goals? How can we plan to meet the contingencies of unanticipated consequences to our programming?

Few new programs and organizations in our society take root in such careful planning. Thus, we are deluged with ineffective and encumbering government bureaucracies, irrelevant educational systems, alienating labor conditions, intransigent church groups, and so on. Charles Silberman, in his best-selling critique of American education, speaks powerfully to our problems:

> By and large, teachers, principals, and superintendents are decent, intelligent, and caring people who try to do their best by their lights. If they make a botch of it, and an uncomfortably large number do, it is because it simply never occurs to more than a handful to ask *why* they are doing what they are doing—to think seriously or deeply about the purposes or consequences of education.[1]

Certainly, religious leaders could fit as neatly as educators in Silberman's statement. He then goes on to place these reflections in a broader cultural context:

> This mindlessness—the failure to think seriously about educational purpose, the reluctance to question established practice—is not the monopoly of the public school; it is diffused remarkably evenly throughout the entire educational system, and indeed the entire society.[2]

It seems to us Silberman is saying we don't plan for the achievement of our objectives. Indeed, we don't even pause to recall our objectives. Peter Berger et al. would see this as a consequence of modernization and an increasingly complex technological social order.[3]

As a society we have failed to recognize and adjust to the reality of our complexity. We decry and fear our bigness. We perpetuate myths about the inevitable dehumanizing consequences of bureaucracy, technology, and planning. And in so doing, we become captives of our myths. But this is not inevitable human destiny.

We fashioned the myths. We can undo them and fashion new ones to serve rather than enslave us. And the churches can play an important role in planning this reconstruction of reality.

Opportunities Lost

A second critical lesson from the Dayton study pivots around the theme of opportunities lost. These do not lend themselves to ready questions of culpability. Rather, they involve many persons at many points missing opportunities which could have resulted in creative utilization of the experimental congregation's presence. Since it is obvious that different policy decisions at the onset would have resulted in a very different experiment, our discussion will consider only actions possible without radical alteration in the nature and membership composition of the Congregation.

When Richard Righter moved to Dayton, he personally visited all the Presbyterian pastors in the metropolitan area. He deliberately did not ask for referrals from their congregations. Thus, this contact was not threatening; he didn't attempt to raid their membership rolls. He sought only to establish his presence in the city, become acquainted, and indicate his openness to cooperative ventures at some later date.

Early in 1969, only a few months after the first organizational meetings, participants in the experimental group established a list of priority issues for study and action. Righter then wrote all the Presbyterian pastors in the city to inform them of the newly formed study groups and invite them and their lay people to join the Congregation for Reconciliation in this endeavor. (Recall that, at this point, study groups and action groups were clearly differentiated.) Righter failed to receive even a single acknowledgment of his letter, much less an inquiry about participation. The evidence from our interviews would suggest that few congregations were even informed of the study projects.

Within six months of arriving in Dayton, Righter had twice contacted every Presbyterian pastor in the city. His willingness, indeed desire, to establish working relationships with other pastors and congregations should have been clear. The interest was not mutual, however. Apparently, conservative pastors wanted nothing to do with the Congregation for Reconciliation, and liberal pastors feared losing members from their own congregations. Thus, except for the congregation which initially provided space to the experimental group for secretarial work, no ties developed. And this congregation later asked the mission to leave because of opposition to their social-action tactics.

The only contact initiated by other pastors or congregations has been a few invitations for Righter to preach or speak to some church group. During his first year, Righter received three invitations to preach and half a dozen opportunities to address couples' or women's groups. The former provided no context to interpret the Congregation's activities, and the latter were typically small audiences. This level of contact remained fairly constant for the first three years but has declined somewhat since, even though it now includes both Presbyterian and United Church of Christ congregations.

The contact with United Church of Christ congregations has been somewhat less than with Presbyterian ones. Early publicity about the Congregation identified it as a Presbyterian group; some UCC pastors, at least, are quite content with that image. One of our questions to pastors was whether they had received any flak from laity because of the Congregation for Reconciliation's activities. One pastor responded bluntly, "Oh, no. My people don't even know they are affiliated with the United Church of Christ. And if I have anything to do with it, they won't find out." Several other pastors also expressed the view that most of their members were unaware of the union status of the Congregation.

At no point has a governing body of a congregation of either denomination invited Righter or a member of his group to engage in dialogue or interpretation of their life-style. The limited contacts with governing bodies have been precipitated by the Congregation for Reconciliation.

We emphasize here that opportunities for interaction and interpretation of the Congregation's life-style were exploited far less effectively than might have been. Many pastors seem quite consciously to have avoided the opportunity. Furthermore, in this context, the kind of presentation of self and impression Righter makes in talking to groups merits recalling. Lay persons and pastors alike told us they were both surprised and impressed. They came prepared for a confrontation with a belligerent radical, not a personally demure, soft-spoken, carefully reasoned pastor articulating a well-grounded theological rationale.

Why, then, did Righter receive so few opportunities to interpret his ministry to other groups? This, of course, necessitates conjecture on our part. Many pastors probably hesitated out of timidity and fear of opposition from conservative lay persons. But also, many probably never even considered that this might be an effective means of broaching issues they themselves had difficulty raising with their congregations.

None of these speaking engagements led to any kind of systematic follow-up, such as an invitation for Righter to return to lead a series of group discussions on a particular topic, an exploration of how interested lay persons in other congregations could develop "less radical" supportive actions, or the formation of study groups. In short, these were one-shot exposures. The opportunity to stimulate discussion and study groups was ignored.

Similarly, our interviews with Dayton pastors revealed that few ever attempted to interpret the controversial activities of the Congregation for Reconciliation. This would have required no direct contact with the Congregation. But ignoring them, pretending they didn't exist, although they were an obvious source of irritation to many Presbyterians in the community, meant missing many opportunities for constructive dialogue. Numerous approaches might have been taken. For example, pastors might have encouraged examination of the issues without considering the tactics of the Congregation. Are their concerns legitimate concerns for people who call themselves Christians? If so, how can Christians make their influence felt? What is the proper stance of the corporate body of the church on social issues? How might we deal reasonably and creatively with the undeniable reality that Christians don't agree on the issue of corporate responsibility? Or pastors might have encouraged careful study of the Congregation for Reconciliation. Are they misguided idealists? Are there theological rationales for their actions? What are the official policies of our denomination on these issues? Such explorations would have generated some tension, but, if skillfully handled, the results could have been positive and creative nonetheless. The very presence of the vigorously active Congregation in the city would have made such essentially educational ministries far more palatable.

The failure of Dayton pastors to utilize the presence of the Congregation for Reconciliation to explore social issues reflects both timidity and the neglect of an opportunity. But our interviews also indicate it suggests the absence of skills to deal with the issues. A great proportion of clergy lack at least two important skills. The first is the ability to deal with any kind of controversial issue. Many pastors simply don't know how to talk about touchy topics. Hence, they tend to confine their views to private conversations among lay persons with whom they sense agreement. Second, many pastors are unable to deal authoritatively with social issues in a group discussion; they lack sufficient information to be a resource person, to present substantive materials on an issue, to defend their own views, or to challenge viewpoints not grounded in fact. Bluntly stated, many are barnyard liberals with neither the skill nor the knowledge to be effective educators.

Many readily acknowledge and decry this. Why, then, do they structure their lives to perpetuate these deficiencies in skill and knowledge which they would like to have and which they believe would bolster their effectiveness in dealing with social issues? In this light, the Congregation for Reconciliation could have served at least two functions. On the one hand, it could have provided a resource in the development of skills in researching social problems and, on the other, it could have been a ready stimulus for underscoring the need for self-study and mutual support in expanding the talents of local clergy.

For five years the Congregation for Reconciliation has manifested religious concern for a wide range of social issues. For five years it has stood as a challenge to other Dayton pastors and congregations to explore possibilities for relating to and becoming involved in the problems of Dayton and our society. The range of potential responses has been limited only by the imagination and the will to act. But in Dayton, not unlike many other communities in America, both imagination and will have lain dormant. Local pastors have either not seen the opportunities offered by the Congregation for Reconciliation or they have lacked the will to take any initiative. They never attempted structures to bring clergy together for discussing specific ways of utilizing either the presence or the resources of the Congregation to educate their lay people or themselves.

There were, of course, other possibilities. But there were also other problems. Presbyterian executives faced structural impediments to their assuming initiative. The Synod mission staff resided in another city. This did not preclude their taking initial action, but it did present organizational difficulties. Again, with the Stated Clerk (executive officer) of the Presbytery, we encounter structural difficulties. From the moment the image of the Congregation took shape, his was a delicate position. Some pastors and lay persons would have opted to squelch the Congregation early in its life, had the Stated Clerk not skillfully provided a protective shield and insulation from hostile criticism in the ecclesiastical environment and thus aided the chances of the Congregation's survival. Had he played a vigorous role in promoting the Congregation and encouraging Congregation-related activities, his credibility as a sober and responsible church executive might have been seriously threatened. Not that his structural position denied promotion of any Congregation-related activities, but the role was risky and he chose not to gamble. Had other pastors contacted him and requested assistance in promoting some program, his position to take initiatives would have been much more secure.

Further initiative might also have come from Righter and the Congregation. Righter made some effort, but the Congregation members themselves, it must be remembered, were largely persons who felt indifference or alienation regarding other churches. They didn't want to spend their energies on white middle-class congregations or pastors and weren't going to encourage Righter in that direction, either. In their defense, though, it might be said that the Presbytery members initiated the experiment and thus probably carried a larger responsibility to watch over their brainchild than vice versa. The newsletter-bulletin circulated by the Cincinnati congregation proved an effective means of communication and interpretation there. Righter certainly knew of the Cincinnati newsletter, but the Dayton group, though it has continuously sent its monthly mailing to all UCC and UPUSA congregations in the Dayton area, made no special effort to tailor this contact as a reconciling force. Had Dayton pastors encouraged any interaction and dialogue, this might have become a viable form of communication.

To consider what might have been is to engage in fantasy. Exploring lost opportunities, we are like Alice roaming the great hall but finding all the doors locked. There is a garden full of surprises beyond the locked doors; Dayton clergy and laity, however, couldn't swallow their timidity and rationalizations long enough to squeeze through the little door and bring their churches into the daylight beyond.

Models and Strategies for Social Action: Pondering the Future

In examining the Congregation for Reconciliation, it seems clear that their activities could not have been easily carried out as a social-action committee within a larger congregation. The role of the pastor as researcher, strategist, and promoter of commitment and group solidarity has been critical. It has been a full-time job. An assistant pastor in a large congregation would almost certainly have found himself under fire. Even the most sympathetic and skillful senior pastor would have had difficulty sheltering this type of group from the wrath of conservative lay people.

On a lesser scale, however, educational and facilitating ministries could be organized within other congregations. The model, of course, would vary depending on the size of the congregation and the cadre of concerned lay people. In larger congregations, a model might resemble the Cincinnati experiment. There is no easy blueprint for this, but certain imperatives do seem evident. First is a sympathetic and skillful senior pastor who will encourage and facilitate, while running interpretive interference with conservative laity. Second is an assistant pastor knowledgeable and political enough to defend the legitimacy and credibility of the group, while heading off abrasive activities and statements by the members. Precarious business, to be sure, but a worthy challenge.

Such *ecclesiola en ecclesia* approaches might eventually develop into action congregations. Governing bodies, not unlike the Miami Presbytery, would have difficulty denying official congregational status. At the same time, efforts toward independence need be charted cautiously. Without first achieving sufficient size and commitment for self-sustenance, autonomy would spell early death.

Let us turn now to the question of the prospects for creating congregations modeled after the Dayton experiment. Our admiration for their accomplishments is tempered by the realization of the conservative tide sweeping through liberal Protestant denominations. We see little hope for a rapid ebb, and thus church leaders face severe restraints in experimenting. To deliberately maneuver to create congregations modeled after the Dayton experiment with denominational funds is to invite discord and reprisal, not reconciliation. Some church governing units might birth and support experimental congregations of this nature without suffering serious retaliation, but their number is few.

Abandonment of the Dayton model would be an equally foolish move. Rather, church leaders need to open ways outside normal denominational funding structures to offer such groups life. We do not suggest clandestine laundering of monies through the National Council of Churches, but rather seeking new sources of support. Some few foundations and philanthropists in America are dedicated to promoting progressive social change. Similarly, there is the possibility of tapping private contributions from progressive well-to-do lay persons. Contributions of $5,000 to $7,000 per year for three or four years from two or three lay persons could launch a Dayton-type venture. Further, a potential pastor's professionally trained wife might subsidize a social-action congregation by assuming the task of family financial support. Outside the church, at least, our society is witnessing some families with women in this role.

The reluctance of the Miami Presbytery to either sanction the Congregation for Reconciliation or deny it permanent status probably forecasts the prospects of other governing bodies' accepting social-action congregations. That this type of group maintain independence from denomination monies becomes critical. We base this analysis on three assumptions. First, the dominant mood among lay people is vehement opposition to social action, especially confrontation-type action, by the churches. Second, church resources expended in opposition to this mood will bring even more serious reprisals than in the late 1960s. And third, such dissension will contribute nothing to the cause.

We believe our assumptions are sound. They are, nonetheless, assumptions and, as such, open to challenge. While we would place our bets on the validity of the first two conjectures, data to support or refute are simply not available. We believe, however, that most of the data available do point to these conclusions. How to assemble adequate data for definite answers ought to be a high priority of church leaders interested in promoting active church participation in social action.

Our third assumption is a conservative sociological bias. We see institutions as terribly precarious structures men create to accomplish goals and transmit and sustain ideologies. While we decry the personalists who would tailor religion into a purely private or group affair sans corporate responsibilities, we also shudder at the prospects of unwitting activists unraveling liberal Protestantism. Our "middle-of-the-road" posture thus expresses *not only* a conclusion as to how Protestant leaders ought to maximize their effectiveness *but also* our theoretical understanding of the social order. Groups like the Congregation for Reconciliation can stimulate change in their communities. They can also be much more effective than the Dayton group in stimulating change within the churches. But the challenge is still one of planning and structuring to limit repercussions.

We will return to this in a moment. Let us first consider further the possibility that our first two assumptions are either wrong or out of focus, and thus our vision clouded. We see conservatism widespread throughout liberal Protestant congregations. Assume, though, that any denomination embodies a sizable number of congregations with a majority of members concerned more with social change, the quality of human life, and a just social order than with personal financial gain and comfort. *If* this should be the case and it is possible to identify these congregations, *then* very different strategy options might emerge. Alone they are too small to fight the conservative tide of the denomination. Together they could explore ways of asserting their will. One prospect might parallel the present struggle within the conservative Lutheran Church, Missouri Synod. As we write, moderates, with their backs pushed to the wall by arch-fundamentalist President

Jacob A. O. Preus, are exploring means of splitting into a separate denomination. This conceivably could be a viable option for action-oriented Christians in liberal Protestantism. It is an idea far more sensible than trying to push a denomination further than its members prefer to go. Even assuming the possibility of activists permanently gaining the upper hand in a liberal denomination, the loss of membership coupled with outstanding property mortgages would be likely to leave them either bankrupt or so preoccupied for years with fiscal matters and litigations that they wouldn't have time, money, or staff to concern themselves with social issues.

To repeat, we view developments along this line as problematic. They fall outside the parameters of our own value presuppositions. Those who must shape the future of liberal Protestantism, however, are not bound by our presuppositions. They are bound by what is structurally and ideologically true. And our central argument is that to change structures and ideologies requires maximum utilization of factual knowledge, theory, imagination, and will. To expect the pieces to fit together with anything less is to leave too much to providence.

Conclusion: A Challenge

During the 1960s liberal church leaders marched gallantly but haphazardly into the political arena. They got caught in a lot of crossfire. For the most part, they have since retreated. Many, like Kelley, now believe the move was ill-conceived or inappropriate from the beginning. This we cannot affirm. But to return and be effective in the ongoing struggle for human justice, the churches must learn from their experiences of the sixties. To us, two points seem paramount.

First, there exist inexorable boundaries beyond which the leaders of voluntary organizations dare not move without the consent of their constituencies. Liberal Protestant leaders drew dangerously close to violating those limits. Second, in doing so, they discovered the next great frontier, the organized church itself. This territory looms even more difficult to tame, for Pogo is right. The challenge, as we see it, is not to make raving radicals of those who prefer to sit in comfortable pews. Rather, the task is to communicate to them the *structural* and *ideological* bases of our continuing cultural turmoil, to convince them that intentional morality is not enough, and, beyond this, to help them develop the faith and courage to participate in the creation of a new social order. Even if the churches can do no more than break down the resistance to change, it will have done a great deal.

It is, of course, easier to suggest that church leaders ought to concentrate on the task of helping their constituencies to understand the social chaos in which we live than it is to face the job. How can we and others be shaped to meet these demands? Most of us lack the spiritual commitment, the psychic strength, and the intellectual competence to muster ourselves to the battles we know must be waged. Deep down inside, we all hear whispers of what our agenda ought really to be. In our soberest, most intimate moments with the self, we know. But mostly we don't dwell so deep in consciousness; how could it be otherwise? The gross discrepancies between our real and ideal selves would shatter the ablest personality were it not for the human dynamics for coping with tensions and conflict. Social psychologists have known this and have described well the mechanisms we employ to temper dissonance.

Often we deny the validity of our own feelings and convince ourselves that an overly vivid imagination is casting shadows larger than our real experience of awareness. Or else we deny the realities we had focused on and offer ourselves excuses of exaggeration or misinterpretation of data. Further, we may choose simply to avoid the "bad news" of information which would reinforce our inner perceptions, or even seek counter evidence as consolation. Sometimes we look to "authorities" to tell us everything is fine: I'm OK, you're OK, and the world's going to be all right too.

Then, of course, by minimizing our own capabilities and viewing problems from a guppy-in-the-ocean perspective, we can offer ourselves another escape. Or else we can rationalize our activities as somehow being relevant to the problem-solving we ought to be about and avoid our own indictments of stopgapping and wheel-spinning. Finally, naturally, in our world of busyness we can manage not to schedule the moments of intense reflection when we might hear an echo inside suggest another road, a different map to lead us to what we really feel is important and worthy.

Now, certainly, all this is human, very human, very understandable—but not necessarily immutable. To take seriously the challenge of today's world is to engage in a most threatening enterprise. The awesomeness of the problems, the dangers of failure, the intensity of needed commitment; the time, the energy, the drudgery—frightening prospects.

The world needs the church and its moral leadership to push, pull, and shove us deep inside ourselves and then out to the front. But the church cannot serve the world in this way until it resolves to carry out its mission to mankind, sans rationalizations and procrastinations. To do this it must put its own house in order and realistically appraise its objective conditions. There are at least three interrelated priorities on which church leaders must focus their attention. First of all, the credibility of the church as a sober and wise spokesman on important moral issues badly needs strengthening. The past has simultaneously witnessed too much reticence from some and unrestrained vigor and rhetoric from others within main-line leadership concerning important moral questions. Contradictory claims to divine wisdom on moral issues will continue. But skill, restraint in selecting issues, and strategic planning to neutralize conflicting claims can revitalize the image of the church as a focal point of moral wisdom.

The second priority must be the reversal of the growing gap between clergy and laity before church leaders find themselves standing alone, an island between two masses of laity, rather than serving as a bridge uniting for a better world. To consider the problem inevitable and insoluble is dangerous nonsense. Both laity who hold tight to orthodoxy and see their pastor as an apocalyptic anti-Christ and those who feel all or most clergy are hopeless refugees from sixteenth-century molds, lost and helpless amid the sophisticated dilemmas of the modern world, must be reached.

The former challenge religious leadership to creative endeavors to work with and bring them along in the creation of a new moral order. Preaching at them will solve nothing, and since they are theologically orthodox they are unlikely to drop out but likely instead to face and fight innovation. In the 1960s, they fought through closing their wallets, and the pain was indeed felt, since this group tends to include a large proportion of the more affluent. Alternatives are few: they must be brought to new expectations of what precisely the church is all about. Though change-oriented clergy shun this task as not central to their endeavors, there can be little doubt that success here would ensure far greater effectiveness for the church in broader society.

Moreover, while church leaders ignore this problem, two very real dangers loom in the background. First, in what might be a rather simple coup, change-resisters might collectively use their resources to purge the church of innovative personnel. Second, and probably even more dangerous, lies the possibility of a massive defection from main-line religion smack into the waiting and welcoming tentacles of conservative religious groups with strong, right-wing, parapolitical leanings. This would deplete already scarce financial resources while swelling the ranks of a political alliance to neutralize, or perhaps overbalance, main-line Protestantism's efforts to effect social change. The forces of resistance would thus have won a major battle in defining the allegiance of God himself.

In addition to working with and winning over change-resisters, the churches need to pour energy into efforts to channel the talents of those who desire social change but lack the structure to make best use of their potential. In some instances this will mean reversing the churches' image for persons who have already abandoned their religious affiliation in frustration. They need new hope or, better, evidence that the church is addressing itself to today's world. America abounds in people willing to give and to work, people not yet convinced that the ideals they hold for humanity are unattainable. If the churches will, there is a natural resource waiting to be tapped, from sea to shining sea.

These tasks cannot be underestimated in either their difficulty or their importance. And the third priority is no simpler. The churches must develop a disciplined organization of highly skilled, change-oriented leaders. Although the decentralized organizational structure of the churches presents severe difficulties for controlling input once professional roles are assumed, numerous possibilities for improving recruitment, training, and socialization await exploration. Clearly, most seminaries will require extensive curriculum revisions to prepare students in solid social theory and analysis of the political, economic, and social institutions of society. Practical politics of parish survival demand attention: the nitty-gritty how-to's for analyzing power, spotting change-seekers, tempering resistance, selecting personnel, augmenting ideas. If the churches are going to have the kind of leadership they need to effect change ten, twenty, or thirty years from now, courses in social theory and basic survival in the stained glass jungle must be given more than a token place in theological training programs.

Further, and equally urgent, is the demand for much stronger support mechanisms for clergy. Though Protestantism, as yet, faces less of a dropout crisis than does Catholicism, the problems of morale and mobility are obvious. As Edgar Mills and his associates have described it, there are too few good jobs, archaic mechanisms for placing men in the most suitable situations, conflicting role expectations, and a variety of other problems which erode commitment and breed sinking morale.[4] Mechanisms of ongoing education and psychic support are urgently needed. If clergy should be expected to avoid hopping on bandwagons and proclaiming jubilation in Jesus-freak and other movements deleterious to the liberal Protestant goals of justice and brotherhood, they need assistance.

When the road gets rough, ministers too need outlets for their frustrations and reinforcement of their commitment. They too need to have the reassurance of their peers trudging along beside them that it's all really worth it. Our own studies, however, indicate that little of this currently exists. Most denominations lack the resources and vision to create these mechanisms; most ministerial alliances, presbyteries, judicatories, and the like do not function in this way.

In all probability, if this need is to be met, it will have to come as a grass-roots movement. We know turned-on children are more effective in educating one another than highly trained professional teachers. We know people who have shared a common problem are more effective in helping one another than are outsiders. Why then shouldn't cadres of clergy join together in trust and commitment to help one another cope with the jobs to be done? For the present moment, at least, solutions are unlikely to come from on high. If, then, church bureaucracies cannot provide, clergy must follow the design of our founding fathers, who never expected much from their government, and do it themselves. Organize. Divide labor. Create reciprocal expectations. Utilize community resources. Build psychic support. Develop the collective strength to purge defense mechanisms and rationalizations, and get on with the work.

Notes

Preface
1. Cited in Richard E. Young, Alton L. Becker, and Kenneth L. Pike, *Rhetoric: Discovery and Change* (New York: Harcourt, Brace & World, 1970), p. 25.
2. Peter L. Berger and Richard J. Neuhaus, *Movement and Revolution* (Garden City, N.Y.: Doubleday, 1970), p. 36.
3. Alvin Toffler, *Future Shock* (New York: Random House, 1970), p. 11.
4. Daniel Patrick Moynihan, *Maximum Feasible Misunderstanding* (New York: Free Press of Glencoe, 1969), p. iv.

Chapter 2   Crucible of Crisis: Background of the Congregation
1. See Warren G. Bennis, *Changing Organizations* (New York: McGraw-Hill, 1966); Warren G. Bennis and Philip E. Slater, *The Temporary Society* (New York: Harper & Row, 1968); Warren G. Bennis, "Post Bureaucratic Leadership," *Trans-action* 6 (July 1969), pp. 45–51; Victor A. Thompson, *Modern Organizations* (New York: Knopf, 1961).
2. This assessment of the "Beyond Bureaucracy" school, an assessment which we essentially share, is made by Charles Perrow in *Complex Organizations: A Critical Essay* (Chicago: Scott, Foresman & Co., 1972).
3. Elihu Katz and S. N. Eisenstadt, "Some Sociological Observations on the Response of Israeli Organizations to New Immigrants," *Administrative Science Quarterly* 5 (1960), pp. 113–33.
4. *Riots, Civil and Criminal Disorders* (Washington, D.C.: Government Printing Office, 1968), pp. 2764–65.
5. The history of the churches' dealing with racial injustice through resolutions is documented in Ernest Q. Campbell and Thomas F. Pettigrew, *Christians in Racial Crisis* (Washington, D.C.: Public Affairs Press, 1959).
6. For a fascinating discussion of *The Confession of 1967* as means whereby clergy acquired status rights to justify their political activities, see John H. Simpson, "A Case Study in Status Politics," *The Christian Ministry,* 1/2 (Jan. 1970), pp. 24–28.
7. *The Proposed Book of Confessions* (Philadelphia: Office of the General Assembly, The United Presbyterian Church in the U.S.A.), pp. 177–86. Used by permission. The Confession of 1967 was actually approved by the General Assembly in 1966.

8. "Strategies for the Development of New Congregations," Board of National Missions, The United Presbyterian Church in the U.S.A. (Sept. 1967).
9. Ibid., p. 3. Used by permission.
10. Ibid., p. 5.
11. Ibid., p. 4.
12. Ibid.
13. Ibid.
14. Ibid.
15. Ibid., p. 6.
16. "A Proposal for a New Congregation for a Ministry of Racial Reconciliation," Committee on National Missions, Presbytery of Miami, Apr. 16, 1968. Used by permission. The Presbytery named the mission "The Congregation *of Racial* Reconciliation." In 1968, however, the group renamed themselves "The Congregation *for* Reconciliation," stating they were *for* something and that their mission was broader than the racial issue.
17. "Rationale and Strategy for the Development of a New Congregation for a Ministry of Racial Reconciliation," Committee on National Missions, Presbytery of Miami, Feb. 7, 1968.
18. "A Proposal for a New Congregation for a Ministry of Racial Reconciliation," loc. cit.
19. Ibid.
20. Ibid.

Chapter 3   In the Beginning: The Genesis of the Congregation

1. We emphasize that our interviews corroborate Righter's recounting of his early organizational efforts for two reasons. First, some people in the community, including clergy, have questioned Righter's credibility. Since our report on Righter's organizational activities draws heavily from his own recounting, we feel it is important to point out that his recollections are in accord with the recollections of others. Second, our assessment of the situation is that Righter received very little, if any, cooperation from Presbytery pastors in organizing the new congregation. Without the assistance of local newspapers, he would have had virtually no leads as to where to recruit members for the congregation. While in the next chapter we are critical of Righter and the Congregation for failing to fulfill the expectations of the Miami Presbytery vis-à-vis development of relations with other congregations, we failed to find much evidence of Presbyterian pastors' opening the door for cooperative ventures.
2. Donald L. Metz, *New Congregations: Security and Mission in Conflict* (Philadelphia: Westminster Press, 1967).
3. "Strategies for the Development of New Congregations," Board of National Missions, The United Presbyterian Church in the U.S.A. (Sept. 1967), p. 6. Used by permission.
4. For partial documentation of this point see Jeffrey K. Hadden, *The Gathering Storm in the Churches* (Garden City, N.Y.: Doubleday, 1969), chapter 5.
5. Some of the more vocal humanists are no longer associated with the Congregation. One former member cited his discomfort with traditional Christian imagery and language as a principal reason for dropping out. He felt he was "nudged" out of the group by the more traditional Christians, and he was rather adamant in expressing the view that it was unchristian to exclude non-Christians from the group. We are not certain how typical this view is, as we were only able to interview a few former members and participants. Two

other observations, however, do seem clear: (1) a sizable minority of those still in the Congregation would more appropriately be classified as secular humanists than as traditional Christians and (2) others have left the group because they felt it was not traditional enough.

6. The terms "member" and "participant" are conceptually distinct in the Congregation's universe of discourse. One need not become a member in order to participate. In many Congregation activities are found both members *and* participants. In spite of this, we have often used the terms interchangeably for the sake of style, believing such usage will not hinder understanding, while making writing a good deal easier for us.

7. "Strategies for the Development of New Congregations," p. 9.

Chapter 4   Parental Disappointment: The Problem of Goals

1. "News and Notes for the Session," *Presbyterian Life* (Mar. 1, 1971), pp. 39–40.

Chapter 5   At War with the Angels: The United People Campaign

1. These were recalled from memory in interviews with Righter and others. There may have been minor projects which escaped memory.

2. While it should be obvious, let us state explicitly that we have only secondhand knowledge of these projects and our perceptions are filtered through others— both within and outside the Congregation. We have also examined the accounts of the news media and interviewed reporters.

3. Statement of Dec. 12, 1968, by United Way of America, and circulated by that organization.

4. Ibid.

5. This action was reported in the Feb. 15, 1970, issue of *The New York Times*.

6. "Fairness Doctrine Complaint Filed Against WLWD-TV by United People Before the Federal Communications Commission," Covington and Burling (Law Firm), Washington, D.C. Case decided June 18, 1971.

7. Social action often produces conflict. With few exceptions, the projects undertaken by the Congregation have produced adversary relationships. Such relationships have a number of distinctive features. Since cooperation and conflict are in some respects two sides of the same conceptual coin, the variables of conflict are inverted variables of cooperation.

   Cooperation is measured by the achievement of a common goal; conflict is marked by the hindrance of often incompatible goals. Effective communication facilitates cooperation; insulation, while functional, often exacerbates conflict. Although conflict is a form of "sociation," the normal flow of interaction tends to be reduced. Cooperation is generally characterized by positive sentiments between parties; conflict normally generates negative or hostile sentiments. Finally, the relative status of cooperating parties contributes a salient dimension to the relationship. The party with higher status often has more to offer in cooperative ventures. Through norms of reciprocity, the obligation incurred is repaid in deference, further reinforcing status. In the conflict relationship relative status translates as relative power. A realistic assessment of advantage and disadvantage is crucial in the pursual of conflict strategy.

   Each of these four factors may vary within and between conflict relationships, and thus they are called variables. First is relative *power*—that is, differing ability can affect interference with the goals of the other or achievement of one's own goals in the face of the other's opposition. Second is *interaction*—that is, the extent and type of mutual contact can shape the conflict situation. Interaction characteristically decreases as conflict increases. Third is *sentiment*—that is, the degree to which negative feelings exist can alter the intensity of conflict. Fourth is *attrition*—that is, cost in whatever value or resource is damaged can measure conflict. Such values may be real, such as lives or property, or symbolic, such as prestige or credibility.

This scheme for analyzing conflict is drawn from Theodore Caplow, *Principles of Organization* (New York: Harcourt, Brace & World, 1964), pp. 326–28. By use of such an equilibrium model, a model from which, incidentally, Caplow has moved away in his recent thinking on organizations, we do not mean to imply that conflict is bad or abnormal. We simply posit the variables as an additional dimension of analysis, helpful in interpreting some of the subtleties of the Congregation's social-action projects.

8. For an illuminating, although occasionally self-serving, discussion of this issue, see Daniel P. Moynihan, *Maximum Feasible Misunderstanding* (New York: Free Press of Glencoe, 1969).

Chapter 6 Gideon's Gang Marches Again: The Gulf Boycott

1. "Minding the Corporate Conscience, 1973," *Economic Priorities Report* 4 (Jan.–Mar. 1973), pp. 10–12.
2. *Africa Today* (July–Aug. 1970).
3. We have put the resolution in proper form but have not altered its content.
4. The Gulf Boycott Coalition was certainly not the first group to be concerned with the Gulf-Angola connection. Several national organizations interested in the broader issue of social justice in Southern Africa have recommended action against Gulf. A pan-African liberation organization has worked steadily for several years on generating a boycott of Gulf products in a number of urban black communities, quite independent of the GBC. By focusing upon the Dayton-based group alone, we may have inadvertently left the impression that it singly mans the barricades against Gulf. Let us hasten to correct that impression.

Chapter 7 The Question of Strategy: Conflict in Context

1. Kenneth Burke, *Permanence and Change* (Indianapolis: Bobbs-Merrill, 1965), p. 244.
2. Our theoretical orientation here is substantially informed by the dramatism model of Kenneth Burke and Hugh Dalziel Duncan. Burke's major works include: *Permanence and Change* (originally published in 1935); *A Grammar of Motives* (Berkeley and Los Angeles: University of California Press, 1969, originally published in 1945); *A Rhetoric of Motives* (Berkeley and Los Angeles: University of California Press, 1969, originally published in 1950); and *Language as Symbolic Action* (Berkeley and Los Angeles: University of California Press, 1968, originally published in 1966). The work of Duncan builds upon that of Burke, especially in dealing with power. Duncan's major works include: *Communication and Social Order* (New York: Oxford University Press, 1968) and *Symbols in Society* (New York: Oxford University Press, 1968). We stress that our work is merely *informed by* the work of these scholars. No attempt is made to present even the most rudimentary propositions of their paradigm.
3. Hugh Dalziel Duncan, *Symbols in Society*, p. 62.
4. *The Proposed Book of Confessions* (Philadelphia: Office of the General Assembly, the United Presbyterian Church in the U.S.A.), pp. 177–86. Used by permission.

5. See, for example, John Kenneth Galbraith, *Economics and the Public Purpose* (Boston: Houghton Mifflin Co., 1973).

6. On this point it may be instructive to recall that it was President Dwight Eisenhower, not Jerry Rubin, who first warned this nation of the danger of the "military-industrial complex." In the public drama, elites are quick to associate the idea with the radical left while social activists have been slow to seek credibility for their claims by pointing to the original source.

7. Alvin W. Gouldner, *The Coming Crisis of Western Sociology* (New York: Basic Books, 1970), pp. 4–5. Used by permission.

Chapter 9   Successful in Life: The Cincinnati Experiment

1. By fortuitous coincidence, we were able to interview the third candidate seriously considered for the Dayton pastorate. Interestingly, his perception of the interview with the New Church Development Committee was that they had envisioned a congregation more nearly resembling the group Holm developed in Cincinnati. Recollections of what one's perceptions were nearly five years earlier may be clouded by developments over those years which serve to alter one's reconstruction of reality. Granting this possibility, our judgment from interviewing this third candidate is that he did correctly recall his perceptions at the time of the interview.

The interesting and, we believe, important observation here involves the respective interviewees' perceptions of the expectations of the committee. As we saw earlier, the committee itself was not of one mind. When we asked the three candidates for the position to name who they felt were the most influential members of the hiring committee, each pointed to individuals whose views about the desired nature of the new congregation paralleled their own interpretation of committee wishes. Righter and Holm had nearly identical lists of influential members. The third candidate, who perceived the committee's expectations in very different terms, had an entirely different list.

The issue is more complex than each interviewee hearing what he wanted to hear. Righter, the activist, heard what he wanted to hear and failed to be very cognizant of other expectations being communicated. Holm, on the other hand, picked up a viewpoint dissident to his expectations and failed to sense much reinforcement in the committee for his own views. Were it not for the availability of the third candidate, we might have concluded that the action-oriented persons on the committee were more forceful in communicating their expectations.

Our interviews with members of the committee lead us to believe both groups clearly stated their expectations. Moreover, when Righter was hired, both groups felt they had gotten "their man." While this is fairly basic social psychology, it is an important dynamic deserving emphasis.

The practical implication is this: When a recruiting committee is divided in what it expects of a candidate, they are unlikely to hire a compromise candidate. While they may consciously label a particular candidate so, in reality both sides will probably feel they got what they wanted. Not until the candidate has assumed the responsibilities of the position will it become clear which side misperceived.

Two further implications follow, one for recruiting committees and one for prospective employees. First, recruitment committees should be more explicit in spelling out their expectations and should attempt to work out any necessary compromises before candidates are interviewed. The practical implication for the interviewee would be to clearly state before all the members of the committee his perception of their expectations, as well as his own. Too often this kind of candor is withheld for fear of losing a desired position. In purely pragmatic terms, something less than complete openness may suffice when the recruiting committee will have little control over the position. But when members of the committee retain some control, whether directly or indirectly, as is usually the case in religious organizations, the deception of silence may come back to haunt the occupant of the position. This is especially true when expectations different from the prospective candidate's are held with some degree of salience. In the absence of candor on the part of the interviewee, that salience may become vocal only after he has violated an influential person's expectations. Such a situation constitutes a formula for a short and unhappy incumbency.

2. Duane Holm, "Presbytery of Cincinnati's Congregation for Reconciliation: a Personal Summary" (Oct. 7, 1972), pp. 2–3. Used by permission.
3. Ibid., p. 2.
4. Robert S. Lecky and H. Elliott Wright, eds., *Black Manifesto: Religion, Racism, and Reparation* (New York: Sheed and Ward, 1969), p. 5. Copyright, 1969, Sheed and Ward, Inc., Publishers.
5. Congregation for Reconciliation Newsletter, Cincinnati, Ohio (Nov. 1971).
6. Duane Holm was kind enough to send us lengthy and insightful remarks. Although they arrived too late to be incorporated in the text, we have paraphrased and summarized them below. We appreciate both his explanations on various points and his bringing us up to date.

A neglected factor influencing the differential development of social-action emphases and styles by the two congregations is cultural receptivity. Important differences in cultural milieu is noted in comparing the two cities. Dayton is a new city with more recent growth and more dynamic industry. It has a relatively liberal business establishment, heavily influenced by Detroit. As in many other "army towns," the expectations generated by the 30,000 Wright-Patterson federal employees are often in tension with the practices of the rest of the community. Dayton, like Cleveland, has a clearly defined ghetto on one side of the river. Like Detroit, many of its factories are located in the black community, where racial unrest can threaten disruption of normal operations.

In contrast, Cincinnati is an older city with a more conservative establishment, no large outside presence, and scattered, separated black communities similar to many old Southern cities. It is less dependent on industry. Further, Cincinnati is a "churchier" town, in which problems do not seem so severe or the need for solutions so urgent. Because of these social and cultural differences some action strategies worked in Dayton which would have been less successful in Cincinnati.

Many in the Cincinnati Congregation held responsible positions in the established institutions and civic life of the city. They were accustomed to running things and checked Holm's strong leadership when it countered their expectations. They refused to allow Holm to involve the Congregation in the grape boycott, in support of California farm workers, for instance. Holm argues they insisted that he make most of the routine housekeeping decisions instead of playing participatory games with them. (Our point was that, in contrast, Righter insisted participation in routine congregational decision-making was not a game. Nor did the Dayton Congregation accept it as such.) Holm insists that members of his flock were not sheepish in exerting their wills, however.

In addition, the Congregation contained a good deal of diversity in political views. Many were open on the issue of race but closed on other matters such as poverty, welfare, and war. Particularly in order to minimize conflict and thereby increase efficiency, the Congregation set out in its first year to establish priorities for action and to agree upon a single project to be emphasized. The Congregation was groping toward one focal social-action issue before the Black Manifesto controversy erupted. It was not until several months afterward, however, that their specific strategy took shape and their drive for selling black economic development to the other Presbytery churches began in earnest.

There are some tentative but hopeful signs that the influence of the Cincinnati Congregation for Reconciliation lingers after its death. First, the Presbytery's increased black investment and black representation apparently have become established policy. Second, the Cincinnati Presbytery's Education Department recently authorized an initial printing of the *Bible in Black and White* curriculum for suggested use in its churches. Third, Congregation ex-members have taken the lead in insisting on a continuing legitimate channel for racial concerns in the form of an Ethnic Affairs Committee in the currently restructuring Presbytery. Finally, Holm was nominated and elected to the General Assembly's (national) Council on Church and Race, where he has pursued the Congregation's concern for curricular and congregational action. These are signs that the experiment, although dead, has not yet been forgotten. Some of its ex-members have at least kept the struggle for racial reconciliation on the Presbytery agenda.

Chapter 10   Toughing Out the Storm

1. J. Howard Pew, "Should the Church 'Meddle' in Civil Affairs?" *Reader's Digest* (May 1966).
2. *The Christian Century* (May 11, 1966), pp. 607–8.
3. "Newspeak" was the official language of the state in George Orwell's celebrated novel, *1984*. The purpose of Newspeak was to make all other modes of thought impossible, as well as to provide a medium of expression proper to the devotees of the Party. It facilitated the process of "Doublethink," the ability to hold two contradictory beliefs simultaneously and accept them both.
4. Dean M. Kelley, *Why Conservative Churches Are Growing* (New York: Harper & Row, 1972).
5. Ibid., p. 86. Used by permission.
6. Ibid., p. 120.
7. Ibid., p. 151.
8. Ibid., p. 164.
9. Ibid., p. 163.
10. Ibid., p. 155.
11. Ibid., p. 134.

Chapter 11   Quo Vadis: Whither Liberal Protestantism?

1. Charles Silberman, *Crisis in the Classroom* (New York: Random House, 1970), p. 11. Used by permission.
2. Ibid.
3. Peter L. Berger, Brigitte Berger, and Hansfried Kellner, *The Homeless Mind: Modernization and Consciousness* (New York: Random House, 1973).
4. Edgar W. Mills, Jr., personal correspondence and communication. Also see Gerald J. Judd, Edgar W. Mills, Jr., and Genevieve Walters Burch, *Ex-Pastors: Why Men Leave the Parish Ministry* (Philadelphia: Pilgrim Press, 1970).